Scott Foresman

Practice Book

Editorial Offices: Glenview, Illinois • Parsippany, New Jersey • New York, New York
Sales Offices: Needham, Massachusetts • Duluth, Georgia • Glenview, Illinois
Coppell, Texas • Sacramento, California • Mesa, Arizona

ISBN: 0-328-14523-8

15 V004 13 12 11

Contents

Contents

Name ____________________

Family Times

Summary

Old Yeller

Fourteen-year-old Travis, his mother, his five-year-old brother Arliss, and a stray yellow dog called Old Yeller are alone at the homestead while his father is away. When Arliss enrages a mother bear by grabbing her cub, Old Yeller must save the boy from the bear's attack.

Activity

Narrate an Adventure Story

Make up an adventure story with your family in which an animal comes to your rescue. Decide on the time and place of the story, which family members are present, and which animal will be the hero. Have each family member take turns describing his or her role in the story.

Comprehension Skill

Setting

The **setting** is the time and place in which a story occurs. Sometimes the author tells you the setting, but sometimes you have to figure it out from the clues in the story.

Activity

Describe a Setting Describe in detail a place that your family is familiar with and see if a family member can guess which place you described. Include colors and sizes and shapes of objects, but do not name them. Include sounds and scents as well.

Lesson Vocabulary

Words to Know

Knowing the meanings of these words is important to reading *Old Yeller*. Practice using these words.

Vocabulary Words

lunging moving forward suddenly
nub a lump or a small piece
romping playing in a rough, boisterous way
rowdy rough; disorderly; quarrelsome
slung thrown, cast, or hurled
speckled marked with many small spots

Grammar

Four Kinds of Sentences

Sentences can be classified in four different ways. A **declarative sentence** tells something. It ends with a period. *For example: I like dogs.* An **interrogative sentence** asks a question. It ends with a question mark. *For example: Do you like animals?* An **imperative sentence** gives a command or makes a request. It ends with a period. *For example: Feed the cat, please.* An **exclamatory sentence** expresses strong feeling. It ends with an exclamation point. *For example: Your iguana is under my bed again!*

Activity

Name That Sentence Write the name of the four kinds of sentences on five note cards each. You will have a total of twenty cards. Mix the cards and place them face down on a table. Have family members take turns choosing a note card and making up a sentence to fit the kind of sentence they picked. Have the rest of the family guess the type of sentence.

Practice Tested Spelling Words

______	______	______	______
______	______	______	______
______	______	______	______
______	______	______	______
______	______	______	______

Name ____________________

Setting

- The **setting** is the time and place in which a story occurs. Sometimes the author tells you the setting, but sometimes you have to figure it out from clues in the story.
- The setting can determine what kind of events happen in a story.
- It can also influence the behavior of characters in a story.

Directions Read the following passage. Then fill in the chart below with elements of the story's setting and how each element affects the events of the story.

It had rained all night long and it was still raining in the morning. Nick called his sheep dog, Jake, to help him move the sheep to the north pasture. He needed to hurry because the stream in the south pasture would soon turn to a raging river. Already, the rain had washed out a part of the main path to the north pasture, so they would have to take the forest path to get to the north pasture. The gold and red trees along the forest path drooped under the heavy rain. The passage between the trees was muddy and slowed their progress. It would take another hour to lead the sheep to the higher ground.

Setting (Time and Place)	Event or Behavior of Character Affected by Setting
Morning, south pasture	1. Heavy rain made Pasture dangerous
2. Morning, main path.	3. Nick must use forest Path
4. Morning, forest path	5. mud slowed progress

Home Activity Your child described the setting in a reading passage. Choose a favorite book or film with your child and work together to describe the elements of the setting and how they affect the story's events.

Name Juan Pereanez

Vocabulary

Directions Choose the word from the box that best matches each definition. Write the word on the line shown to the left.

Check the Words You Know
✓ lunging
✓ nub
✓ romping
✓ rowdy
✓ slung
✓ speckled

nub **1.** a lump or small piece

lunging **2.** moving forward suddenly

speckled **3.** covered with small spots

slung **4.** thrown, cast, or hurled

rowdy **5.** rough and disorderly

Directions Choose the word from the box that best completes each sentence below. Write the word on the line shown to the left.

slung **6.** At the end of the school day, Susan ____ her books into her locker.

speckled **7.** The bird's nest held three pale, ____ eggs.

romping **8.** The boys liked ____ around during recess.

rowdy **9.** The ____ neighborhood kids ran down the block, shouting and laughing.

nub **10.** The pencil eraser was worn down to a ____.

Write a Journal Entry

On a separate sheet of paper write a journal entry you might make after you hiked in the woods and saw a bear. Use as many vocabulary words as you can.

School + Home **Home Activity** Your child identified and used vocabulary words from *Old Yeller.* Work with your child to identify familiar people or things to whom each word might be applied.

Name ____________________

Vocabulary • Word Structure

- Sometimes the ending *–ed* or *–ing* is added to a verb. This ending can change the verb's meaning.
- Remember that *–ed* makes a verb show action that happened in the past and *–ing* makes a verb show action that is happening in the present.

Directions Read the following passage about bears. Then answer the questions below. Look at the structure of the words as you read.

If you ask an American to imagine a bear, the black bear is almost certainly the one they will think of. Black bears are not often seen in American forests. Since Colonial times, their numbers have been seen to be shrinking because humans have hunted them and moved into their territory. But it is still a good idea to avoid them. Films often show bear cubs romping in the woods. However, brown bears are much more dangerous than they are cute. They eat everything from grass to animals and are very protective of their young. Food left lying around campsites may attract them. If you do see a bear, lunging away is not a good idea. Any sudden movement will cause the bear to chase you. Park rangers often recommend loud singing or rowdy conversation while you are hiking. Bears avoid humans when they can. If a bear hears you coming, it will vanish into the woods before you arrive.

1. How does the *–ing* in *shrinking* change the meaning of the root word?

____

2. What is the root word of *lunging?*

____

3. What tense is formed by adding *–ing* to the verb *romp?*

____

4. How does the *–ed* in *hunted* change the meaning of the root word?

____

5. How does the passage give clues to the meaning of *rowdy?*

____

____

Home Activity Your child used word endings to understand new words in a passage. Read a newspaper or magazine article with your child, identifying words with endings that change their meanings.

Name______________________________________

Cause and Effect

Directions Read the following passage. Then answer the questions below.

The pioneers traveled to the western frontier for many reasons. Some wanted better land for farming. They traveled West in wagons looking for good and inexpensive farm land. Homesteading allowed some pioneers to settle on free land if they cleared, farmed, and lived on the land for five years. After five years the land would be theirs. But this was very hard work. Homesteaders had to clear rocks and trees. They had to build a shelter. They had to plow the field and plant a crop. It took the first two years just to clear the land and build a shelter. A homesteader's first year's crop was usually very small because of the back-breaking work to clear the land for planting. The first shelter was usually only a lean-to, a house that looked like a three-sided shed. The open side faced the camp fire. It was not easy to stay on this land for five years. Many homesteaders failed to make a living from the land.

1. Why did some pioneers settle on homestead land?

____

____

2. Give two of the conditions necessary for homesteaders to gain ownership of the land.

____

____

3. Explain why a second-year crop would be larger than a first-year crop.

____

____

4. Why was it so difficult to stay on homestead land for five years?

____

____

5. On a separate sheet of paper, write a journal entry describing a typical day on the homestead.

Home Activity Your child has read information about pioneers and answered questions about cause and effect. Read a newspaper or magazine article with your child and ask him or her to identify causes and effects of events in the article.

Name ____________________

Setting

- The **setting** is the time and place in which a story occurs. Sometimes the author tells you the setting, but sometimes you have to figure it out from clues in the story.
- The setting can determine what kind of events happen. It can also influence the behavior of characters in a story.

Directions Read the following passage. Then answer the questions below.

The icy feel of the wind and the gathering clouds meant snow was on its way. The cows needed to be put in the barn, water needed to be brought in the house from the well, and enough firewood had to be cut to keep the family warm during the storm. James would take care of the cows and his brother Jack would bring in the water. Their father would take care of the firewood. According to their grandfather, this was going to be a big storm. His knees always ached when a big storm was on the way. James and Jack didn't mind a big snow storm because they would be warm and snug in their cabin. Because the family could not go out during the storm, they would sing and play games and eat their mother's freshly baked cookies in front of the fire.

1. How do you know this story takes place in winter?

2. Where and during what time in history does this story take place? How do you know this?

3. How does the weather affect the grandfather?

4. How do James and Jack feel about the coming storm?

5. Visualize the scene described in the passage's final sentence. List three sensory details from your visualization.

Home Activity Your child identified the setting and the characters' reactions to the setting. Tell your child a story about a storm that affected you. Have your child visualize the storm and determine how it would affect him or her.

Setting

- The **setting** is the time and place in which a story occurs. Sometimes the author tells you the setting, but sometimes you have to figure it out from clues in the story.
- The setting can determine what kind of events happen. It can also influence the behavior of characters in a story.

Directions Read the following passage. Then fill in the chart below with elements of the story's setting and how each element affects the events of the story.

The storm during the night had left everything covered in a thick coat of ice. By morning, Ellen had to kick the front door hard to break the ice that sealed it shut. Her house was on a hilltop, and she could see the whole valley sparkling with ice. The beautiful view filled her with joy. When she went outside again that afternoon, General Hammond, her dog, dashed out the door and into the yard. The fast-moving dog couldn't stop as it reached the edge of the hill. Soon it was sliding down the slope, barking wildly. Ellen laughed. "Silly dog," she said. She carefully stepped off the porch and went after him.

Setting (Time and Place)	Event or Behavior of Character Affected by Setting
Morning, house on a hilltop in winter	**1.** Ellen must
2.	**3.** Makes Ellen feel
4.	**5.** General Hammond

Home Activity Your child identified the setting of a reading passage. Read a short story or magazine article with your child and have your child identify the setting. Then have your child draw a picture of the setting.

Name ______________________________________

Graphic Organizer

Graphic organizers are story maps, semantic maps, pictorial maps, webs, graphs, frames, charts, time lines, and other devices that help you to view and construct relationships among events, concepts, and words.

Directions Complete the graphic organizer to understand the setting of a story by using the following information.

The story you read is set in a log cabin in the 1800s. A fireplace is used for heat and a cast iron wood stove for cooking. The furniture includes a straw bed and a table with four chairs.

Name ____________________________________

Directions Fill in this semantic organizer with information about the vocabulary word ***speckled.***

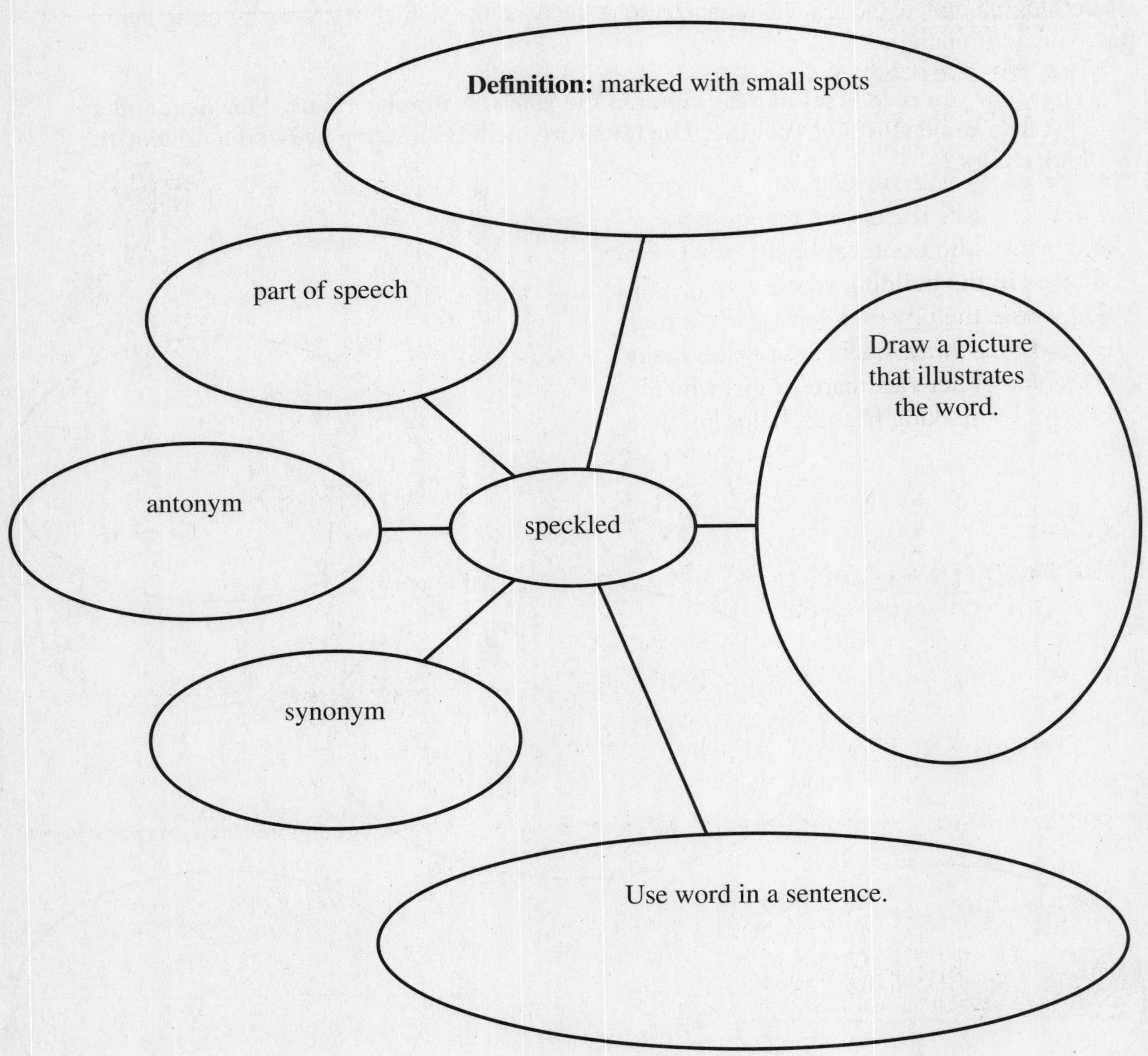

School + Home

Home Activity Your child learned about using graphic organizers as a way to organize and understand information. Read a story with your child and create a graphic organizer to help him or her visualize and understand the setting or characters of the story.

Name

Family Times

Summary

Viva New Jersey

Lucinda recently moved from Cuba to New Jersey with her family. She hasn't made any friends yet, and she longs to be back in Cuba. Lucinda rescues an abandoned dog and brings him home, although pets are not allowed in the building where she lives. The dog causes the power in her building to go off and runs away. Lucinda searches for the dog. One of her classmates, a girl who also has trouble making friends, helps her. They become friends.

Activity

The People We Meet Think about some of your closest friends and how you met them. Write a short account of how you met one of your friends and read it to a family member. Recall as many details about your first encounter as you can.

Comprehension Skill

Compare and Contrast

To **compare and contrast** is to tell how two or more things are alike and how they are different.

Activity

Same Difference With a family member, compare and contrast two people in your family. Think of characteristics to compare. For example, compare and contrast hair, clothing, height, favorite foods, and hobbies.

Lesson Vocabulary

Words to Know

Knowing the meanings of these words is important to reading *Viva New Jersey*. Practice using these words.

Vocabulary Words

corridors long hallways; passages in a large building into which rooms open
destination place to which someone or something is going or is being sent
groping feeling about with the hands
menacing threatening
mongrel animal of mixed breed, especially a dog
persisted kept on; refused to stop or be changed
pleas requests or appeals

Grammar

Independent and Dependent Clauses

A **clause** is a group of related words that has a subject and a predicate. If a clause makes sense by itself, it is an **independent clause.** *We wear our winter coats* is an example of an independent clause because it can stand on its own. If a clause does not make sense by itself, it is a **dependent clause.** *When it is cold outside* is an example of a dependent clause because it cannot stand on its own as a sentence.

Activity

Complex Sentence With a family member, make a two-column chart. Write five independent clauses in one column. In the other, write five dependent clauses. Cut the chart into two lists and give one list to each of you. Take turns reading clauses from your lists. The second clause must join with the first clause to make a complex sentence. Once you have created five sentences, switch the order in which you read independent and dependent clauses.

Practice Tested Spelling Words

______	______	______	______
______	______	______	______
______	______	______	______
______	______	______	______
______	______	______	______

Name ______________________

Vocabulary • Context Clues

- When you are reading and see an unfamiliar word, use **context clues**, or words around the unfamiliar word, to figure out its meaning.
- Context clues include definitions, explanations, and synonyms.

Directions Read the following passage about dogs. Then answer the questions below. Look for context clues as you read.

Walking down one of her usual streets, Officer Laura heard the whimpering pleas of a puppy. She looked around and realized the puppy had fallen into a storm drain. She reached down, but found that she could not reach down far enough. Officer Laura persisted and kept groping for the puppy, but it was just out of reach. She called the fire department for more help. When the fire fighters arrived, they lowered a special hook with a looped rope to lift the puppy. The puppy did not like the rope, and everyone heard its menacing growl. They carefully worked the rope around the puppy, and it was finally lifted to safety. The mongrel pup was wet, dirty, and looked like a cross between a cat and a poodle! Officer Laura laughed at the sight. She held the puppy up to show the crowd who had gathered to watch. The crowd applauded and continued on to their final destinations. Officer Laura and the puppy walked together down the street. Officer Laura realized she had found a new partner.

1. What are *pleas*? What sound did this puppy make?

____

2. What does *persisted* mean? What clues help you to determine the meaning?

____

3. What does *groping* mean? What clues help you to determine the meaning?

____

4. What does *mongrel* mean? What clues help you to determine the meaning?

____

____

5. What word in the passage is a synonym for *threatening*?

____

Home Activity Your child identified and used context clues to understand new words in a short passage. Work with your child to identify unfamiliar words in an encyclopedia article about dogs.

Name ____________________________

Character

Directions Read the following passage. Then answer the questions below.

JASON: Why can't I go to the game tonight?

MOM: I told you. I need you to babysit your little sister.

JASON: Why can't somebody else in this family watch Jessie?

MOM: I told you before. Your dad and I are going to see Grandma in the hospital, and Sally needs to go to the library to work on a project.

JASON: But that's not fair! Jeff and I made plans weeks ago to go to the game.

MOM: I'm sorry, but there's nothing else we can do. We didn't plan on Grandma getting sick.

(Sally enters the room.)

SALLY: What's all the moaning about, Jason?

JASON: I planned to go to the game tonight with Jeff, but now I have to babysit because you have to go to the library.

SALLY: What if I go to the library a little earlier? They have a storyteller for preschool kids in the afternoon. Maybe Jessie would like to hear the story while I study?

MOM: Great idea, Sally.

JASON: Yeah, Sally. Thanks!

1. How do you know Jason is upset?

____

2. Why is Jason upset?

____

____

3. Why does Jason think the situation is unfair?

____

____

4. How is Jason more selfish than Sally?

____

____

5. On a separate sheet of paper, rewrite the scene with Jason being less selfish.

Home Activity Your child has read a short passage and answered questions about a character. Read a short story with your child. Ask your child questions about the character's motives in the story.

Name ____________________

Compare and Contrast

- To **compare and contrast** is to tell how two or more things are alike and how they are different.

Directions Read the following passage. Then answer the questions below.

Cubans who choose to come to the United States often face some difficult changes. Cuba's average temperature is between 70°F and 80°F. Even in the winter, it rarely gets below 70°F. Although it's usually warm in Cuba, some months are very rainy. Cuba's summers are hot and humid.

Some Cuban immigrants settle in New Jersey. New Jersey's climate is much different from Cuba's. Although summers can be hot and humid, the winters are very cold.

Besides getting used to the weather, Cubans must also get used to differences in the culture and language. This is something that almost all immigrants must get used to in their new country, regardless of where they come from. However, most new immigrants eventually find things to love about their new home.

1. What is the difference in climate between Cuba and New Jersey?

____

2. What is a similarity between the climate of Cuba and New Jersey?

____

3. How do you think new Cuban immigrants to New Jersey feel about these differences?

____

4. What challenge is faced by almost all immigrants who come to a new country?

____

____

5. Write a summary of this passage in one or two sentences.

____

____

Home Activity Your child read a short passage and compared and contrasted the climates of two countries. Have your child compare and contrast the climate of two cities in the United States.

Name ______________________

Compare and Contrast

- To **compare and contrast** is to tell how two or more things are alike and how they are different.

Directions Read the following passage. Then complete the diagram by listing California and Costa Rica's similarities in the intersection of the circles and their differences on the outsides.

When Cecilia moved to California from Costa Rica, the first thing she noticed was the ocean. She had lived near the ocean in Costa Rica, so this was a welcome sight. One big difference, though, was the large number of buildings on the shore. In her part of Costa Rica, there were not as many buildings to clutter the view of the water. The food was different too. She liked to eat fresh papayas in Costa Rica. In California she had been introduced to oranges and grapes. Cecilia believed that California, like Costa Rica, had many good things to offer.

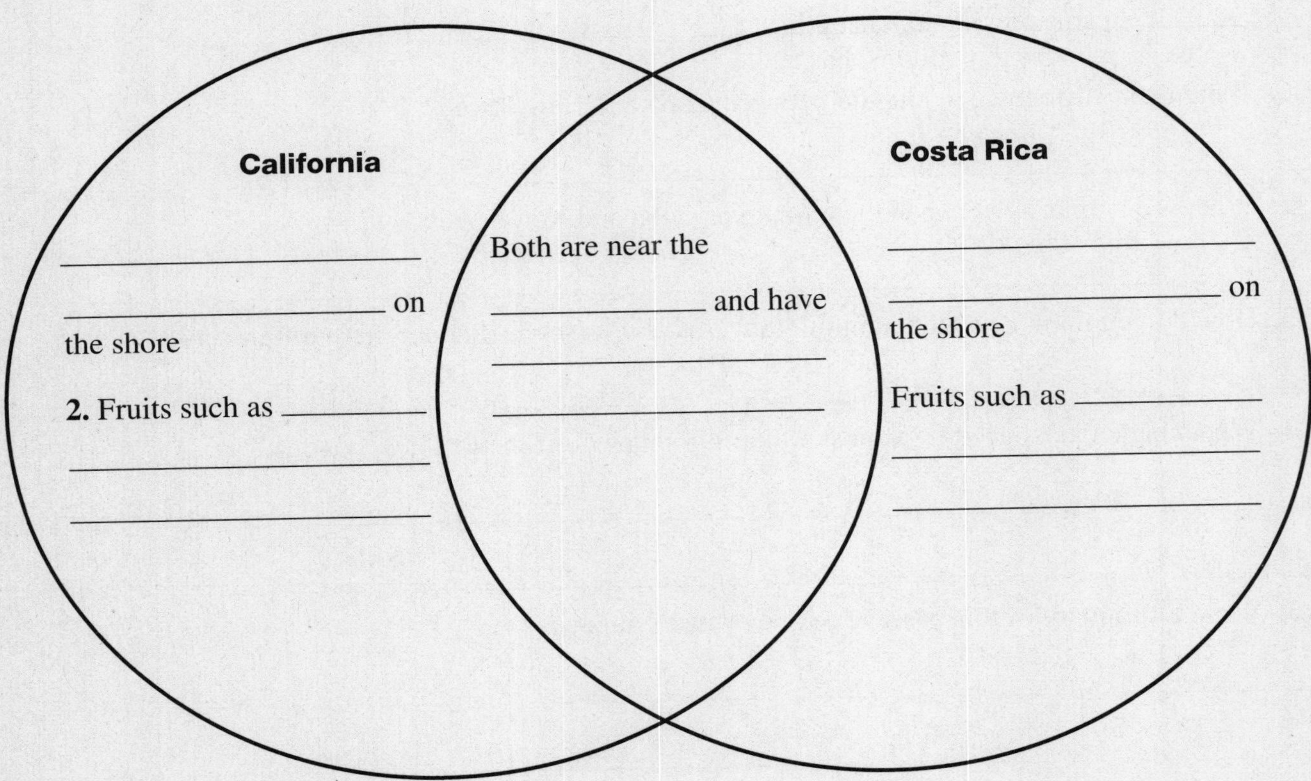

School + Home **Home Activity** Your child read a short passage and compared and contrasted two different places. With your child, write two lists comparing and contrasting two different stores you frequently shop at.

Name______________________________

Magazine/Periodical

Magazines contain an **index**, which is much like a table of contents. The index is usually in the first few pages. Many magazines also have recurring **sections** devoted to certain subjects (news, entertainment, fashion, sports, or finance, for example). Magazines present information by order of interest and present important articles of high interest first. Article titles are like chapter titles, letting readers know what they are about. Most magazine articles follow the five W's and H format. A reader learns the Who? What? When? Where? Why? and How? in the first few paragraphs.

Directions Use this index from a news magazine to answer the questions below.

1. What are the titles of the three main sections?

____

____

2. What are the titles of the two articles in the NATION section?

____

____

3. On what page is the article about car leases?

____

4. What is the title of the article in the BUSINESS section?

____

5. The YOUR TIME section contains two articles. What are their titles?

____

____

Name ______________________________

Directions Read this article from a news magazine article. Then answer the questions below.

Village at Risk

Shishmaref is melting into the ocean. Since the mid-1970s, this Inupiaq village, perched on a slender barrier island 625 miles north of Anchorage, has lost half its coastline. As Alaska's climate warms, the permafrost beneath Shishmaref's beaches is thawing, and the sea ice is thinning, leaving its 600 residents increasingly vulnerable to violent storms. One house has collapsed, and eighteen others had to be moved to higher ground, along with the town's bulk fuel tanks. Giant waves have washed away the school playground and destroyed $100,000 worth of boats, hunting gear, and fish-drying racks. The remnants of multimillion-dollar sea walls, broken up by the tides, litter the beach. "It's scary," says a village official. "Every year we agonize that the next storm will wipe us out."

6. **Who** is this article about?

____

____

7. **What** is this article about?

____

____

8. **Where** does this take place?

____

9. **When** do events in this article take place?

____

10. **Why** is this happening?

____

____

Home Activity Your child learned about using magazines as resources. Look at a magazine index together. Ask your child to locate an article you are both interested in. Then read the article and find the five W's and H in each.

Name ______________________________

Family Times

Summary

Saving the Rain Forests

There is more than one kind of rain forest. Yet they all face similar risks, and many of these risks are caused by humans. Humans depend on the rich resources of rain forests, but every year we put them more and more at risk. Some humans, however, want to help. There are many ways to help save the rain forest.

Activity

It Starts at Home Recycling paper products is an easy way to help save the rain forests. With your family, come up with a plan for your household to recycle paper products. You may need to look into your local recycling program.

Comprehension Skill

Fact and Opinion

Statements of fact can be proved true or false. They can be proved by reading, observing, or asking an expert. **Statements of opinion** are judgments or beliefs. They cannot be proved true or false.

Activity

The *Real* Story Ask each member of your family to write a short description of an event that you all were involved with. Gather everyone's descriptions and make a list of what is factual in each description and what is opinion. You might be surprised at how differently people remember the same event.

Lesson Vocabulary

Words to Know

Knowing the meanings of these words is important to reading *Saving the Rain Forests*. Practice using these words.

Vocabulary Words

basin all the land drained by a river and the streams that flow into it

charities organizations for helping those in need or the environment

equator an imaginary circle around the middle of Earth

erosion process of gradually wearing away by glaciers, running water, waves, or wind

evaporates changes from a liquid to a gas

exported sent goods out of one country for sale and use in another

industrial engaged in or connected with business, trade, or manufactured goods

recycled processed or treated so it can be used again

tropics regions near the equator that are also the hottest parts of Earth

Grammar

Compound and Complex Sentences

A **compound sentence** contains two simple sentences joined with a comma and a conjunction. *For example: Tim had a ticket, but he forgot to bring it with him.* A sentence that has one independent clause and one or more dependent clauses is called a **complex sentence.** *For example: After the driver stops at the stop sign, she may drive forward.*

Activity

Thought Addition With a family member, make a two-column chart. Write five simple sentences (such as *Mom goes to work*) in one column and five dependent clauses (such as *after we leave for school*) in the other column. Take turns joining two of the simple sentences to form a compound sentence and a dependent clause with a simple sentence to form a complex sentence. How many compound and complex sentences can you make?

Practice Tested Spelling Words

____________	____________	____________	____________
____________	____________	____________	____________
____________	____________	____________	____________
____________	____________	____________	____________
____________	____________	____________	____________

Fact and Opinion

- A statement that can be proved true or false is called a **statement of fact.**
- A statement that tells a person's thoughts, feelings, or ideas is called a **statement of opinion.** Statements of opinion cannot be proved true or false.

Directions Read the following passage. Then complete the graphic organizer below.

Rain forests make up only seven percent of the land surface of our planet. However, some scientists say they think that they contain more than half of Earth's plant and animal species. A large percentage of rain forest animals are insects, and a large percentage of those insects are beetles. Scientists are still not sure how many animal species exist on Earth because they have only been able to identify a small fraction of rain forest insects. One scientist said, "I believe that as many as thirty million kinds of insect live in the rain forests."

Statement of Fact

1.

2.

3.

Statement of Opinion

4.

5.

Home Activity Your child identified statements of fact and opinion in a short passage. Tell your child a story about a friend or family member that contains both statements of fact and opinion. Have him or her tell you which statements are which.

Name______________________________________

Vocabulary

Directions Choose the word from the box that best matches each definition. Write the word on the line.

Check the Words You Know
___basin
___charities
___equator
___erosion
___evaporates
___exported
___industrial
___recycled
___tropics

____________________ **1.** an imaginary line around the middle of Earth

____________________ **2.** changes from a liquid to a gas

____________________ **3.** regions of the world near the equator

____________________ **4.** processed to be used again

____________________ **5.** sent to a different country for sale or trade

Directions Circle the word or words that have the same or nearly the same meaning as the first word in each group.

6. charities	organizations that help	groups of writers	clubs for children
7. basin	hill near the sea	land drained by a river	mountain with snow
8. erosion	building up	covering over	wearing away
9. industrial	for use in business	for help in education	for ideas at home
10. evaporates	disappears	melts	boils

Write a Weather Report

On a separate sheet of paper, write a weather report for a tropical area. Include as many vocabulary words as you can.

Home Activity Your child identified and used vocabulary words from *Saving the Rain Forests.* Have a discussion with your child about the selection. Encourage him or her to use the vocabulary words during the discussion.

Name____________________________________

Vocabulary • Word Structure

- An **ending** is a letter or letters added to the end of a base word.
- The endings *–s* and *–es* are added to singular nouns to make them plural.
- The ending *–ed* is added to a verb to make it past tense. The ending *–ing* is added to a verb to make it tell about present or ongoing actions. The ending *–s* is added to a verb to show present action in the third person. Recognizing an ending will help you figure out a word's meaning.

Directions Read the following passage. Then answer the questions below.

Many people in the United States eat bananas. A banana plant needs a hot, wet climate to grow. That is why they grow in the tropics near the equator. Millions of tons of bananas are exported and are shipped to the United States every year. Many charities that provide food like to receive bananas because they are a good source of vitamin C, fiber, and potassium.

1. *Bananas* and *tropics* both have the same ending. What are their base words? How does *–s* change the meaning of their base words?

____

____

2. What is the difference between *–s* at the end of *tropics* and *–s* at the end of *needs?*

____

____

3. What letters are added to the word *charity* to make it plural?

____

4. *Exported* and *shipped* both have the same ending. What are their base words? How does *-ed* change the meaning of their base words?

____

____

5. Choose a noun or a verb from the passage. What is its base word? Add a new ending to it. How has the meaning of the word changed?

____

____

Home Activity Your child identified endings to understand new words in a passage. Write a note with him or her to another member of your family. Have your child identify the endings of words your child used in the note.

Name ________________________________

Graphic Sources

Directions Study the precipitation graph of the rain forest in Campa Pita, Belize. Then answer the questions below.

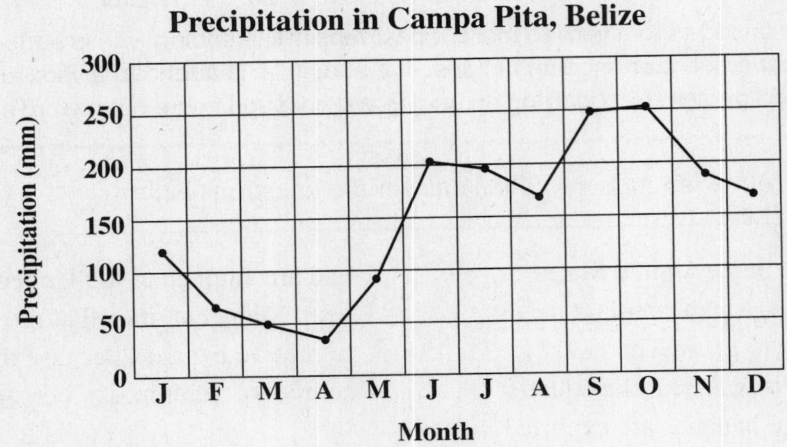

1. Which month had the least amount of precipitation? About how much precipitation fell in that month?

____

____

2. Which month had the greatest amount of precipitation? About how much precipitation fell in that month?

____

____

3. The rainiest months in Campa Pita correspond with which season in North America?

____

4. The driest months in Campa Pita correspond with which season in North America?

____

5. Explain how a graph of precipitation in your area might be different from the graph above.

____

____

____

Home Activity Your child has interpreted information from a graph. Find a graph in a newspaper or magazine article. Ask him or her to interpret the information in it.

Fact and Opinion

- A statement that can be proved true or false is called a **statement of fact.**
- A statement that tells a person's thoughts, feelings, or ideas is called a **statement of opinion.** Statements of opinion cannot be proved true or false.
- Statements of opinion may be either *valid* or *faulty*. Valid statements of opinion are supported by facts. Faulty statements of opinion are not supported by facts.

Directions Read the following passage. Then answer the questions below.

After David heard a news story about the shortage of landfills, he asked his teacher if he could write about recycling for his report. During his research, he found out that recycling just one can will save enough energy to power a TV for three hours. He learned that an aluminum can could be recycled an unlimited number of times. David considered what he had learned for a moment. It would be great, thought David, if he and his classmates could save a lot of energy by recycling cans. The news report also said that over two hundred million trees could be saved each year if all the newspaper was recycled. David wondered if his class could recycle paper as well. He felt his class could make a difference in saving energy and natural resources.

1. Underline a statement of fact in the passage.
2. How do you know that the sentence you identified above is a statement of fact? How would you prove it?

____

____

3. Circle a statement of opinion in the passage.
4. How do you know that the sentence you identified above is a statement of opinion?

____

____

5. Explain why the opinion you identified is valid or not valid.

____

____

Home Activity Your child read a short passage and identified the statements of fact and opinion. Read a newspaper editorial with your child. Ask him or her to underline statements of fact in the editorial once and statements of opinion twice.

Name ______________________________________

Fact and Opinion

- A statement that can be proved true or false is called a **statement of fact.**
- A statement that tells a person's thoughts, feelings, or ideas is called a **statement of opinion.** Statements of opinion cannot be proved true or false.

Directions Read the following passage. Then complete the graphic organizer below.

Trees in the rain forest are amazing to study. They have thinner and smoother bark than trees in other kinds of forests. If their barks were thicker, they would hold in too much moisture. Many rain forest trees have leaves with thin tips. This allows water to run off quickly so fungus and bacteria cannot grow on them. I think that without their special characteristics, rain forest trees would probably not survive their extreme living conditions.

Statement of Fact

1. They have ______________________________

2. If their barks were ______________________________

3. ______________________________

Statement of Opinion

4. Trees from the rain forest are ______________________________

5. ______________________________

Home Activity Your child identified statements of fact and statements of opinion in a short passage. Look at pictures in a newspaper or magazine with your child. Have him or her make a statement of fact and a statement of opinion about each picture.

Name ______________________

Graph

A **graph** is a pictorial representation of data. Graphs show how any one piece of information compares with other pieces. A graph can show information more quickly than a verbal explanation and can reveal how something changes over time. There are bar graphs, circle graphs, line graphs, and pictographs. Titles and labels on a graph will help you interpret the data in the graph.

Directions Use this bar graph to answer the questions below.

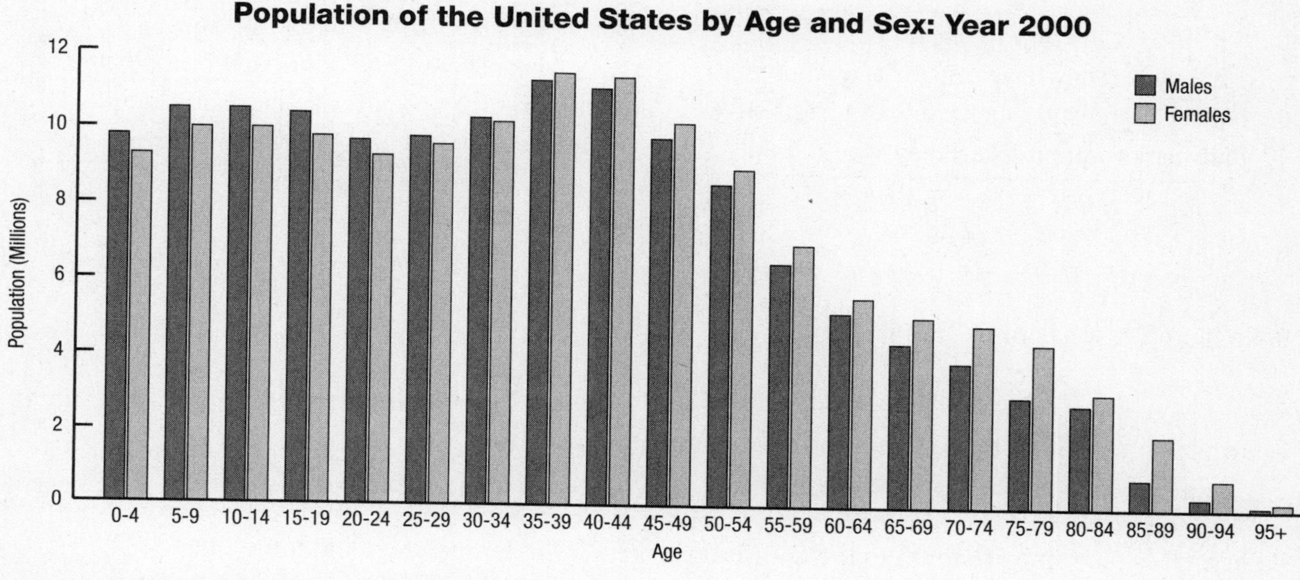

1. What information is given in this graph?

____

____

2. What two groups are compared in this graph?

____

3. Which group had a greater population from birth to age 4?

____

4. Using the data in this graph, what conclusion can you draw about people over 60 years old?

____

____

5. What generalization can you make about human lifespans based on the data in the graph?

____

____

Name ____

Graph

Directions Use the following graphs to answer the questions below.

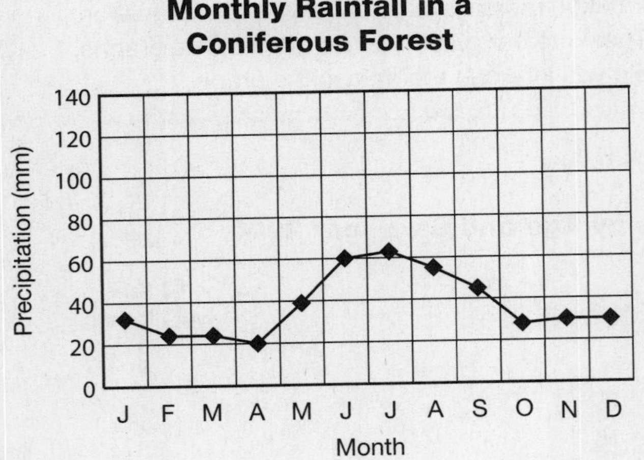

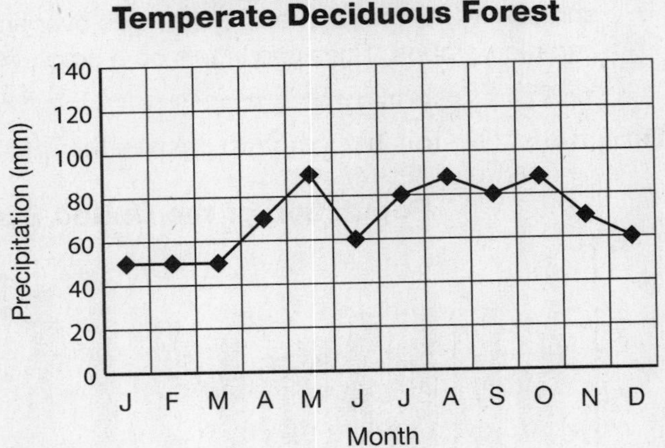

6. Which forest has more rain in May?

____

7. In which month do both forests have the same amount of rain?

____

8. Which is the rainiest month in the coniferous forest? The temperate deciduous forest?

____

9. What conclusion can you draw about precipitation in the coniferous forest for October, November, and December?

____

____

10. What conclusion can you draw about precipitation when you compare the data from both forests?

____

____

Home Activity Your child learned how to read and understand data on graphs. Find a graph in a newspaper or magazine. Discuss it with your child and draw conclusions about the data.

Name

Family Times

Summary

When Crowbar Came

The Craig family often took in wild animals in need of help. Many of these animals became pets. One pet was a crow the Craigs named Crowbar. Crowbar ate with them at the table, walked with the kids to the bus stop, and even picked up coins from the schoolyard and deposited them in the gutter of the bank building. After a few years, however, Crowbar migrated with other crows and was never seen again.

Activity

Wild Things With members of your family, imagine a wild animal you might like to have as a pet. Why do you think this animal would make a good pet? How do you think the animal would have to change in order to be a pet? Remember, wild animals are not meant to be pets and are usually not happy when living outside their natural homes.

Comprehension Skill

Fact and Opinion

Statements of fact can be proved true or false. Facts can be proved by reading, observing, or asking an expert. **Statements of opinion** are judgments or beliefs. Opinions cannot be proved true or false. Sometimes statements express both a fact and an opinion.

Activity

A Matter of Fact Find an editorial from a newspaper or magazine. With a family member, read the column and circle the statements of fact the writer cites in support of his or her opinion. How many facts does the writer offer as support? Do you think the writer's argument is strong?

Lesson Vocabulary

Words to Know

Knowing the meanings of these words is important to reading *When Crowbar Came*. Practice using these words.

Vocabulary Words

aggressive taking the first step in an attack
detect discover or find out
dubiously uncertainly; filled with doubt
frustration a feeling of helplessness or anger caused by failure
imprinted learned as a baby animal to identify and follow a parent
materialize appear or suddenly be seen
migration the act of going from one region to another with the change in seasons
secretive having the habit of secrecy; not frank or open
tolerated allowed or permitted

Grammar

Common and Proper Nouns

A **common noun** names any person, place, or thing. *For example: teacher, bus stop, book.* A **proper noun** names a particular person, place, or thing. *For example: Mrs. Riley, the White House, the Astrodome.* **Abbreviations** are shortened forms of words. People often abbreviate proper nouns, including titles in front of names (e.g., *Mr., Mrs.*), the names of the days (e.g., *Mon., Tues.*), and the names of some months (e.g., *Sept., Jan.*). These abbreviations begin with capital letters and usually end with a period.

Activity

Properly Done With a family member, make a list of a dozen common nouns. Try to think of a mix of people, places, and things. Cut the nouns into strips of paper and put them in a hat or cup. Take turns selecting nouns from the cup and changing the common noun into a proper noun. For example, change the common noun *city* to the proper noun *Chicago.*

Practice Tested Spelling Words

________	________	________	________
________	________	________	________
________	________	________	________
________	________	________	________
________	________	________	________

Name____

Fact and Opinion

- **Statements of fact** can be proved true or false. They can be proved by reading, observing, or asking an expert.
- **Statements of opinion** are judgments or beliefs. They cannot be proved true or false, but they can be *supported* by facts and logic.

Directions Read the following article. Then complete the diagram by identifying statements of fact and statements of opinion.

Blue jays are large birds that are easily noticed in many areas of the United States. Some people think blue jays are beautiful birds because of their bright blue color. Other people think they are very destructive because they eat other birds' eggs and damage some gardens by eating seeds. Still others like that blue jays eat insects and help control the insect population. Blue jays are related to crows and are very noisy. However, it is difficult to distinguish them by their sound because they sound like many other birds.

Blue Jays are large birds that are easily seen in many areas of the United States.

Which part of statement is opinion?

1.

Which part of statement is fact?

2.

How to support?

3.

How to prove?

4.

5. Write another fact or opinion you read in the article. Which kind of statement is it?

____

Home Activity Your child read a short article and identified statements of fact and statements of opinion. Read a short article with your child about a familiar animal. Ask him or her to identify statements of fact and opinion. Ask how the facts can be proven and the opinions can be supported.

Name ______________________________

Vocabulary

Directions Choose the word from the box that best matches each definition. Write the word on the line.

Check the Words You Know
___aggressive
___detect
___dubiously
___frustration
___imprinted
___materialize
___migration
___secretive
___tolerated

________________ **1.** the act of moving from one region to another with the change in the seasons

________________ **2.** a feeling of anger and helplessness caused by failure

________________ **3.** allowed or permitted

________________ **4.** taking the first step in an attack

________________ **5.** fixed firmly in the mind

Directions Choose the word from the box that best matches each clue. Write each word in the puzzle.

Across

6. to become visible

Down

7. not frank or open

8. uncertainly, doubtfully

9. learned as a baby animal to follow a parent

10. discover, notice

Write a Description

Using a separate sheet of paper, describe what a flock of birds might look like. Use as many vocabulary words as you can.

Home Activity Your child identified and used vocabulary words from *When Crowbar Came.* Read an article about birds with your child. Have him or her point out unfamiliar words. Try to figure out the meaning of each word by using words that appear near it.

Name ________________________________

Vocabulary • Word Structure

- A **suffix** is a word part added to the end of a base word to change its meaning or the way it is used in a sentence. The suffix *–ly* means "in the manner of"; *–tion* means "the act of"; and *–ize* means "to make or cause to be."

Directions Read the following passage. Then answer the questions below.

Lin loved to watch the ducks gather in the pond on her grandfather's farm. Winter was comng on quickly and she knew it was soon time for their migration south. Usually her dog Ace and the ducks tolerated each other pretty well. For some reason, one of the ducks had become aggressive with Ace. When Ace approached the flock, it would rush at Ace with its wings flapping wildly. Ace retreated and just watched the ducks in frustration. This continued for about a week as the ducks continued to gather on the pond. It appeared that this duck could detect when Ace approached, and it would rush and flap and quack wildly. This game between Ace and the duck continued until the ducks finally began their migration south.

1. How does the suffix *–ly* change the meaning of the base word *quick* in the word *quickly?*

____

2. How does the suffix *–tion* change the meaning of the base word *migrate* in the word *migration*?

____

3. How does the suffix *–ize* change the meaning of the base word in the word *modernize?*

____

4. How does the suffix change the meaning of the base word in the word *frustration?*

____

____

5. Think of another word that ends with either *–ize* or *–tion*. Use it in an original sentence that makes its meaning clear.

____

____

Home Activity Your child read a short passage and identified suffixes at the ends of words. Read a story with your child and identify the suffixes *–ness* and *–tion* at the ends of words in the story. Ask your child how the suffix changed the meaning of the word.

Name ____________________

Author's Purpose

Directions Read the article. Then answer the questions below.

It is easy to identify one of America's most popular birds, the cardinal. Its beautiful bright red color and crested head make it easy to spot. Cardinals prefer to build nests in evergreen trees or thick bushes. If you don't have these, you can attract them to your backyard by providing the food they like. Their cone-shaped beaks help them eat seeds, their favorite food. They seem to prefer sunflower seeds, but they will also eat fruits and insects. Cardinals mate for life, and a male and female will usually be seen together at a feeder. If you continue to provide the food they like, you can enjoy the beautiful sight of a pair of cardinals all year long.

1. What has the author informed the reader about?

____

____

2. What has the author hoped to persuade the reader to do?

____

____

3. Were you persuaded by the author? If so, what did you find persuasive? If not, how could the author have written the article so that it would have persuaded you?

____

____

____

4. What words did the author use to make the cardinal an appealing bird to have at your feeder?

____

____

5. On a separate sheet of paper, write a short passage that would persuade someone to build a bird feeder.

Home Activity Your child has read a short passage and identified the author's purpose. Watch a few commercials on television or look at some newspaper ads with your child. Ask him or her what the purposes of the commercials were and whether they were successful.

Name ______________________________

Fact and Opinion

- **Statements of fact** can be proved true or false. They can be proved by reading, observing, or asking an expert.
- **Statements of opinion** are judgments or beliefs. They cannot be proved true or false, but they can be *supported* by facts and logic.

Directions Read the following passage. Then answer the questions below.

JOE: Did you know there are two major league baseball teams that are named after birds, the St. Louis Cardinals and the Baltimore Orioles?

EMILY: I've heard of the teams, but I've never thought about the birds they are named after.

JOE: I like the Baltimore Orioles. They are named after Maryland's state bird, and the team's uniforms are orange and black, just like the colors of the oriole.

EMILY: What about the Cardinals? I thought the state bird of Missouri was the bluebird, not the cardinal.

JOE: Yes, but the state bird of Illinois is the cardinal. Maybe there is some connection because St. Louis is so close to Illinois.

EMILY: Maybe. Anyway, I like the red color in their uniforms.

1. State one fact presented in this scene.

____

2. How would you prove this fact?

____

3. State another fact presented in this scene.

____

4. How would you prove this fact?

____

5. State one opinion presented in this scene. How do you know it is an opinion?

____

____

Home Activity Your child read a short passage and identified statements of fact and opinion. Read an article in a newspaper or magazine together and identify the statements of fact in the article. Then ask your child how he or she could prove the facts.

Name ______________________________

Fact and Opinion

- **Statements of fact** can be proved true or false. They can be proved by reading, observing, or asking an expert.
- **Statements of opinion** are judgments or beliefs. They cannot be proved true or false, but they can be *supported* by facts and logic.

Directions Read the following passage. Then complete the diagram by identifying statements of fact and statements of opinion.

Marnie loved hummingbirds. She first saw one while visiting her grandmother. Her grandmother had a hummingbird feeder hanging next to her window. Marnie could watch the tiny birds for hours. She thought they were so colorful and pretty. She could hardly believe they were only a few inches in length.

She was captivated by their amazing ability to hover like helicopters at the feeder. She was delighted that they could fly backwards and straight up and down. When Marnie looked up hummingbirds in her grandmother's encyclopedia, she found out that they can beat their wings as fast as 80 beats per second.

Marnie was captivated by the hummingbirds' amazing ability to hover like helicopters.

Which part of statement is opinion?

1. ______________________________

Which part of statement is fact?

2. ability to ______________________________

How to support?

3. Ask people if they think ______________________________

How to prove?

4. Research ______________________________

5. Write another statement of opinion you read in the passage.

____

Home Activity Your child identified the statements of fact and the statements of opinion in a reading passage. Research a type of bird together and then have your child make statements of opinion about the bird.

Name ____________________

Card Catalog/Library Database

A **card catalog** and **library database** provides information you need to find a book in the library. The card catalog has drawers with cards in them. The cards provide information about a book, including its **author, title, subject,** and its **call number.** You can search a catalog by author, title, or subject. A library database is the online version of a card catalog.

Directions Look at the starting search screen for a library database. Then answer the questions below.

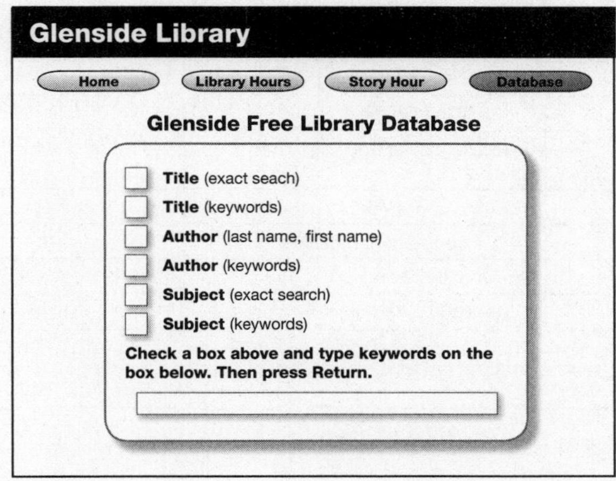

1. Which box would you check to find a book about crows? Which keywords would you type?

____

2. Which box would you check to find the novel titled *Watership Down*? Which keywords would you type?

____

____

3. Which box would you check to find a book by Jean Craighead George? Which keywords would you type?

____

____

4. Which box would you check to find a book with *crows* in its title? Which keywords would you type?

____

5. Which box would you check to find a book about the migration of crows? Which keywords would you type?

____

____

Name ______________________________

Directions Look at the search results from a library database. Then answer the questions below.

Glenside Library

Home | Library Hours | Story Hour | Database

Glenside Free Library Database

Search results for **Title** containing **crows**

8 entries found Results page **1** of 1

Number	Title	Year	Status
1	Crows	1985	on shelf
2	The Crows and the Serpent	1996	on shelf
3	Crows Can't Count	1992	checked out
4	Crows, Jays, Ravens, and Their Relatives	1977	on shelf
5	A Crow's Journey	1996	reserved
6	Crow's Long Scratch of Sound	1966	on shelf
7	Crows of the World	1996	checked out
8	Crows Over a Wheatfield	1988	on shelf

6. These results are from a search for a title containing the word *crows.* How can you tell?

____

7. How many entries were found for this search? How many are shown on this page?

____

8. If you wanted to check out *Crows of the World* today, would you be able to? How do you know?

____

____

9. Which book is reserved? What do you think it means for a book to be reserved?

____

____

10. Why does *When Crowbar Came* not appear on this list?

____

____

Home Activity Your child learned about using a library database. Go to the library or check online for a library database with your child. Then search a topic you are both interested in.

Name

Family Times

Summary

The Universe

Scientists have new ways of studying stars, planets, and solar systems. They can observe planets forming and stars being born. Beyond the Milky Way galaxy, scientists think that there are at least one hundred billion galaxies. Eventually, even the mysteries of black holes and quasars may be understood.

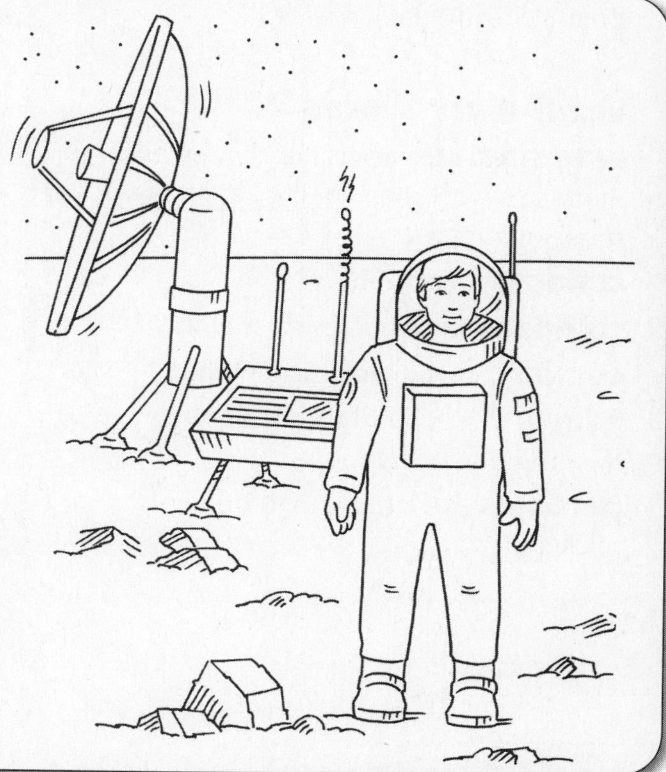

Activity

Galaxy Greetings Imagine that you could travel anywhere in outer space. What would you want to see? What are you most curious about? What do you think you would learn? Talk over these questions with your family and compare your responses.

Comprehension Skill

Main Idea and Details

Find the **topic** of a paragraph or article by asking what it is about. Find the **main idea** by looking for the most important idea about the topic. To help find the main idea, notice supporting **details** that tell more. Details are smaller pieces of information about the main idea.

Activity

The Big Idea Play an idea game with your family. Have one player choose a topic and then give pieces of information that all relate to that topic. See who can guess the topic first.

Lesson Vocabulary

Words to Know

Knowing the meanings of these words is important to reading *The Universe*. Practice using these words.

Vocabulary Words

astronomers experts in the science that deals with the sun, moon, planets, stars, and galaxies

collapse to cave in

collide to strike violently together

compact firmly packed together

galaxy a group of billions of stars forming one system.

particles extremely small units of matter

Grammar

Regular and Irregular Plural Nouns

You can form regular **plural nouns** by adding *–s* or *–es* to the singular noun. However, some plural nouns are formed in unusual ways. For example, some words, such as *knife*, form the plural by changing *f* to *v* and adding *–es*: *knives.* Other words form the plural by changing a vowel or staying the same. Because there is no easy way to predict how these irregular plurals change their spelling, they must be memorized instead. *For example: man/men, sheep/sheep, child/children, cactus/cacti.*

Activity

Pick Plurals Play a game with your family in two teams. Each team should make a list of singular nouns for the other team to make plural. See how well you score. Use the dictionary to judge the answers.

Practice Tested Spelling Words

Name ____

Main Idea and Details

- The **topic** is what a paragraph or article is about.
- The **main idea** is the most important idea about the topic.
- **Details** are pieces of information that explain or support the main idea.

Directions Read the following passage. Then complete the diagram with the topic, the main idea, and details from the passage.

The North Star has been and still is an important tool for travelers. Before navigational instruments were developed, many sailors used the North Star to navigate. Measuring angles between themselves and the star allows people to determine their location at sea. Hikers and other outdoor enthusiasts still use the North Star to find their way in the wilderness. The North Star is easy to see if you know where to look in the sky. It is quite bright and is the last star in the tail of the Little Dipper.

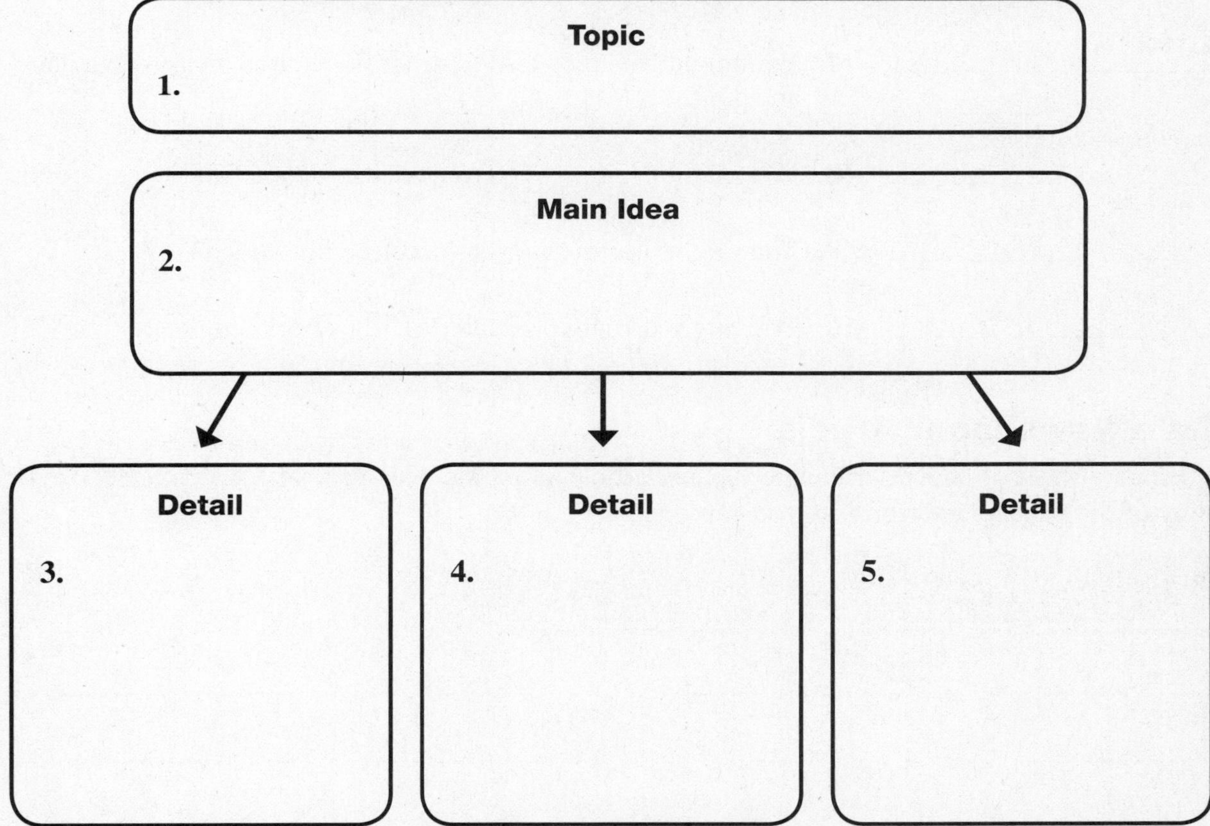

Home Activity Your child identified the main idea and details of a nonfiction passage. Work with your child to identify the main idea and details of each paragraph in an article about stars or planets.

Name ___________________________________

Vocabulary

Directions Choose the word from the box that best matches each definition. Write the word on the line.

Check the Words You Know

- ___astronomers
- ___collapse
- ___collide
- ___compact
- ___galaxy
- ___particles

_________________ **1.** firmly packed together

_________________ **2.** to cave in

_________________ **3.** to hit or strike violently together

_________________ **4.** extremely small units of matter

_________________ **5.** scientists who study the sun, moon, planets, stars, etc.

Directions Choose the word from the box that best matches each clue. Write the word on the line.

_________________ **6.** You might use this word to describe something packed together.

_________________ **7.** You might use this word to describe what two cars do in an accident.

_________________ **8.** You might use this word to describe what a folding chair does.

_________________ **9.** You might use this word to describe the Milky Way.

_________________ **10.** You might use this word to describe specks of dust.

Write a Newspaper Article

On a separate sheet of paper, write a newspaper article about the discovery of a new planet. Use as many of the vocabulary words as you can.

School + Home **Home Activity** Your child identified and used vocabulary words from *The Universe.* Make up a story with your child about outer space. Use as many of the vocabulary words as you can.

Name ______________________________

Vocabulary • Word Structure

- Many words in English are based on **Greek** and **Latin roots.** Sometimes you can use these roots to figure out the meaning of an unfamiliar word.
- The Greek root *astro-* means "star." The Greek root *geo-* means "earth." The Greek root *–ology* means "the study of." The Greek word *nautes* means "sailor." The Latin word *spiritus* means "soul, courage, vigor." The Latin root *–mit* means "send." The Latin prefix *trans-* means "across, over."

Directions Read the following passage. Then answer the questions below.

Until astronauts are able to safely visit Mars, we are able to familiarize ourselves with "the red planet" from images sent to Earth by satellites and from the Mars exploration rovers, *Spirit* and *Opportunity*. The two rovers are clever robots that function like geologists on the surface of Mars. As the rovers move over Mars's surface, they take pictures and transmit them back to Earth. The pictures are of hills and valleys, rocks and boulders, and even particles of sand. An important discovery made by the rovers is that Mars probably had water on its surface a very long time ago.

It won't be long before the two rovers wear out. There is no way to return them to Earth to be fixed. Even though they won't last forever, *Spirit* and *Opportunity* have helped us know more about the galaxy beyond our own planet.

1. What can you tell about the meaning of *astronaut* from its Greek roots?

____

2. How do you think the definition of *spiritus* relates to the rover named *Spirit*?

____

3. What do the Latin prefix and root in *transmit* tell you about the word's meaning?

____

____

4. Based on the meanings of the Greek roots of the word, what do you think the Mars rovers do to function as *geologists*?

____

5. Write as many words as you can think of that use the roots *astro-*. If you cannot think of any words by yourself, use the dictionary for help.

____

Home Activity Your child identified and used Greek and Latin roots to understand new words in a passage. Work with your child to identify unfamiliar words in an article by examining their Greek or Latin roots.

Name ______________________________

Generalization

Directions Read the article. Then answer the questions below.

Many people are fascinated by outer space. School children learn about our solar system in school. Television and radio announcers tell us what to watch for in the night sky. They tell us when the planets are brightest and which ones we can see with the naked eye. For years, people have thought that there might be life on one of the other planets. However, space explorations have not found life on other planets—yet.

Mars seems to be one of the planets people are most fascinated by. It is the fourth planet from the sun and is one of the smaller planets. People often call it the red planet because of its color. Science fiction writers have often used Mars as a setting for their stories. More fantastic than fiction, the Mars rover expedition has sent two robots to explore the surface of Mars. Now we can see actual pictures of the surface of another planet.

1. State one generalization given in the beginning of the passage.

____

____

2. State one fact that supports this as a valid generalization.

____

____

3. State another fact that supports this as a valid generalization.

____

____

4. State another generalization in this passage.

____

____

5. Is this a valid generalization? Why or why not?

____

____

Home Activity Your child has identified generalization in a short passage. Read a short story or article about astronomy with your child. Ask him or her to identify the generalizations and to decide if they are valid or faulty.

Main Idea and Details

- The **topic** is what a paragraph or article is about.
- The **main idea** is the most important idea about the topic.
- **Details** are pieces of information that explain or support the main idea.

Directions Read the following passage. Then answer the questions below.

NASA selects astronaut candidates with both civilian and military backgrouds. Once a candidate is chosen, he or she must go through a very challenging training program for one year. After completing the training course, the candidate joins the astronaut corps. About one year later, he or she may be assigned to a flight.

Once an astronaut has completed the basic training, he or she trains in a specialized area. The astronaut can train as a pilot astronaut, a mission specialist, or a payload specialist. The pilot is in charge of the shuttle, crew, and mission. The mission specialist monitors the shuttle's food, water, and fuel. He or she also conducts experiments and spacewalks. The payload specialist is in charge of equipment unique to the shuttle and its mission.

1. Write the topic of this passage in two or three words.

____

2. What is the main idea of the passage?

____

____

3. What are two or three key words that helped you determine the main idea?

____

4. What are some details that support the main idea?

____

____

5. Write a sentence about why you think an astronaut must go through so much training.

____

____

Home Activity Your child identified the main idea and supporting details of a short passage. He or she picked out key words that helped to determine the main idea. Read an article about space exploration with your child and pick out the key words that help identify the main idea.

Name ______________________________

Main Idea and Details

- The **topic** is what a paragraph or article is about.
- The **main idea** is the most important idea about the topic.
- **Details** are pieces of information that explain or support the main idea.

Directions Read the following passage. Then complete the diagram with the topic, the main idea, and details from the passage.

Our solar system is part of the Milky Way galaxy. When we look up on a clear, dark night, we see some of the billions of stars that are part of this galaxy. There are three major parts in this galaxy. The disk contains newer stars such as the sun. The halo contains the oldest stars in the galaxy. The center of the galaxy is obscured by dust. Recent interest in the center has focused on the possibility of a massive black hole there. This galaxy still holds many surprises for us to discover in the future.

Topic

1. ______________________________

Main Idea

2. The Milky Way ______________________________

____

Supporting Detail

3. There is a disk that contains ______________________________.

Supporting Detail

4. There is a halo ______________________________.

Supporting Detail

5. There is a ______________________________.

Home Activity Your child identified the main idea and supporting details of a nonfiction passage. Read an encyclopedia or magazine article about the Milky Way. Have your child identify the main ideas and supporting details in two of the paragraphs.

Name ______________________

Skim and Scan

To **scan** is to move one's eyes quickly down the page, seeking specific words and phrases. Scanning is used to find out if a resource will answer a reader's questions. Once a reader has scanned a document, he or she might go back and skim it. To **skim** a document is to read the first and last paragraphs as well as using headings, summaries, and other organizers as you move down the page. Skimming is used to quickly identify the main idea. You might also read the first sentence of each paragraph.

Directions Scan the phone book entries. Then answer the questions below.

ICE & ICE CUBES

Ken's Locker
2001 S. Maplewood Dr. 555-9001

Mack's Ice of Homewood
319 E. Harvey Ave. 555-0902

ICE SKATING RINKS

See Skating Rinks and Parks

ILLUSTRATORS

See Artists, Commercial

IMPORTERS

Safari Imports
938 W. River Dr. 555-3434

INCOME TAX PREPARATION

See Accountants, Certified Public; Accountants, Public; Tax Preparation Services

IN-HOME CARE SERVICES

See Home Health Care and Services

1. What do you need to do if you want to find an illustrator?

____

2. What do you have to do to find the number and address of the nearest ice skating rink?

____

3. Where can you buy ice on Harvey Ave.?

____

____

4. Where would you go if you wanted to buy a gift imported from another country?

____

____

5. Can you find the phone number for a Certified Public Accountant on this page? Where would you look?

____

____

Name ____________________

Directions Skim the passage by reading the headings and the first sentence of each paragraph. Then answer the questions below.

MERCURY

Mercury is the second smallest of the planets. It is not much larger than our moon. It even looks like our moon. At night Mercury can only be seen for a brief time before sunrise and after sunset. Because it is so close to the sun, its temperatures soar to over 800 degrees Fahrenheit.

Mercury has many craters like our moon. It has a huge basin called the *Caloris Basin.* It was formed when a meteorite crashed into it billions of years ago.

VENUS

Venus is similar in size to Earth. It is very bright and is seen as a morning star and an evening star. Venus is so bright because it is covered with clouds that reflect the sunlight very well.

Venus comes closer to Earth than any other planet. Its atmosphere is very different than Earth's.

6. Which two planets is this passage about? How can you tell?

____

____

7. Will this passage help you answer questions about Pluto? Why or why not?

____

____

8. Will this passage help you answer questions about Earth? Explain.

____

____

9. If you were looking for information about craters, would this passage help? Explain.

____

____

10. If you needed to find information to compare the size of Venus and Mercury, would this passage help you? Explain.

____

Home Activity Your child learned about scanning and skimming to help find a main idea or information. Look at a newspaper or magazine with your child and have him or her skim it to find the main idea. Then ask your child to scan it for a particular piece of information.

Name

Family Times

Summary

Dinosaur Ghosts

In 1947, scientists uncover the bones of dozens of *Coelophysis* dinosaurs in New Mexico. However, the cause of the dinosaurs' death is a mystery. The scientists rule out mudslides, volcanoes, asteroids, poisoned water, floods, and drought. Then they find a theory that works: a drought followed by a flood.

Activity

Back in Time Imagine that you can go back in time more than 200 million years. What do you think the world would be like? What is the value of finding out? With members of your family, talk over these questions and compare your responses.

Comprehension Skill

Main Idea and Details

The **topic** of a piece of writing is what the entire piece is about. Usually the topic can be expressed in just a few words. The **main idea** is the most important idea about this topic. Sometimes an author will state a main idea directly. If it is not given, you must figure it out yourself. Supporting **details** are smaller pieces of information that tell more about the main idea.

Activity

The Big Idea With a member of your family, take turns telling fables or short stories that contain a moral or a lesson. At the end of your story, ask your audience, "What do you think is the big idea?" Have them identify the main idea, as well as several supporting details from the story.

Lesson Vocabulary

Words to Know

Knowing the meanings of these words is important to reading *Dinosaur Ghosts*. Practice using these words.

Vocabulary Words

fragile easily broken, damaged, or destroyed

poisonous containing a dangerous substance; very harmful to life and health

prey animal or animals hunted and killed for food by another animal

sluggish lacking energy or vigor

specimens examples of a group; samples

treacherous very dangerous while seeming to be safe

volcanic of or caused by a volcano

Grammar

Possessive Nouns

Possessive nouns show ownership or that a quality belongs to someone or something. They can be either singular or plural. You can make most singular nouns possessive by adding *–'s. For example: canyon/canyon's.* For plural nouns that end in *s*, form the possessive by adding an apostrophe. *For example: scientists/scientists'.* For plural nouns that do not end in *s*, add *–'s. For example: children/children's.* Never use an apostrophe to form a plural noun. An apostrophe shows ownership, not number.

Activity

Possessive Collage With a family member, clip several singular and plural nouns from newspaper or magazine headlines. Make a collage by gluing these words onto a sheet of poster board. Near each word in the collage, write the noun's possessive form.

Practice Tested Spelling Words

____________	____________	____________	____________
____________	____________	____________	____________
____________	____________	____________	____________
____________	____________	____________	____________
____________	____________	____________	____________

Name ______________________________

Main Idea and Details

- The **topic** of a piece of writing can usually be stated in a few words.
- In a piece of writing, the **main idea** is the most important idea about the topic. Sometimes the main idea is given in a sentence. If it is not, you must figure it out on your own.
- **Details** are pieces of information that explain or support the main idea.

Directions Read the following passage. Then complete the diagram below.

When dinosaurs roamed Earth, the climate was very different from what it is today. The day was slightly shorter because Earth revolved at a faster pace. Earth received less radiation from the sun, and the atmosphere had a greater level of carbon dioxide in it. The carbon dioxide caused Earth's temperature to be warmer than it is today. At the beginning of the Mesozoic era when the first dinosaurs developed, the continents were joined together. The single ocean was much higher, and there was no ice at the poles.

Main Idea

1.

Details

2.

3.

4.

5.

Home Activity Your child read a short passage and identified its main idea and supporting details. Work with your child to identify the main idea and supporting details of individual paragraphs in a magazine article or encyclopedia article.

Name ______________________________

Vocabulary

Directions Choose the word from the box that best matches each definition. Write the word on the line.

Check the Words You Know

- ___fragile
- ___poisonous
- ___prey
- ___sluggish
- ___specimens
- ___treacherous
- ___volcanic

______________ **1.** containing a dangerous substance

______________ **2.** lacking energy or vigor

______________ **3.** very dangerous while seeming to be safe

______________ **4.** of or caused by a volcano

______________ **5.** easily broken, damaged, or destroyed

Directions Choose the word from the box that best completes each sentence. Write the word on the line.

6. The hungry tiger saw its ______________ running away through the high grass.

7. John collects ______________ of all types of butterflies.

8. Until she broke out in a rash, Joan did not realize that the plant was ______________.

9. Without water, Jackie became ______________ at the end of the long race.

10. She was afraid the ______________ chair would break under his weight.

Write a Friendly Letter

On a separate sheet of paper, write a letter to a friend describing a fossil you found while hiking. Use as many vocabulary words as you can.

School + Home **Home Activity** Your child identified and used vocabulary words from *Dinosaur Ghosts*. Read a newspaper, magazine, or encyclopedia article about volcanoes. Work with your child to identify unknown words and use context clues to determine their meaning.

Name ______________________

Vocabulary • Word Structure

- A **suffix** is a word part added to the end of a base word to change its meaning or the way it is used in a sentence. You can use suffixes to help you figure out the meanings of unfamiliar words.
- The suffix *–ic* means "related to," as in *democratic;* the suffix *–ous* means "full of," as in *courageous.*

Directions Read the following passage. Then answer the questions below.

Steve and Jose were preparing their project for the Academic Olympics. The competition was being held the next day. They were preparing a display of poisonous plants with descriptions of each plant. To collect specimens, they had gone on a hike through treacherous terrain. They were very careful not to touch any of the plants they found with their bare hands. The most unusual plant was quite fragile and was growing in volcanic soil. With this plant, they thought, they were sure to win first place.

1. *Academic* and *volcanic* both end with the same suffix. How does *–ic* change the meaning of the base words?

____

____

2. What part of speech is *volcano*? What part of speech does it become when you add the suffix *–ic*?

____

3. *Poisonous* and *treacherous* both end with the same suffix. How does *–ous* change the meaning of the base words?

____

____

4. What part of speech is the word *poison*? What part of speech does it become when you add the suffix *–ous*?

____

5. Think of a noun or verb that can be changed into an adjective by adding *–ous* or *–ic*. Write a sentence that uses both the base word and the word with the suffix.

____

____

Home Activity Your child read a short passage and identified suffixes. Read a story or article with your child, and ask him or her to point out words that have suffixes. Ask how the suffix changes the word.

Name ____________________

Graphic Sources

Directions Study the graph. Then answer the questions below.

Mesozoic Era—The Era of Reptiles

Activity	Dinosaurs Begin	Dinosaurs Expand	Dinosaurs More Diverse, Then Die Out
Period	Triassic	Jurassic	Cretaceous

Millions of Years: 250 240 230 220 210 200 190 180 170 160 150 140 130 120 110 100 90 80 70 60

1. What information is given about dinosaurs on the time line?

2. During what period were the dinosaurs more diverse?

3. How long was the age of reptiles from beginning to end? What was this era called?

4. Which was the longest period in the era? How long was it?

5. If dinosaurs appeared on Earth about 225 million years ago, about how many years ago did they disappear?

School + Home **Home Activity** Your child has used a time line to answer questions. Find a time line or graph in a newspaper or magazine, and work with your child to determine what information is presented in it.

Name

Main Idea and Details

- The **topic** of a piece of writing can usually be stated in a few words.
- In a piece of writing, the **main idea** is the most important idea about the topic. Sometimes the main idea is given in a sentence. If it is not, you must figure it out on your own.
- **Details** are pieces of information that explain or support the main idea.

Directions Read the following passage. Then answer the questions below.

Acid rain is a result of air pollution. It is formed when gases are released that combine with water in the atmosphere to form an acid. The airborne acids eventually fall to earth in the form of acid rain. Acid rain damages the soil by making it acidic, and causing tree growth to slow. Acid rain can pollute water and poison plants. In addition, it can burn holes in the waxy coating on tree leaves and needles, causing photosynthesis to slow. The trees become more vulnerable to disease and insect damage.

1. In one or two words, what is the topic of the passage?

2. What is the main idea of the passage?

3. What is one important detail that supports the main idea?

4. List a second detail from the passage that supports the main idea.

5. What is a fact you already knew about air pollution or acid rain that you could use to support the main idea of the passage?

Home Activity Your child read a short passage and identified its main idea and supporting details. Select a magazine or newspaper article to read with your child. After you read, identify the main idea and supporting details in the article.

Name ____________________

Main Idea and Details

- The **topic** of a piece of writing can usually be stated in a few words.
- In a piece of writing, the **main idea** is the most important idea about the topic. Sometimes the main idea is given in a sentence. If it is not, you must figure it out on your own.
- **Details** are pieces of information that explain or support the main idea.

Directions Read the following passage. Then complete the diagram below.

When you look at the moon at night, it's hard to believe that it doesn't give off its own light. What you see is sunlight bouncing off the moon. When the moon is between Earth and the sun, the back part of the moon is lit. We can't see that part from Earth. At that time, the part of the moon facing Earth is dark, so that you can't see the moon when you look at the sky.

Main Idea

1. The moon is visible or hidden from Earth ____________________

____

Details

2. The moon does not ____________________

3. We see the moon because ____________________

4. The moon appears dark ____________________

5. When the moon cannot be seen from Earth, ____________________

School + Home

Home Activity Your child identified the main idea and its supporting details in a short passage. Work with your child to write a paragraph containing a main idea and three supporting details about a local environmental issue.

Name ______________________________

Order Form/Application

Order forms and **applications** are charts with columns and spaces in which you can write or type. An order form is the means by which a person can purchase merchandise by completing a form and emailing or sending it to a company. An application is a form by which a person can apply for a job. Application forms ask for identifying information such as name, address, and phone number, and also ask for the person's educational and job history.

Directions Answer the questions below about the following order form.

Search [ ]

MYSTERY HOUSE ORDER FORM

Click SUBMIT when you have completed this form.

Item Number	Item	Quantity	Price
13715	Big Bracelet		$
20166	Big Ring		$
			+ $5 shipping and handling
		TOTAL PRICE	$

BILLING ADDRESS

* Name
* Street Address
* City
* State   * ZIP
* Country
Phone
* Email address

PAYMENT METHOD

* Type of Credit Card
* Account Number
* Expiration Date

SHIPPING ADDRESS

☐ Check this box if same as billing address

* Name
* Street Address
* City
* State   * ZIP
* Country
Phone

Your comments and messages here.

* REQUIRED FIELD

Submit

1. Why is there space for two names and addresses on this order form? When would you provide only one?

____

____

2. If you are buying an item, what information do you need to specify on the order form?

____

3. If you wish to submit an online order at Mystery House, what payment options do you have?

____

4. How is ordering an item online different from ordering an item from a mail-order catalog?

____

____

5. If you are ordering from this web page, what information is optional?

____

Name ______________________________

Directions Fill out the following application.

<table>
<tr><td colspan="2">1. PERSONAL INFORMATION
Name ____________________
Address ____________________
____
Telephone ____________________</td><td></td></tr>
<tr><td colspan="2">2. EDUCATION
Name of school ____________________
____
Highest grade completed ____________________</td><td>Include the name of your school and the last grade you completed.</td></tr>
<tr><td>3. EXPERIENCE
Job title ____________
____
Employer ____________
____________</td><td>Duties ____________
Dates of Employment
____
____________</td><td>Include information about jobs you may have had such as babysitting, mowing lawns, and raking leaves. You may also include volunteer experience.</td></tr>
<tr><td>4. REFERENCE
Name ____________
____
Relationship
____________</td><td>Telephone ____________
____
Number of years known
____________</td><td>A reference is a person who can tell about the kind of person you are. List someone who knows you well enough to explain that you are a good worker.</td></tr>
<tr><td colspan="2">5. WHY DO YOU WANT THIS JOB?
____
____________________</td><td>Pretend you are applying for a job selling books at a local book fair. Explain why you would like that job.</td></tr>
</table>

School + Home **Home Activity** Your child learned about filling out an order form and an application form. Practice filling out an order form with your child either online or in a catalog.

Name

Family Times

Summary

A Week in the 1800s

A group of modern children step into a historic settlement in Canada to see what life is like in the 1800s. They use the language of the time, dress in typical clothing of the era, and do work that would be expected of them. At the end of a week, they all have a new appreciation for life today.

Activity

Things to Do Yesterday Imagine that you were alive two hundred years ago. Write out a schedule that shows what your day might be like. Then create a list of items from your everyday life today that did not exist in the 1800s. Compare your schedule and list with those of a family member, discussing how different life was two centuries ago.

Comprehension Skill

Graphic Sources

Graphic sources such as charts, graphs, and time lines show information visually. Previewing graphic sources in a text will help you identify and understand the topic. As you read, compare the graphic sources with information in the text. Sometimes creating your own graphic sources while you read will help you understand and remember the material in the text.

Activity

Pictures and Words Find a newspaper article that contains text and a graphic source. After looking over the graphic source, read the article aloud with a family member. Talk about how the graphic source helps you understand the article's topic.

Lesson Vocabulary

Words to Know

Knowing the meanings of these words is important to reading *A Week in the 1800s.* Practice using these words.

Vocabulary Words

counselor person who gives advice; an advisor
identity who or what you are
physical of or for the body
surplus amount over and above what is needed
technology the use of scientific knowledge to control physical objects and forces

Grammar

Action and Linking Verbs

An **action verb** tells what a subject does. *For example: The boy works.* "Works" is an *action verb* because it tells what the boy *is doing*. A **linking verb** joins a subject with a word or words in the predicate that tell something about the subject, such as what the subject is or how the subject feels. *For example: The boy is a student.* "Is" is a *linking verb* because it links "boy" (the subject) to "a student" (the predicate). Linking verbs include forms of *be* (*am*, *are*, *is*, *was*, *were*), as well as *seem*, *feel*, and *become*.

Activity

Verb Trade Play this game with two family teams. Take turns picking short sentences out of a story. If the verb in a sentence is an action verb, change it to a linking verb. If the verb is a linking verb, change it to an action verb. Use the same subject for your new sentence, but add or subtract other words as needed to give the new sentence meaning. *For example: Tom visited the blacksmith; Tom was the blacksmith in his town.*

Practice Tested Spelling Words

____	____	____	____
____	____	____	____
____	____	____	____
____	____	____	____
____	____	____	____

Name____________________

Graphic Sources

- **Graphic sources**, such as charts, diagrams, and time lines, show information visually.
- As you read, compare written words to the graphic sources for a better understanding.

Directions Study the time line below about inventions. Then answer the questions.

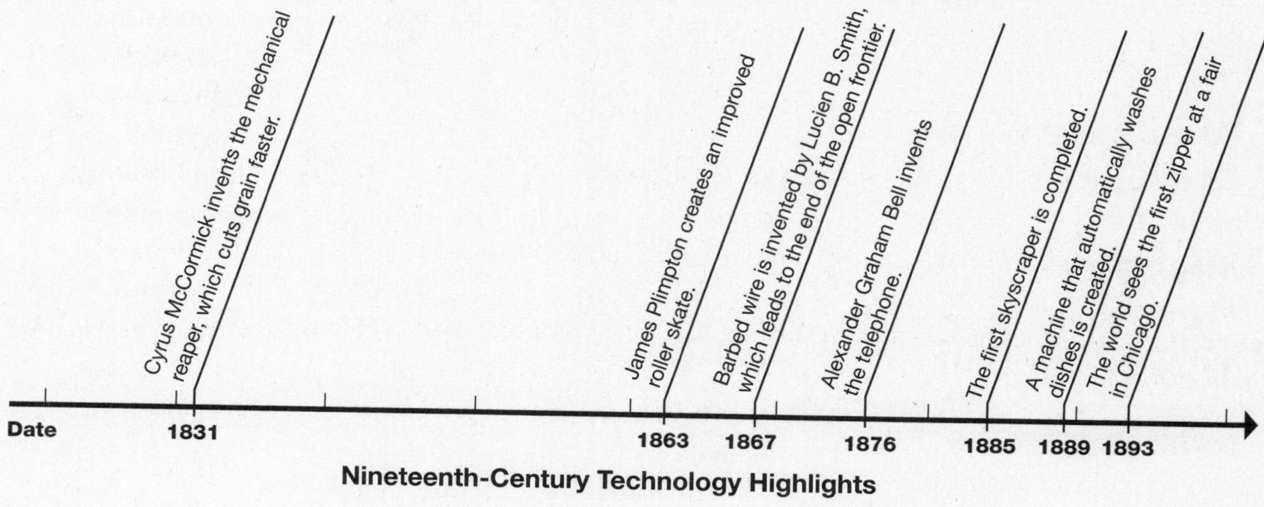

Nineteenth-Century Technology Highlights

1. What information is shown on this time line? Would you find technology invented in 1912 on this time line? Why or why not?

____

____

2. Do you think this time line includes all of the technology invented in the nineteenth century? Why or why not?

____

3. How many years passed between the invention of the reaping machine and the invention of the dishwasher?

____

4. Which invention do you think is the most useful to people today? Why do you think so?

____

5. How do you think an author would structure a magazine article that includes this time line?

____

____

Home Activity Your child used a time line to learn information visually. Look in an encyclopedia for an article about an invention. Look at any graphic sources that accompany the article and discuss how the graphic sources help you understand the article.

Name ______________________________

Vocabulary

Directions Choose the word from the box that best matches each definition. Write the word on the line.

Check the Words You Know

- ___counselor
- ___identity
- ___physical
- ___surplus
- ___technology

______________ **1.** person who gives advice

______________ **2.** the use of scientific knowledge to control physical objects and forces

______________ **3.** who or what you are

______________ **4.** of or for the body

______________ **5.** amount over and above what is needed

Directions Choose the word from the box that best completes each sentence. Write the word on the line shown to the left.

______________ **6.** The store had too many toys because they received a ___ shipment.

______________ **7.** Margaret kept her ___ a secret at the costume party.

______________ **8.** There is a lot of ___ work to be done on a farm.

______________ **9.** He visited a ___ to get some good advice about handling stress.

______________ **10.** As ___ improved, it became easier to get work done on the farm.

Write a Journal Entry

On a separate sheet of paper write a journal entry you might make after a long day of working on a farm in the 1800s. Use as many vocabulary words as you can.

Home Activity Your child identified and used vocabulary words from *A Week in the 1800s*. Read an article with your child about the Civil War. Ask your child to point out unfamiliar words. Help your child guess their definitions, and then check the meanings using a dictionary or glossary.

Name ____________________

Vocabulary • Dictionary/Glossary

- A **dictionary** is a book of words and their meanings.
- A **glossary** is a short dictionary at the back of a book. It includes definitions of words used in the book.

Directions Read the following passage. Then use a dictionary to answer the questions below.

Farmers in the 1800s did not have an easy job. Farming required a great deal of hard, physical labor. A harvest might provide just enough food for the farmer's family with very little surplus. Today, new technology helps make farming more efficient. Using mechanical farm equipment can result in less physical labor and a surplus of crops. Because a farmer's identity is closely linked to the success of his or her farm, many farmers are eager to take courses in argriculture. These courses can help them to learn how to improve their farms. To find the right courses, they can visit a college counselor who knows about the courses that are being offered.

1. Find *physical* in a dictionary. What part of speech is it?

____

____

2. Find *surplus* in a dictionary. What does it mean? Why do you think it is better for farmers to have a surplus of crops?

____

____

3. Find the word *identity* in a dictionary. Which meaning fits this passage?

____

____

4. Find *agriculture* in a dictionary. What does it mean?

____

____

5. Find *counselor* in a dictionary. What synonym could replace *counselor* in this passage?

____

Home Activity Your child used a dictionary to understand new words in a passage. Work with your child to identify unfamiliar words in an article or story. Look up these words in a dictionary. Go over the pronunciation, part of speech, and meaning of these words with your child. See how many new words your child can learn.

Name______________________________

Compare and Contrast

Directions Read the article. Then answer the questions below.

People on the frontier did many things for themselves that we don't have to do today. To make sure their homes were heated, they gathered and chopped wood, carried it home, and burned it in a fireplace or stove. Today we don't leave our homes to find fuel because we just turn on the heater.

People on the frontier did not have prepared and packaged foods they could buy at the market. If they wanted some cornbread and there was no general store nearby, they had to grow and dry the corn, grind it, and mix it with the other ingredients, which they had to make themselves. They couldn't just open a box of cornbread mix! Also, they churned their own butter and pressed their own apples for cider.

Can you imagine all this work? Life on the frontier was definitely more time consuming!

1. What are the differences between how people on the frontier heated their homes and how we heat our homes today?

____

____

2. How do you think changes in the weather affected the lives of people on the frontier?

____

____

3. Compare the way people prepare food today with the way they did on the frontier.

____

____

4. Think of a favorite food. How do you think you would make this food if you lived on the frontier?

____

____

5. Interview an older relative about what school was like during his or her childhood. On a separate sheet of paper, compare and contrast your relative's experiences with your own.

Home Activity Your child read a short passage and compared and contrasted modern life with life on the frontier. Discuss with your child what it was like when you were growing up. How is your childhood similar or different from your child's?

Name ____________________

Graphic Sources

- **Graphic sources**, such as charts, diagrams, and time lines, show information visually.
- As you read, compare written words to the graphic sources for a better understanding.

Directions Study the illustration below. Then answer the questions below.

In the 1800s, settlers moved themselves and their belongings across the country in covered wagons such as the **prairie schooners**. Covered wagons were pulled by oxen, horses, or mules.

1. In what type of article might you find this illustration?

____

____

2. How does the caption help you to understand the illustration?

____

____

3. How does the illustration enhance the information in the caption?

____

4. What do you think was the purpose of the falling tongue and the neck yoke?

____

____

5. If you were writing an article using this illustration, how would you structure it?

____

____

Home Activity Your child studied an illustration and caption and answered questions about it. With your child, discuss how graphic sources help us read and learn.

Name ______________________________

Graphic Sources

- **Graphic sources**, such as charts, diagrams, and time lines, show information visually.
- As you read, compare written words to the graphic sources for a better understanding.

Directions Study the map. Then answer the questions below.

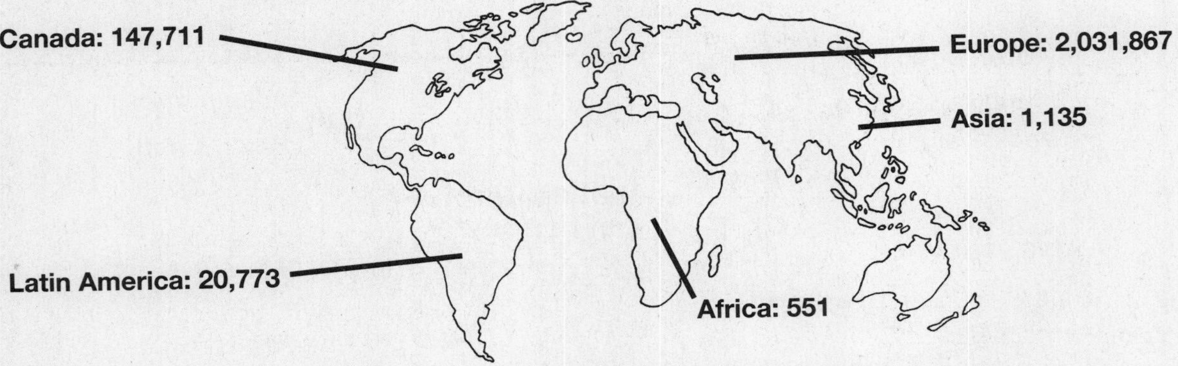

Foreign-Born Population of the United States in 1850

1. What does this map tell you?

____

____

2. What type of article might include a map like this?

____

____

3. From which continent did the most people come to the United States? From which continent did the fewest?

____

4. What does this map tell you about the United States in 1850?

____

____

5. A lot of the information on this map could be shown in a table, graph, or chart. What do you know because it is shown on a map instead?

____

____

Home Activity Your child used a map to answer questions. With your child, research information about a favorite activity. Create a graphic source to show that information.

Name ____________________

Almanac

An **almanac** is a reference source that is published every year and contains up-to-date statistics. It also contains country profiles, information about weather, key events in world history, and lists of recent prize winners in science, literature, and sports.

Directions Study the almanac page below. Use the information on the page to answer the questions that follow.

The United States of America in 2004

POPULATION

Many people live in the United States. It was estimated that 293,655,404 people lived in the country in 2004. About 144,537,408 were males and 149,117,996 were females.

See below for the age breakdown:

Age	Percent of Population
0–14 years	20.7%
15–64 years	66.9%
65 and older	12.4%

GEOGRAPHY

The United States is a large country. The total area is listed below.

The total area of the United States
98,826,630 sq km

The total land area
9,161,923 sq km

The total water area
664,707 sq km

ECONOMICS

People from the United States do business in foreign countries. See below for the percent of the total goods exported and imported to and from other countries to the United States in 2004.

Country	Percent Exported	Percent Imported
Canada	23.4%	17.4%
Mexico	13.5%	12.5%
Japan	7.2%	10.7%
United Kingdom	4.7%	9.3%
Germany	4%	5.3%

Name ____________________

1. In general, what does this almanac page tell you?

2. In what situation do you think you would use an almanac?

3. Why do you think the almanac gives the land and the water area of the nation?

4. What is the difference between the percentage of people over 65 years old and those people between 0 and 14 years?

5. If you were 16 years old, would you be in the largest age group percentage or the smallest?

6. What country imported the least amount of goods from the United States?

7. How much more did Canada export than import?

8. What other information do you think you might find about a country in an almanac?

9. Almanacs are packed with information. How do you think you would find the information quickly?

10. If you wanted to find out how people in the 1800s made their food, would an almanac be a good place to look? Why or why not?

Home Activity Your child learned about using almanacs as resources. Together, imagine you have to add a page in the almanac about your community. What kind information would you include on your page?

Name ______________________________

Family Times

Summary

Good-bye to the Moon

Kepler Masterman is taking a trip from his home on the moon to the strange environment of Earth. He misses his friends, and the trip is a bit strange. However, when he lands he is excited to explore Earth.

Activity

Fast-Forward Imagine that you are living in the future and traveling to another planet. How might you feel on your journey? With a member of your family, brainstorm a list of words to describe your thoughts and feelings about approaching a new world.

Comprehension Skill

Compare/Contrast

To **compare and contrast** is to tell how two or more things are alike and how they are different. Clue words such as *like*, *similarly*, *instead*, *but*, *although*, and *however* are often used to signal comparisons or contrasts.

Activity

Side by Side Place two examples of an object side by side—for example, two pens or two cups. With a family member, compare and contrast these two items.

Lesson Vocabulary

Words to Know

Knowing the meanings of these words is important to reading *Good-bye to the Moon*. Practice using these words.

Vocabulary Words

combustion act or process of burning

dingy lacking brightness or freshness; dirty-looking

negotiate to talk over and arrange terms; confer; consult

traversed passed across, over, or through

waft a breath or puff of air, wind, scent

waning going through its regular reduction in the amount of its visible portion, such as the moon.

Grammar

Subject-Verb Agreement

A **subject** and **verb** must **agree,** or work together in a sentence. In the present tense, a singular subject is paired with a singular verb. *For example: The spaceship moves quickly.* Most singular verbs end in *–s* or *–es.* A plural subject is paired with a plural verb. *For example: Spaceships move quickly.* Plural verbs usually do not end in *–s.* Collective nouns, such as *family* or *class,* are considered singular. *For example: The class goes to the museum every year.* The singular verb form "goes" is used, instead of the plural verb form "go." In sentences with a helping verb and a main verb, the helping verb (a form of *be*) agrees with the subject. *For example: The men are painting.*

Activity

Let's Agree List five verbs that agree with each of the following subjects: *travelers, water, children, father*. Then, with a family member, take turns saying a subject aloud and having the other person supply two or three verbs that agree with it.

Practice Tested Spelling Words

______	______	______	______
______	______	______	______
______	______	______	______
______	______	______	______
______	______	______	______

Name ____________________

Compare and Contrast

- When you **compare and contrast,** you tell how two or more things are alike and how they are different.
- Clue words such as *like, as,* and *similarly* can show similarities. Clue words such as *however* and *instead* can show differences.

Directions Read the following passage. Then complete the diagram below by giving details that compare and contrast the characteristics of Earth and its moon.

If you ever travel to the moon, you will experience low gravity. As you know, both Earth and its moon are spheres. Yet the moon, with a diameter of about 2,000 miles, is only one-quarter the size of Earth. As a result, the moon's gravity is much lower. In fact, it has only one-sixth of Earth's gravity. For that reason, walking on the moon is like bouncing on a mattress.

In 1969, astronauts were delighted to learn how easily they could leap and bounce upon the lunar surface. The difference in gravity also affects how much objects weigh. Objects on Earth weigh six times as much as they do on the moon. In other words, if a person weighs 120 pounds on Earth, he or she would weigh only 20 pounds on the moon!

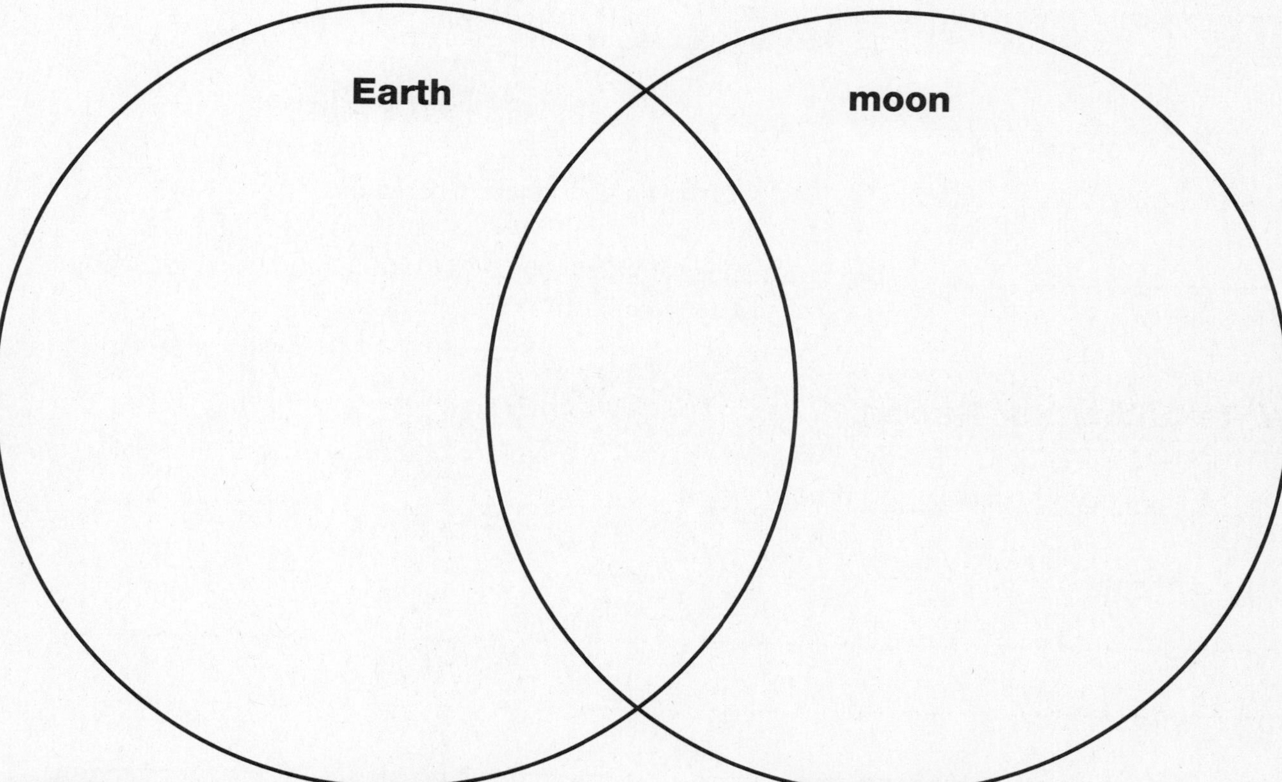

Home Activity Your child used details from a nonfiction passage to compare Earth and its moon. Work with your child to compare and contrast details of individual paragraphs in a magazine article about outer space. Challenge your child to ask questions to clarify points and check understanding.

Name ______________________________

Vocabulary

Directions Choose the word from the box that best matches each definition below. Write the word on the line.

Check the Words You Know

- ___combustion
- ___dingy
- ___negotiate
- ___traversed
- ___waft
- ___waning

__________ **1.** going through its regular reduction in the amount of its visible portion

__________ **2.** passed across, over, or through

__________ **3.** act or process of burning

__________ **4.** lacking brightness or freshness; dirty-looking

__________ **5.** to talk over and arrange terms; confer; consult

Directions Choose the word from the box that best matches each clue below. Write the word on the line.

__________ **6.** This occurs when something burns.

__________ **7.** This might describe a dirty, dark room.

__________ **8.** An example of this is a small breath of perfume.

__________ **9.** This is what you do to make a bargain.

__________ **10.** This happens to the moon as its visible bright side gradually faces away from Earth.

Write a Weather Report

On a separate sheet of paper, write a weather report you might make the day after an unusual weather event. Use as many vocabulary words as you can.

Home Activity Your child identified and used vocabulary words from *Goodbye to the Moon*. Read a story or nonfiction article with your child. Have him or her point out unfamiliar words. Work together to figure out the meaning of each word by using other words that appear near it.

Vocabulary • Context Clues

- When you are reading and see an unfamiliar word, you can use **context clues**, or words around the unfamiliar word, to figure out its meaning.
- Context clues include definitions, explanations, examples, and synonyms.

Directions Read the following passage about outer space. Then answer the questions below.

Gil was at the controls of the space shuttle, and he was under pressure because Governor Otis of the Moon and his son were on board. Suddenly, the smell of combustion reached him. A waft of a burnt odor was coming from the back of the craft. Gil inched his way to the dingy, dirty engine room to check the status. If necessary, he was prepared to consult with Mission Control to negotiate for emergency repairs. As he traversed, or crossed, the space shuttle to the food court, he saw the problem. A meal was burning in the service cell.

"How's everything going?" called the Governor.

"Just great!" Gil answered with a smile as he hurried back to the controls.

1. What does *combustion* mean? What clues help you to determine the meaning?

____

2. What is a *waft*? What clues help you to determine the meaning?

____

____

3. How do context clues help you determine the meaning of *dingy*?

____

____

4. What does *negotiate* mean as it is used in this text? How can you use context clues to determine this meaning?

____

____

5. What does *traversed* mean? What clues help you to determine the meaning?

____

____

Home Activity Your child identified and used context clues to understand unfamiliar words in a passage. Work with your child to identify unfamiliar words in an article or fiction story. Have him or her find context clues to help clarify the meanings of the unfamiliar words.

Name________________________________

Sequence

Directions Read the following story. Then answer the questions below.

On his first lunar trip, Todd took his pet dog aboard the spacecraft. About halfway through the day-long journey, the captain of the shuttle scolded Scout for barking. He said dogs were a nuisance on the moon, but it was too late to send Scout back to Earth.

After they touched down on the moon, Todd and Scout were issued thermal suits to protect them from extreme temperatures. After they got off the spacecraft, they bounced along the dusty lunar surface, enjoying the lack of gravity. Todd was amazed by the craters, ridges, and mountains of the moon's landscape. He threw a ball up in the air for Scout to retrieve, but boy and dog then had to wait for what seemed like minutes for the ball to land! With the low gravity, it took a long time. What fun it was to play in this bouncy place!

Eventually the captain of the shuttle took a turn tossing the ball to Scout too. After this bit of exercise and fun, he said that dogs belonged on the moon after all.

1. What is the first event that happens in this story?

____

2. What happens next? What words help you clarify the sequence of events?

____

____

3. Tell the next three events in sequence.

____

____

____

4. What is the last thing that happens in the story?

____

____

5. On a separate sheet of paper, list the words that give clues to sequence in the story.

Home Activity Your child identified the sequence of events in a fiction story. Together, read a short story. Work together to order the events in sequence, using clue words as well as your prior knowledge.

Name ______________________________

Compare and Contrast

- When you **compare and contrast,** you tell how two or more things are alike and how they are different.
- Clue words such as *like, as,* and *similarly* can show similarities. Clue words such as *however* and *instead* can show differences.

Directions Read the following passage. Then answer the questions below.

Last night, my sister Kara dreamed about life in the year 2120. She saw many wonderful things. For example, in 2120 people wear a wrapping of wire around their heads. These wire wrappings, called personal techno-units, keep people in constant contact with all sources of entertainment and information. No longer is there any need for headphones or portable radios!

People's homes are unlike those of the twenty-first century, as well. In the future, homes are built underground to make the most of solar energy. Also, unlike cars that Kara knows from the present, supersonic shuttles transport people to their destinations in an instant.

Kara and I both wished she could have brought home just one of the inventions of the future!

1. How would you compare the way people get entertainment in the present and in 2120?

____

____

2. How would you contrast a personal techno-unit with a pair of headphones?

____

3. Contrast transportation in the story with transportation now.

____

4. How do homes in the future contrast with homes today?

____

5. Write two good questions you could ask to check your understanding of the story.

____

____

Home Activity Your child compared and contrasted details in a fiction passage. Together, read magazine articles about two distinct historical periods. Work together to compare and contrast the two time periods.

Name ______________________________

Compare and Contrast

- When you **compare and contrast,** you tell how two or more things are alike and how they are different.
- Clue words such as *like, as,* and *similarly* can show similarities. Clue words such as *however* and *instead* can show differences.

Directions Read the following passage. Then complete the diagram by adding details that compare and contrast Diego's activities on Earth and Mars.

If Diego were back home on Earth, he would be hiking and biking. Here on Mars, at least for the moment, he was sitting in the cramped darkness of a space capsule. Nevertheless, he was excited about this space mission with his parents, who were both astronauts. Sure, Diego missed his old friends at home, but in the coming weeks a dozen young people—new friends!—would arrive to join him at the colony on Mars.

Diego had to admit, he longed for the taste of "real" food. One of the only things he dreaded about the time on Mars was three meals a day of freeze-dried food bricks. He was curious about the atmosphere on Mars. The air was thick with dust and wind, and often the temperature soared over one hundred degrees. He remembered that the thermometer at home rarely topped seventy. His usual clothing was jeans, a shirt, and a jacket. Here on Mars, he could play outside, but he would have to remember to wear his insulated oxygen suit.

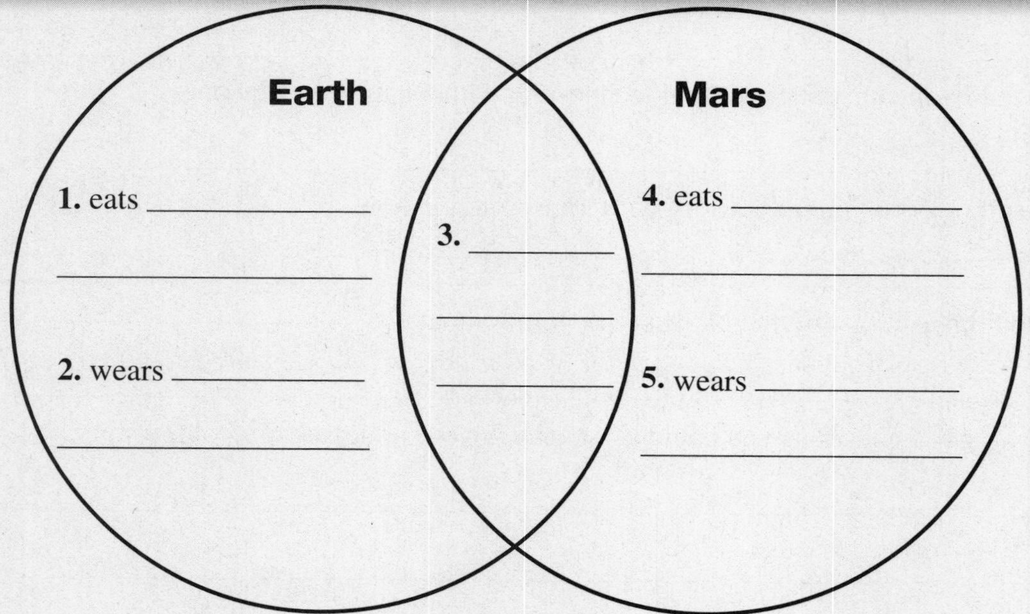

Home Activity Your child compared and contrasted details of a fiction passage. Work with him or her to compare and contrast details from your own lives with details in a story about the past.

Name ______________________________

Dictionary and Glossary

A **dictionary** is a book of words and their meanings. Words are listed in alphabetical order, and each entry shows a word's spelling, syllable parts, pronunciation, and parts of speech. Many entry words contain more than one definition and more than one part of speech. A **glossary** is a short dictionary at the back of some books. It includes definitions of words used in the book. Often it tells the page number where the word can be found. Entry words in dictionaries and glossaries are usually printed in boldface. Using guide words can help you find entry words quickly. Pairs of guide words appear at the top of each page and show the page's first and last entry words.

Directions Use the following glossary entries to answer the questions below.

oppose to be against (page 289)
orbit to travel in an orbit or circle (page 231)
orbiter a person or object that travels in an orbit (page 231)
organism a living thing (page 38)

1. Under which pair of guide words—*operate* and *orient, oak* and *oral*, or *orchard* and *outer*—would you find the four glossary entries shown above?

____

2. In what order are these four entry words presented?

____

3. Which of these four words appears earliest in the main text? On what page does the word appear?

____

4. Why is only one definition listed for each entry word above?

____

____

5. To find out all possible parts of speech for the word *orbit*, what resource could you use?

____

____

Name ________________________________

Directions Use this dictionary entry for *orbit* to answer the questions below.

or•bit (ôr' bit) **n.** 1. eye socket; 2. the path of a heavenly body or spacecraft revolving around a heavenly body; 3. the scope of a person's activity; **v.** 1. to travel in an orbit or circle; 2. to put into motion in a circle in space SYN path, course [<Latin *orbita*, path <*orbis*, a circle]

6. How many definitions are listed in this entry?

7. Which parts of speech for *orbit* are listed? What is a synonym for *orbit?*

8. Which definition listed above best fits the meaning of *orbit* in the sentence, "Mars, Neptune, and Pluto orbit the sun"?

9. How many syllables does orbit have? Where do the syllables divide? Which syllable is accented?

10. What is the origin of the word *orbit*? How does this origin relate to the meaning of the word?

Home Activity Your child learned about using dictionaries and glossaries as resources. Look at a dictionary together. Ask your child to locate several entries, using guide words. Discuss the elements of the entry, including pronunciation, word history, part(s) of speech, and definition.

Name

Family Times

Summary

Egypt

Ancient Egypt was an important civilization with a fascinating history and interesting traditions. The land produced abundant crops and swarmed with animals that live no more. Egyptians created their own type of writing (hieroglyphics), unique burial customs, and astounding pyramids.

Activity

Thinking of Links Play an association game with your family. Start by saying a word related to ancient Egypt, such as *pyramid.* The next person says a word they associate with the first word. Continue until everyone has had a few turns. Then start again with another word relating to Egypt.

Comprehension Skill

Graphic Sources

Graphic sources, which show information visually, include charts, graphs, and time lines. Preview a selection's graphic sources before you read it to understand what you read more deeply. Sometimes creating your own graphic source—such as a diagram, outline, or time line—as you read can help you understand a text better.

Activity

Picture Yourselves Team up with family members to create graphic sources relating to your life. First, make a map showing the location of your home, schools, and places of work. Then create a diagram (often called a family tree) that lists the names and relationships of your ancestors. Finally, draw a time line of memorable events in your life and the lives of other family members.

Lesson Vocabulary

Words to Know

Knowing the meanings of these words is important to reading *Egypt*. Practice using these words.

Vocabulary Words

abundant more than enough; very plentiful
artifacts things made by human skill or work, especially tools or weapons
decrees official decisions or laws
eternity all time; time without beginning or ending
immortal living forever; never dying
receded moved backward
reigned ruled

Grammar

Past, Present, and Future Tenses

All verbs have **past, present,** and **future tenses.** The future tense is formed with the helping verb *will. For example: will make, will write.* The past tense of **regular verbs** is formed by adding *–d* or *–ed* to the present tense. *For example: settled, farmed.* **Irregular verbs,** however, change spelling for the past tense. You must memorize irregular verb forms, such as *wrote, rang,* and *became,* or use a dictionary to help you.

Activity

Time Travel Work with a family member to "translate" a newspaper or magazine article into the past, present, and future tenses. Select an article together, then read aloud a short section of it three times. The first time, read it with all its verbs in the future tense. The second time, read it with all its verbs in the present tense. The third time, read it with all its verbs in the past tense. Notice how in many cases an article about a single event will use a mixture of verbs in all three tenses.

Practice Tested Spelling Words

______	______	______	______
______	______	______	______
______	______	______	______
______	______	______	______
______	______	______	______

Name ____________________

Graphic Sources

- **Graphic sources** are used to show information visually. Maps, charts, graphs, pictures, and schedules are some examples of graphic sources.

Directions Study the following graphic source. Then answer the questions.

Structure	Height
Petronas Tower: Kuala Lumpur, 1998	**452 m**
Eiffel Tower: Paris, 1889	**324 m**
Great Pyramid: Giza, about 2600 B.C.	**147 m**
Big Ben: London, 1856	**96 m**
Taj Mahal: Agra, 1648	**74 m**
Leaning Tower of Pisa: Pisa, about 1350	**56 m**
Statue of Liberty: New York, 1886	**46 m**

1. Which is the tallest of these famous structures? Which is the oldest?

2. Which is the second tallest? The third?

3. The Great Pyramid in Egypt was the world's tallest structure for 4,000 years. How tall is the Great Pyramid?

4. How does the Great Pyramid compare with the Statue of Liberty and Big Ben? Be specific.

5. Write a one-sentence summary of what this graphic source shows.

Home Activity Your child used a graphic source to answer questions. Work together to identify the purpose of a graphic source in a magazine. Challenge your child to answer questions based on the graphic source.

Name ______________________________

Vocabulary

Directions Choose the word from the box that best matches each definition below. Write the word on the line.

Check the Words You Know

- ___abundant
- ___artifacts
- ___decrees
- ___eternity
- ___immortal
- ___receded
- ___reigned

______________ **1.** more than enough; very plentiful

______________ **2.** living forever; never dying

______________ **3.** moved backward

______________ **4.** ruled

______________ **5.** all time; time without beginning or ending

Directions Choose the word from the box that best matches each clue. Write the word on the line.

______________ **6.** This is the longest possible period of time.

______________ **7.** This is what kings and pharaohs did.

______________ **8.** This describes gods rather than people.

______________ **9.** These are made by kings or other authorities.

______________ **10.** Tools, art, and weapons from a past civilization are examples of this.

Write a Narrative

On a separate sheet of paper write a narrative about a ruler from ancient times. Use as many vocabulary words as you can.

Home Activity Your child identified and used vocabulary words from *Egypt*. Read a story or nonfiction article about Egypt together. Point out unfamiliar words concerning details about the country and its people. Use the context to try to figure out what the words mean.

Vocabulary • Word Structure

- When you are reading and see an unfamiliar word, check to see if you recognize any **Greek** or **Latin roots**. These can help you figure out meaning.
- Latin roots include *ars* for "skill, knowledge," *factum* for "made," *cedere* for "to go away," *abundare* for "abound," *regnare* for "to rule," and *mortis* for "death."

Directions Read the following passage. Then answer the questions below.

When the flood waters receded, the archaeologists started to dig along the Nile River. Their efforts were richly rewarded. They found abundant artifacts from an ancient civilization. Much of the jewelry and artwork dated back to the time when pharaohs reigned over the lands. The pharaohs' tombs contained gifts pharaohs had made to the gods in an attempt to become immortal and live for eternity.

1. How does knowing the Latin root *cedere* help you to determine the meaning of *receded?*

____

____

2. Which Latin root do you think *abundant* comes from? How does this root help you to determine the meaning?

____

____

3. How does the meaning of *artifacts* combine the meanings of two roots, *ars* and *factum?*

____

____

4. How would using Latin roots help you determine the meaning of the word *reigned?*

____

____

5. *Immortal* combines the prefix *im–,* meaning "not," with the Latin root *mortis*. How can this word structure help you to determine the meaning of the word?

____

____

Home Activity Your child identified and used Latin roots to understand new words of a passage. Work with your child to identify unfamiliar words of an article. Then see if he or she recognizes any Latin roots that can help in understanding the new words. Confirm the meanings with your child.

Name ___________________________________

Main Idea and Details

Directions Read the article. Then answer the questions below.

In ancient Egypt, scribes were writers, and there was much writing to be done. The ability to read and write made scribes highly respected members of society. Scribes were among the small minority of Egyptians who had a formal education. Because most people did not go to school, only about one in a hundred could actually read and write. Scribes were skilled in using the Egyptians' complex system of writing, hieroglyphics. Their job was to write documents, letters, and contracts, as well as keep records for rulers. However, their education could lead them to become accountants, doctors, priests, or government officials. Scribes had their own god, and one scribe even became a pharaoh. Scribes had status and authority in ancient Egypt.

1. What is the main idea of this article?

____

____

2. What is one detail that supports this main idea?

____

____

3. Give another detail that supports the main idea.

____

____

4. What is a third detail that supports the main idea?

____

____

5. On a separate sheet of paper, write a summary of the article.

Home Activity Your child has read information about Egyptian scribes and identified the main idea and supporting details. Read a short article with your child. Challenge him or her to identify the main idea and supporting details in the article using a graphic organizer that he or she created.

Name____

Graphic Sources

- **Graphic sources** are used to show information visually. Maps, charts, graphs, pictures, and schedules are some examples of graphic sources.

Directions Look over the following graphic source. Then answer the questions below.

Ancient Egyptian Spoken Languages

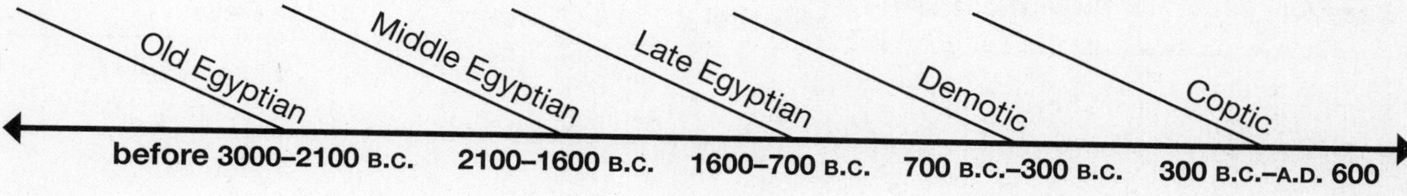

Date

1. What kind of graphic source is this? What is it about?

____

2. What does it tell you about the number of ancient Egyptian languages and when they were used?

____

____

3. What was the first stage of Egyptian language? The second?

____

____

4. What language was spoken in 400 B.C.? In A.D. 100?

____

____

5. In one sentence, summarize the information that this graphic source conveys.

____

____

____

Home Activity Your child identified information in a graphic source and wrote a summary of it. With your child, look through a magazine or newspaper for an interesting graphic source. Discuss it, and then ask your child to give a short summary of the information it shows.

Name ______________________________

Graphic Sources

- **Graphic sources** are used to show information visually. Maps, charts, graphs, pictures, and schedules are some examples of graphic sources.

Directions Read the following chart. Then answer the questions that follow.

Ancient Egyptian Calendar				
Season	**Pronunciation**	**Number of Months**	**Days per Month**	**Approximate Dates**
Inundation	akhet	4	30	June 21–October 21
Emergence	peret	4	30	October 21–February 21
Harvest	shemu	4	30	February 21–June 21

1. What kind of graphic source is this? What is it about?

____

2. What does it show about the number of seasons in the ancient Egyptian calendar?

____

3. How many months were there in a year? How many days were there in each month?

____

4. The calendar was based around the flooding of the Nile, which occurred during the Inundation. When was that season?

____

5. The Egyptian year started with the appearance of the star Sirius on June 21. What season did June 21 begin? In what season was March 1? November 1?

____

____

School + Home **Home Activity** Your child identified information in a graphic source. With your child read an article in a magazine or newspaper. Challenge him or her to design a graphic source that could accompany the article.

Reference Book

A **reference book** is a kind of **manual.** A manual usually contains instructions for immediate use or for reference. It usually has a table of contents, an index, sections, illustrations, and explanations.

Directions Use this excerpt from a grammar reference book to answer the questions.

Simple Tenses
Verbs have three simple tenses: present, past, and future.

Present tense of a verb is the same as the name of the verb.

try jump use

Past tense for regular verbs is formed by adding *–d* or *–ed.* (Sometimes the spelling changes.)

tried jumped used

Future tense is formed by placing *will* or *shall* before the present tense verb.

will try shall jump will use

Irregular Verbs
Irregular verbs do not follow the usual pattern for past tense. These are some examples of irregular verbs:

bring/brought sing/sang
write/wrote eat/ate

Learn irregular verbs. You can also find verb forms for irregular verbs in a dictionary. These are common irregular verbs:

begin	fall	know	see
break	go	lie	speak
come	have	ride	take
drink	hide	ring	throw

1. Which sections of the grammar reference book are shown here?

____

2. What might you look up in the index to find this information?

____

3. What does this manual tell you about how to form the past tense of a regular verb?

____

4. If you wanted to know what irregular verbs were, what could you learn from this manual? What are four examples of irregular verbs?

____

____

5. Would a grammar reference book be a good source to find information about how to study for English tests? Explain.

____

____

Name ____________________

Directions Use this excerpt from a manual to answer the questions.

How to Read Hieroglyphics

Hieroglyphics is the ancient Egyptian system of writing. You can learn to read hieroglyphics yourself.

Sometimes hieroglyphic writing is supposed to be read from left to right, and sometimes it's supposed to be read from right to left. You can always tell which way to read a set of hieroglyphics because the animal and people symbols face toward the beginning.

In hieroglyphics, some symbols are picture symbols and others are sound symbols. These are the four types of symbols you'll find:

1. Alphabet signs — Each symbol represents a sound. Some Egyptian signs such as *th* and *kh* differ from English sounds.

2. Syllable signs — These represent combinations of consonant sounds.

3. Word pictures —These are pictures used as the signs for objects.

4. Determiners — These give the reader clues to how a sign is being used.

Consult the charts in this manual for alphabet, syllable, word, and determiner signs. If you put sounds and pictures together, you'll have a good idea of how to read hieroglyphics.

6. Which section of the manual is shown here? What would you look up in the index to find this information?

____

____

7. Which way should you read hieroglyphics—left to right or right to left?

____

____

8. Which hieroglyphic signs are pictures of what they represent?

____

9. Which hieroglyphic signs represent a single consonant sound?

____

10. Summarize the instructions in this manual section.

____

____

Home Activity Your child learned about using grammar reference books and manuals as resources. Look at a grammar reference book together. Ask your child to locate information and examples of the following: *possessives, clauses,* and *pronouns.*

Name

Family Times

Summary

Hatchet

Lost in the woods after his plane crashes, Brian finds shelter in a cave. During the night, a porcupine wanders in, scaring Brian and shooting him with its quills. After Brian recovers, he decides he must find a way to make fire to survive. After several hours of trying to make fire with a hatchet and birch bark, he succeeds.

Activity

Survival Journal Imagine you are lost in the wilderness like Brian. Write one or two journal entries about your experiences. Share your journal entries with a family member.

Comprehension Skill

Sequence

Sequence is the order in which things happen in a story. You can recognize sequence by looking in the text for references to time of day, as well as clue words such as *first*, *then*, *finally*, *before*, and *after*. Sometimes events occur at the same time. In these cases, an author may include clue words such as *during* and *while*.

Activity

Then What Happened? Together with a family member, take turns reading a story aloud. While one person reads a paragraph or two, the other person jots down any important events that occur in that section of text. At the end of the story, work together to number the events in sequence.

Lesson Vocabulary

Words to Know

Knowing the meanings of these words is important to reading *Hatchet*. Practice using these words.

Vocabulary Words

hatchet a small ax with a short handle, for use with one hand

ignite to set on fire

painstaking very careful; particular; diligent

quill a stiff, sharp hair or spine like the pointed end of a feather

registered to have had some effect; to have made an impression

smoldered burned and smoked without flame

stiffened to have been made or became rigid; fixed

Grammar

Principal Parts of Regular Verbs

A verb has four **principal parts.** The first part is the **present.** It is the form of the verb that is listed in a dictionary entry. *For example: talk, burn.* The second part is the **present participle,** which is formed using a helping verb and the *–ing* ending. *For example: am talking, is burning.* The third part is the **past,** which is usually formed using the *–ed* ending. *For example: talked, burned.* The fourth part is the **past participle,** which is formed using a helping verb and the verb's past part. *For example: was talking, have burned.*

Activity

Name That Part Select an article in a magazine or newspaper. Which of the four principal verb parts do you think will appear most often in the article? With a family member, circle all the verbs in the article and identify which part of the verb they were. Was your prediction correct?

Practice Tested Spelling Words

________	________	________	________
________	________	________	________
________	________	________	________
________	________	________	________
________	________	________	________

Name ____________________

Sequence

- **Sequence** is the order in which things happen. Clue words such as *next, then,* and *yesterday* help to indicate the sequence in which events occur.
- Some events in a story happen simultaneously, or at the same time. Clue words such as *meanwhile* and *at the same time* signal simultaneous events.

Directions Read the following passage. Then complete the diagram below.

Janie and Finn walked down the campground road to get some fresh water. It was getting dark, but Janie remembered the way to the water pump—a left at the fork in the road and then a right. When they got there, Janie pumped the cool water while Finn held the bucket. Then Finn started to splash Janie with the water. Janie was furious, and yelled at him to put the bucket down and let her get the water. Janie refilled the bucket. Meanwhile, Finn ran away. Janie called his name, but there was no response. She raced back to the campground to tell her mother that Finn was lost, all the while worried about him. To her surprise, Finn had already made it back and was sitting quietly by the fire.

End

4. ____________________

3. ____________________

2. ____________________

1. ____________________

Beginning

5. What did you visualize Janie's face to look like at the end of the story?

____

Home Activity Your child identified the sequence of events in a story. Discuss a time when someone or something got lost. Together, identify the sequence of events in the memory.

Name ____

Vocabulary

Directions Choose the word from the box that best matches each definition. Write the word on the line.

Check the Words You Know
___hatchet
___ignite
___painstaking
___quill
___registered
___smoldered
___stiffened

______________________ **1.** to set on fire

______________________ **2.** to have been made or became rigid

______________________ **3.** a stiff, sharp hair or spine

______________________ **4.** very careful

______________________ **5.** burned and smoked without flame

Directions Choose the word from the box that best matches each clue. Write the letters of the word on the blanks. The boxed letters spell out one of the words from this selection.

6. ___ ___ ___ ___ ___ ___ [ ] ___ ___

[e]

[g]

7. ___ ___ [ ] ___ ___

[s]

8. ___ ___ [ ] ___ ___ ___ ___

[e]

[r]

9. ___ ___ ___ ___ ___ [ ]

[d]

6. This happened to a match after it was blown out.
7. This is on a porcupine.
8. You might use this to chop wood.
9. You use a match to do this to a pile of wood.
10. The mystery word is: ______________________

Write a News Report

On a separate sheet of paper, write a news report about a sixth grade student who managed to survive after being marooned on a deserted island. Use as many vocabulary words as you can.

Home Activity Your child identified and used vocabulary words from *Hatchet.* Together, create a crossword puzzle and clues with the words in the selection.

Vocabulary • Word Structure

- An ending is a letter or letters added to the end of a base word. For example, the ending *–ed* can be added to verbs to show past action, and *–ing* can be added to verbs to show ongoing or current action.
- Sometimes the *–ed* or *–ing* form of the verb is used as an adjective.

Directions Read the following passage. Then answer the questions below.

Joseph took his hatchet with him into the thick forest. He had to find the plant before the skin on his palm stiffened and became crusty. Moments before he had been walking past his fading campfire, which had smoldered for a half-hour. He had tripped and landed hands-first in the still-hot embers. When it finally registered with Joseph that his right palm was badly burned, he cried out in pain. He knew the only cure for the burn was a special plant that grew deep in the forest. It was a painstaking task to locate this single plant in so much vegetation, but he had no choice. The pain was now throbbing in his palm. It was unbearable. Finally, Joseph saw the long stems of the plant among some bushes in front of him.

1. What is the base word in *stiffened*? What does it mean?

____

2. What is the ending in the word *smoldered*? What does the word mean?

____

3. Is there a word ending in *painstaking*? Why or why not?

____

4. *Registered* is in what tense? Rewrite the sentence using the *–ing* ending instead of *–ed* for *registered*.

____

____

5. Write a word that can change from a verb to an adjective when the ending *–ing* is added. Use the word in a sentence.

____

____

Home Activity Your child identified word endings to determine the meanings of words. While reading an article with your child, have your child underline word endings. Use the endings to help your child define the words.

Name ______________________________

Plot

Directions Read the story. Then answer the questions below.

We ran out of gas just as we crossed the bridge. I got out of the car and helped my dad push it to the side of the road. All around us were rows and rows of corn. My dad got the map to see where we were. It looked like the next town was at least five miles away. My dad told me that I could wait with the car or go with him. Since walking was better than staying by myself, I grabbed my backpack from the car and we were on our way. About thirty minutes into the walk, my legs started to get tired. I was wondering if I'd ever make it. I didn't tell my dad though because he'd say I should've stayed with the car. I tried my hardest to forget about my legs, until we came to a hill that practically finished them off. Just then, I got an idea. I turned on my dad's cell phone. On top of the hill, it had good reception. My dad was able to call information and get a taxi service that came to get us. I was never so grateful for the invention of the cell phone as I was then.

1. What is the first event in the plot of the story?

____

____

2. How does this first event set up the story's action?

____

____

3. Why do you think the narrator tells you that he or she is getting tired of walking?

____

____

4. What is the resolution in this story?

____

____

5. On the back of this page, summarize the plot of this story in your own words.

School + Home **Home Activity** Your child has answered questions about the plot in a story. Discuss with your child memorable plotlines from your favorite stories. Answer this question: What makes the plots exciting or interesting?

Name ____________________

Sequence

- **Sequence** is the order in which things happen. Clue words such as *next, then,* and *yesterday* help to indicate the sequence in which events occur.
- Some events in a story happen simultaneously, or at the same time. Clue words such as *meanwhile* and *at the same time* signal simultaneous events.

Directions Read the following passage. Then answer the questions below.

Kaila knew they needed to build shelter before the storm hit, so she gathered the others and worked as quickly as possible. First, she scouted around for a dry spot. They didn't want to build their shelter where it would sink into the mud. Next, she and Brian hoisted a fallen tree off the ground and rested it in the crook of a nearby standing tree. This was the main support beam for their tent-like shelter. Meanwhile, several of the others gathered smaller branches, grass, and leaves. Then they took the bare branches and rested them against the main beam. After the basic structure was up, everyone took the leaves and grasses and covered up the holes. In the end, they had a dry and sturdy shelter from the storm.

1. What was the last step in making the shelter?

2. Why did they have to find a dry spot before building the shelter?

3. What two events happened at the same time?

4. Was the sequence of the events crucial to your understanding of the passage?

5. On a separate sheet of paper, draw the shelter you visualized while reading.

Home Activity Your child identified the sequence of events in a passage and visualized the details. With your child, read about a process (such as cooking a meal, making a craft, or fixing a car). Have your child visualize each step of the process and describe the pictures in his or her mind.

Name ______________________________

Sequence

- **Sequence** is the order in which things happen. Clue words such as *next, then,* and *yesterday* help to indicate the sequence in which events occur.
- Some events in a story happen simultaneously, or at the same time. Clue words such as *meanwhile* and *at the same time* signal simultaneous events.

Directions Read the following passage. Then complete the diagram by telling the sequence of events.

Harold started to scream for help, but he knew it was useless. There was no one around. Just then, he heard the sound of a helicopter far off in the distance. He quickly started a fire and added as many leafy palms as he could to make it smoky. Then, he took out his red blanket from his backpack and laid it on the ground. He had to make himself visible. Harold searched his pockets for something that he could use as a reflector. A stick of chewing gum would do the trick. He took the gum wrapper and placed it in the sun's rays. As the helicopter flew overhead, Harold reflected the rays as best he could toward it. He could do nothing now but hope it worked.

End

4. Harold made ______________________________

3. Harold placed the red ______________________________

2. Harold built ______________________________

1. Harold started ______________________________

Beginning

5. Describe how you visualize Harold as he gets ready for the helicopter.

____

Home Activity Your child identified the sequence of events using a graphic organizer. Read a story with your child. Place the events of the story on a time line in the order in which they occurred.

Name________________________________

Posters/Announcement

An **announcement** makes something known to the public. A **poster** is a type of announcement that gives specific facts about an event. It should answer the questions *Who? What? When? Where?* and *Why?*

Directions Read the poster below.

If you were stranded on a deserted island, would you know how to survive? We would!

On Friday, February 5 at the Yukon Memorial Library, the Survival Enthusiasts of Tri-City are hosting their annual *Be Smart: Learn All There Is to Know About Survival* seminar. Eight mini-sessions will teach you how to prepare yourself for just about anything.

The chart below gives you just a sampling of what is in store for you at the seminar.

Name	Description	Time	Location
Survival Kits	Learn what items everyone must have in order to make a survival kit for almost any circumstance. Make your own survival kit during the session.	**8:00 A.M.– 8:45 A.M.**	Hendricks Room
Natural Disasters Awareness	Have you ever witnessed a hurricane, tornado, or earthquake? If so, then come to this session to learn what you need to do to prepare yourself for these natural disasters.	**9:00 A.M.– 10:00 A.M.**	Conference Room B

If you're interested in joining us for a hands-on look at how to survive just about any situation, then please **call us at 555-2000** to get more information or to request the registration form. You may send the form directly to the *Survival Enthusiasts of Tri-City, P.O. Box 580, Yukon, Minnesota, 55509*, with your check made out to the organization for the seminar fee of $150. The price of the seminar includes the mini-sessions, a survival kit, lunch, and your very own *Learn How to Survive* packet. The **deadline for registration** is **January 20**. Hope to see you there!

Name ____________________

Directions Use the poster to answer the following questions.

1. What event is this poster announcing?

2. Where is this event being held?

3. When is it too late to register for the event?

4. What will you learn about in Conference Room B at 9 A.M.?

5. How does this poster try to get your attention?

6. How would you get more information about the event?

7. Where would you post this poster if you were part of the organization putting on the event?

8. Why do you think the poster tells you what is included in the registration price?

9. What kind of people might be interested in this event?

10. What might you add to this poster to make it more appealing?

Home Activity Your child learned about posters and announcements. Have your child create a small announcement or poster that describes an upcoming event in your family (such as a birthday party, special dinner, or gathering).

Name

Family Times

Summary

When Marian Sang

Marian Anderson was not allowed to attend music school because she was African American. Though she performed in Europe with great success, in the United States it was nearly impossible for her to sing in public. People supported Anderson, and eventually she performed at the Lincoln Memorial and at the Metropolitan Opera House.

Activity

Never Give Up With one or more members of your family, discuss a time in your life when you did not give up, even though you were facing a seemingly impossible challenge. What did you think and how did you feel about your situation? How did you manage to persist and finally to succeed?

Comprehension Skill

Generalize

To **generalize** is to make a broad statement or rule that applies to several examples. Sometimes authors signal a generalization by using clue words such as *most, all, always, never, many*, or *in general.* Valid generalizations are accurate, but faulty generalizations are not accurate. You can use information from the text to help you decide which generalizations are valid and which are faulty.

Activity

Creating Generalizations With a family member, make generalizations about something you know well. *For example: Most of the buildings on this street are made of wood.* Take turns judging whether the other person's generalizations are valid or faulty.

Lesson Vocabulary

Words to Know

Knowing the meanings of these words is important to reading *When Marian Sang*. Practice using these words.

Vocabulary Words

application a request for something, such as employment, an award, or a loan

dramatic like a drama; of or about plays

enraged made very angry; made furious

formal according to set customs or rules

momentous very important

opera a play in which music is an essential and prominent part, featuring arias, choruses, and with orchestral accompaniment

prejudice unreasonable dislike of an idea or group of people

privileged having some special rights, advantage, or favor

recital a musical entertainment, given usually by a single performer

Grammar

Principal Parts of Irregular Verbs

Like regular verbs, **irregular verbs** have four parts. Unlike regular verbs, however, irregular verbs change spelling for the past and past participle forms. You must memorize these forms, or use a dictionary to help you. The first part is the **present** (such as *throw*). The second part is the **present participle** (*is throwing*). The third part is the **past** (*threw*). The fourth part is the **past participle** (*had thrown*). Remember that for both regular and irregular verbs, the present and past participles include helping verbs.

Activity

Which Verb Part? Cut out twelve squares of paper. On each square, put one of the four principal parts of the verbs *come*, *go*, and *see*. Fold the squares and put them in a mug or bowl. Take turns with a family member choosing a square and saying the name of the verb part that appears.

Practice Tested Spelling Words

________	________	________	________
________	________	________	________
________	________	________	________
________	________	________	________
________	________	________	________

Generalize

- Sometimes authors **generalize**, or make a broad statement or rule that applies to many examples. Often, clue words such as *most, all, sometimes, always, usually, generally, seldom,* and *never* help to identify generalizations.
- Generalizations supported by facts and logic are called valid generalizations. Faulty generalizations are not always supported by facts.
- Generalizations should always be supported with facts.

Directions Read the following passage. Then complete the diagram below.

Robert was a talented actor. When he was young, neighbors came to see him put on plays with his siblings in the backyard. As Robert grew older, he wanted to become a professional actor. At the time, African Americans were rarely given roles. Robert knew his goal would be hard to reach, but he was determined to do it.

First, Robert moved from his town to a big city where there were more opportunities. He tried out for all kinds of roles, but he was never offered a part. Often it was clear to Robert that he was a better actor than the people who were given parts. Several times he asked directors to explain their choices, but it never changed the outcome. Robert waited for the next audition and tried again. It was difficult to stay confident and to avoid feeling bitter, but he was determined to meet that challenge.

Robert began to hear stories about African American actors finding work in theaters in Europe. Robert decided to make the big move across the sea. Nothing was going to stop him.

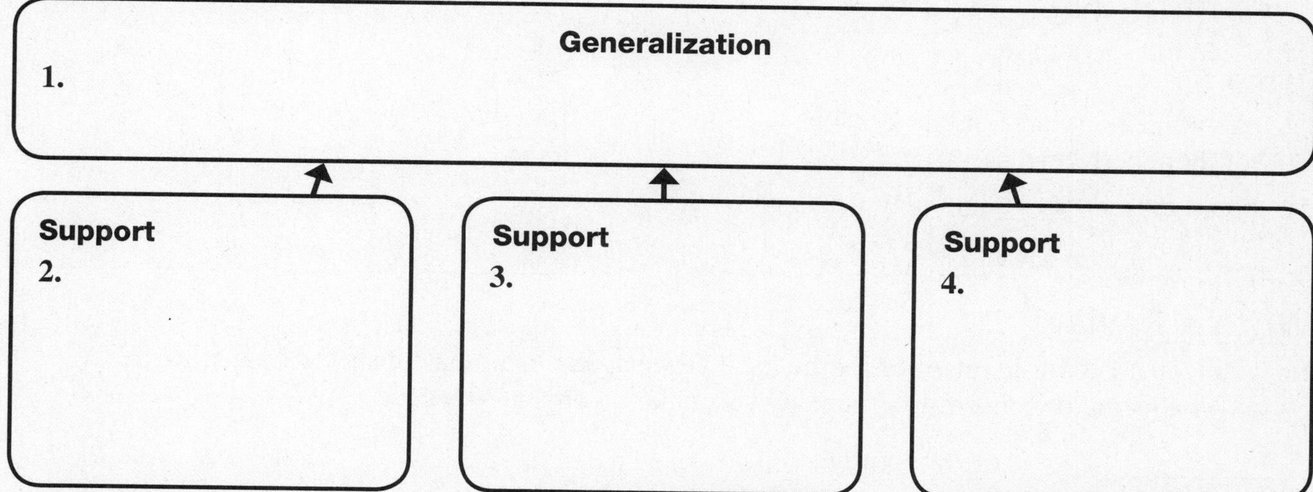

5. What is one question you generated while completing the diagram?

Home Activity Your child made a generalization and supported it with details. Read a story together. Make a generalization about a character based on details from the story.

Name ______________________________

Vocabulary

Directions Choose the word from the box that best matches each definition. Write the word on the line.

Check the Words You Know
___application
___dramatic
___enraged
___formal
___momentous
___opera
___prejudice
___privileged
___recital

______________ **1.** unreasonable dislike of an idea or group of people

______________ **2.** according to set customs or rules

______________ **3.** having some special rights, advantage, or favor

______________ **4.** a request for employment, a loan, etc.

______________ **5.** very important

______________ **6.** a musical entertainment, given usually by one performer

Directions Choose the word from the box that best matches each clue. Write the letters in the crossword puzzle.

Down

7. made very angry or furious

8. This is a play in which the words are sung instead of spoken.

Across

9. A violinist or pianist might give one of these performances.

10. like a drama; of or about plays

9 7

8

10

Write a Review

Imagine you are a music reviewer for the local newspaper. On a separate sheet of paper, write a review of a recital or concert. Use as many vocabulary words as you can.

School + Home **Home Activity** Your child identified and used vocabulary words from *When Marian Sang*. Together, create a crossword puzzle with the vocabulary words from this selection.

Name____

Vocabulary • Word Structure

- A **suffix** is a word part added to the end of a base word to change its meaning or the way it is used in a sentence.
- The suffix *–ic* means "pertaining to or associated with," as in *artistic*. The suffix *–ous* means "full of," as in *poisonous*. The suffix *–ation* means "the state of being," as in *frustration*. You can use suffixes to figure out the meanings of words.

Directions Read the following passage. Then answer the questions below.

Autumn desperately wanted to be in an opera. She had attended a few with her aunt, and she loved the way the singers' voices resonated throughout the grand theaters. The downtown opera house was offering a summer camp for young singers, so Autumn found the application online and printed it out.

She was a little worried, because she had no formal singing experience. Autumn did have dramatic experience, though. She was in all the school plays, and she even took acting classes on the side.

When the application was complete, Autumn sent it in. All she could do now was dream about how joyous she would feel singing such beautiful music on an opera stage. How momentous that day would be!

1. What is the suffix in *application*? What does the word mean?

____

2. How does the suffix change the meaning of the base word in *dramatic*?

____

____

3. Define the word *joyous* in terms of its suffix.

____

4. How can the suffix help you to figure out the meaning of *momentous*?

____

____

5. Describe a moment in your life that you would call *momentous*. Use the word in context.

____

____

Home Activity Your child identified suffixes in order to determine the meanings of words. Together, make a list of other words that use the suffixes *–ic, –ation,* and *–ous*. Have your child guess at their meanings based on their suffixes. Then use a dictionary to confirm the meanings.

Name ____________________________________

Draw Conclusions

Directions Read the following passage. Then answer the questions below.

In 1952, Janet was eight years old. She was old enough to do many things by herself, yet she was too young to leave the neighborhood on her own. She was old enough to understand many things, yet she didn't understand what her mother meant when she said that many people in town were prejudiced towards African Americans like her.

One day Janet went over to her friend Jim's house. She asked Jim if he would go into town with her to get a soda. Jim grabbed some change he had in his piggy bank and they headed for town. Janet and Jim found a drugstore that sold sodas, and they walked inside. They went up to the counter and waited for the attendant to help them. He was drying cups and putting them away. Five minutes passed, and still he dried the cups without paying attention to them. Janet and Jim thought this was strange, because they were standing right in front of him, obviously waiting to be waited on. Then Janet remembered her mother's warning about prejudiced people.

1. What conclusion can you draw about the time period described in the passage?

____

____

2. What is one detail in the passage that supports this conclusion?

____

____

3. What conclusion can you draw about Janet's personality?

____

____

4. What is one detail that supports your conclusion?

____

____

5. On another sheet of paper, describe a time in your life when you discovered something about the world that you did not know before.

Home Activity Your child drew conclusions and used details from a passage to support them. With your child, discuss some aspect of your childhood. Have your child draw a conclusion about your experience, using details from your conversation.

Generalize

- Sometimes authors **generalize**, or make a broad statement or rule that applies to many examples. Often, clue words such as *most, all, sometimes, always, usually, generally, seldom,* and *never* help to identify generalizations.
- Generalizations supported by facts and logic are called valid generalizations. Faulty generalizations are not always supported by facts.
- Generalizations should always be supported with facts.

Directions Read the following passage. Then answer the questions below.

Andy had never been to an opera. He had heard that all operas were long and boring, so he was never interested in going to one. When his parents told him that the whole family was going to attend an opera downtown, Andy complained.

At the opera house, Andy was prepared for boredom, but instead he got a surprise. The opera's words were Italian, but his father was right—somehow he could understand the meaning of the story. Andy didn't know the Italian words, but the singer's expressions and tones of voice helped Andy to understand.

As the family left the opera house, Andy shared his new belief: all operas are amazing. In fact, he couldn't wait to see and hear another one.

1. What generalization does Andy make before he goes to the opera?

____

2. Is this generalization valid or faulty? How do you know?

____

____

3. What generalization can you make about Andy?

____

4. What generalization does Andy make after the opera? Explain why it is valid or faulty.

____

____

5. What question(s) did you ask yourself to find out if Andy's generalizations were valid or faulty?

____

____

Home Activity Your child identified generalizations and supporting details. Together, read an article in the opinion section of a newspaper. Then identify one generalization and look for supporting details in the text. With your child, ask questions that help you determine whether the author's generalization is valid or faulty.

Generalize

- Sometimes authors **generalize**, or make a broad statement or rule that applies to many examples. Often, clue words such as *most, all, sometimes, always, usually, generally, seldom,* and *never* help to identify generalizations.
- Generalizations supported by facts and logic are called valid generalizations. Faulty generalizations are not always supported by facts.
- Generalizations should always be supported with facts.

Directions Read the following article. Then complete the diagram below.

It is not easy to succeed as a professional musician. Many musicians cannot depend on getting their income from performing, so they must find other work to make up for it. Also, musicians must be flexible. Some musicians have to travel far in order to arrange a job or to give a concert. They may have to work hard to advertise themselves, so that people become interested in them and will want to attend their shows. Advertising may involve putting out a high-quality CD and then finding radio stations to play it regularly. Only a tiny number of professional musicians rise to the level of celebrity stardom. However, if you have the talent and the willingness to work hard, you may be able to make a career as a working musician.

Generalization

1. Most musicians must

Support
2. Musicians might have to get

Support
3. To get work, musicians often must

Support
4.

Support
5.

Home Activity Your child made a generalization based on details in an article. Discuss what makes a generalization valid or faulty. Together, share a few generalizations that you believe are faulty. Then talk about a few other generalizations that you believe are valid.

Name____

Readers' Guide to Periodical Literature

- The ***Readers' Guide to Periodical Literature*** is a set of books that lists, alphabetically by author and subject, the articles that are published in more than 200 periodicals. Each entry provides an article's title, author, volume, pages, and date.
- Volumes of the *Readers' Guide* are indexed by time period. You can find a *Readers' Guide* in most libraries.

Directions Read the following page, which is similar to one you would find in the *Readers' Guide to Periodical Literature*. Then answer the questions on the next page.

Volume, April 2003–January 2004

AFRICAN AMERICANS

See also

Africa

Culture

Art

African American Art Expo. W. Carter. *American Artists* v73 p86–92 Jy '03

Artists to Watch 2004. K. Jackson. *African American Art* v36 p112–15 D '03

History

From Slavery to Congress [a look at African American history]. T. Weatherby. *Historical Happenings* v204 p21–8 Ap '03

We Shall Overcome [Civil Rights movement]. S. Barnes. *African Americans Today* v59 p60–7 My '03

Performing Arts

The Academy Finally Responds [Academy Awards given to African American actors]. P. Ames. *That Is Entertainment* v276 p9–15 Jy '03

The Fabulous Josephine Baker. O. Rather. *Appearing Nightly* v39 p90–101 Au '03

Jazz's Finest Players. E. Douglass. *Jazz Now* v73 p43–55 O '03

Revisiting the Career of Marian Anderson. *The Performers' Magazine* v75 p88–95 S '03

Politics

The African American Vote. R. Cooper. *Politics and You* v23 p65–8 O '03

African Americans in Congress. C. Johnson. *Washington Today* v54 p19–27 S '03

Name ______________________________

1. What kinds of sources are listed in a *Readers' Guide*?

____

2. Why would it be useless to look in this volume for an article published in February 2004?

____

____

3. How are the articles arranged on this sample page?

____

4. What is the purpose of the note directing the reader to see also "Africa" and "Culture"?

____

____

5. When did K. Jackson's article appear in a magazine?

____

6. What article appeared in *Jazz Now*?

____

7. What is the purpose of the brackets after some of the articles' titles?

____

____

8. If you were researching Martin Luther King, Jr., what magazines might you consult?

____

9. If you needed the latest information on a topic, how would you go about selecting a volume of the *Readers' Guide* to use?

____

____

10. How can using the *Readers' Guide* save you time when researching a subject?

____

____

____

Home Activity Your child answered questions about the *Readers' Guide to Periodical Literature*. Have him or her explain the different parts of a *Readers' Guide* page to you. Then plan a trip to the library to take a look at a real *Readers' Guide* in order to conduct research for an upcoming report.

Name ______________________________

Family Times

Summary

Learning to Swim

Kyoko doubts her swimming ability. Eventually, with her mother's help, she learns to swim two strokes. Later Kyoko and her mother enjoy jumping in the waves of the Sea of Japan. They realize that they have drifted far from shore. Kyoko's mother tells her to swim strongly to some rocks, and they make it safely there. Kyoko no longer doubts herself.

Activity

Striving for Success With a family member, discuss an important physical or mental goal you wish to accomplish. Together, make a list of the steps you might take to reach this goal. Try to be as specific as possible.

Comprehension Skill

Sequence

Sequence is the order in which events occur in a story. Try to recognize sequence in a text by looking for words relating to time of day, as well as clue words such as *first*, *then*, *finally*, *before*, and *after*. If events occur at the same time, an author may include clue words such as *during* and *while*.

Activity

Good Directions Write a list that gives instructions on how to do something you know well (such as shooting a free-throw or drawing a cartoon). Be specific about the sequence of steps in your instructions. Try to use clue words to help the reader understand the sequence. Have a family member read the paragraph and try to perform the task. Then switch roles and repeat the activity.

Lesson Vocabulary

Words to Know

Knowing the meanings of these words is important to reading *Learning to Swim.* Practice using these words.

Vocabulary Words

customary according to custom; usual

emphasized stressed; called attention to

frantic very much excited; wild with rage, fear, pain, or grief

stunned to have been dazed, bewildered, shocked, overwhelmed

treaded to have kept the body straight in the water with the head above the surface by moving the arms and legs

Grammar

Verbs, Objects, and Subject Complements

A **direct object** is a noun or pronoun that follows an action verb and tells who or what receives the action of the verb. *For example: Alex wrote the letter.* "The letter" is the *direct object* of the *action verb* "wrote." An **indirect object** is a noun or pronoun that tells to whom or from whom the action of the verb is done. *For example: Alex wrote the letter to Hannah.* "Hannah" is the *indirect object* of "wrote." A **subject complement** follows a linking verb and refers to the subject of the sentence. *For example: Alex was happy to write the letter.* "Happy" is the *subject complement* of the *linking verb* "was."

Activity

Colorful Sentences Gather three colored pencils or crayons. Assign one color to each of the objects and complements described above. Choose an article in a magazine to read with a family member. As you read, identify the different sentence parts and circle them with the correct colors.

Practice Tested Spelling Words

____________	____________	____________	____________
____________	____________	____________	____________
____________	____________	____________	____________
____________	____________	____________	____________
____________	____________	____________	____________

Name

Sequence

- In both fiction and nonfiction, **sequence** is the order of events.
- The time of day and clue words such as *before* and *after* can help you determine the order in which things happen.

Directions Read the following passage. Then complete the diagram by writing the main events in sequence on the time line.

Raj was determined to learn all the swimming strokes in one summer. First he learned how to swim the front crawl. After two weeks, Raj had mastered the stroke. Next came the backstroke. Floating on his back was something Raj learned as a child, so this stroke came easy to him. The breaststroke, his next challenge, was even easier, and Raj barely had to practice it. Raj thought he'd have no problem mastering the last and final stroke, the butterfly. Immediately, though, Raj struggled with getting the timing of his arm and leg movements right. Somehow, he just couldn't seem to get it. His teacher told him to feel the rhythm and to relax. Raj was so busy trying to learn all the strokes that he had forgotten the main principle—to have fun!

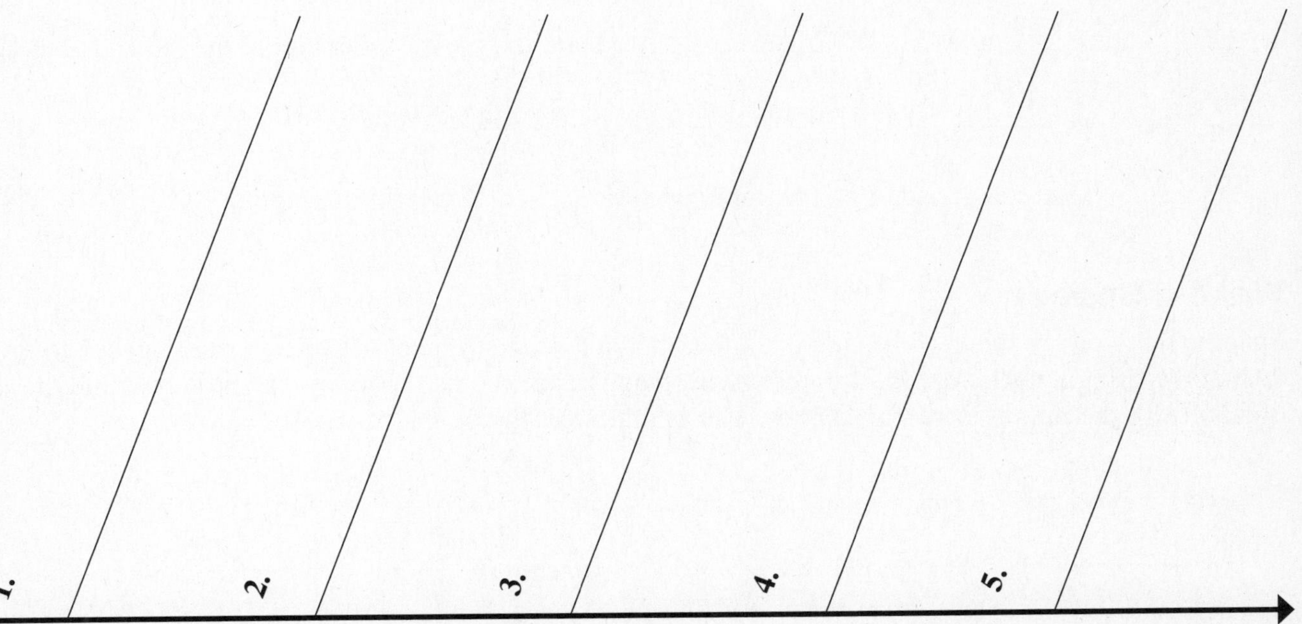

School + Home **Home Activity** Your child identified the sequence of events in a story. Together, discuss the sequence of events in a scene from a favorite movie or television program.

Name____________________________________

Vocabulary

Directions Choose the word from the box that best matches each definition. Write the word on the line.

Check the Words You Know
___customary
___emphasized
___frantic
___stunned
___treaded

______________________ **1.** stressed; called attention to

______________________ **2.** dazed

______________________ **3.** kept the body straight in the water with the head above water by moving the arms and legs

______________________ **4.** usual; according to custom

______________________ **5.** very much excited

Directions Choose the word from the box that best completes each sentence. Write the word on the line shown to the left.

______________________ **6.** During the swimming test, he ______ water for three minutes.

______________________ **7.** The teacher ______ the importance of never swimming alone.

______________________ **8.** It was ______ to learn the crawl stroke before the butterfly stroke.

______________________ **9.** She was ______ by the size of the wave.

______________________ **10.** Try not to become ______ if caught in a riptide.

Write a Speech

Imagine that you are the head lifeguard at a beach. On a separate sheet of paper, write a speech to give to the other lifeguards before the summer swimming season begins. Your speech should remind the lifeguards of the importance of their jobs. Use as many vocabulary words as you can.

School + Home **Home Activity** Your child identified and used vocabulary words from *Learning to Swim*. Together, write a story about a day at the beach. Include as many vocabulary words from the selection as possible.

Name ____

Vocabulary • Context Clues

- **Synonyms** are words that have the same or similar meanings.
- When you read, you may come across a word you don't know. Look for synonyms as clues to the unknown word's meaning.

Directions Read the following passage. Then answer the questions below.

It was customary that all lifeguards must pass a test before being hired to work at the beach. Ally was aware of this usual procedure, so she made sure to prepare for the test well ahead of time. Every day, she practiced swimming against a current in the lake, and she treaded water for several minutes at a time. Ally reminded herself not to get too frantic, or excited, during the test. In that case, of course, she wouldn't be able to concentrate. All her life, her swimming teachers emphasized, or stressed, that lifeguards need to stay calm in all situations. Ally was stunned when she first heard this. She was also astonished at how serious this summer job really was.

1. What synonym for the word *customary* appears in the passage?

____

2. What does the word *frantic* mean in this passage? How do you know?

____

____

3. What is the meaning of *emphasized*? How can you tell?

____

____

4. What synonym for *stunned* is included in the passage? Name a second synonym for *stunned*.

____

5. Another synonym for *customary* is *traditional*. Explain why this word is not an appropriate synonym for *customary* as it is used in this passage.

____

____

Home Activity Your child identified synonyms using context clues. Together, read an article in a magazine or newspaper. Have your child choose a few unfamiliar words from the article and look up synonyms for them in a thesaurus. Together, rewrite the sentences by adding the synonyms in order to help clarify the meaning of the unfamiliar words.

Name ______________________________

Generalize

Directions Read the following article. Then answer the questions below.

Just like most activities, swimming has certain rules that should always be followed. These rules are designed to assure the safety and protection of swimmers. Of course, sometimes swimming rules must be adapted to a particular pool or beach you are using.

First of all, it is important never to swim alone. This rule applies even to strong, experienced swimmers. No swimmer can predict when an unexpected wave or current or a personal health problem could overcome him or her. This rule promotes safety by providing a companion who can help a swimmer or go to get additional help, if necessary.

Second, it is important to know how deep the water is before diving into it. Again, this rule applies to all swimmers, not just beginners. Diving into shallow water can seriously injure a person. Many such diving injuries involve the head, neck, and spine. They are among the most dangerous of all injuries.

Finally, it is important not to swim in water during any type of storm. Lightning is dangerous when you are on the ground, and even more so when you are in the water.

1. What generalization does the writer make in the first paragraph?

____

2. What clue word helps you identify this generalization?

____

3. Is this generalization valid or faulty? Explain.

____

____

____

4. What generalization does the writer make in the third paragraph?

____

____

5. Is this generalization valid or faulty? Why?

____

____

Home Activity Your child has analyzed generalizations in a nonfiction passage. Discuss one or more rules in your home that are based on generalizations. Share ideas about why these generalizations are valid.

Name ______________________

Sequence

- In both fiction and nonfiction, **sequence** is the order of events.
- The time of day and clue words such as *before* and *after* can help you determine sequence.

Directions Read the following passage. Then answer the questions below.

We arrived at the cabin just in time to take the canoe out on the lake before dark. Oscar and I dragged the canoe from the storage shed. We buckled on our safety jackets, grabbed the paddles, and shoved off from shore. Some ways off, we spotted a plastic bag floating in the water, and we decided to retrieve it. Meanwhile, the sun was beginning to set. When we came nearer to the bag, Oscar leaned toward the water in order to grab it. Suddenly the canoe tipped over, dumping us in the water.

Luckily our safety jackets kept us afloat. In a minute or so, we managed to flip the canoe over again. Then Oscar tried to climb in, but he tumbled back into the water. It was going to be too difficult to get back into the canoe, and it was almost dark. What would we do now?

1. How do the references to the time of day help you follow the sequence of events?

2. What did the narrator and Oscar do before going out on the water?

3. What two events happened at the same time? How do you know?

4. If the characters had *not* put on their safety jackets, how might the story have changed?

5. Predict what will happen next in the story.

Home Activity Your child identified the sequence of events in a passage and made a prediction. Read a new story with your child. While reading, focus together on identifying the sequence of events, using clue words when possible. Before you reach the conclusion of the story, you may wish to share predictions about how it will end.

Name ____

Sequence

- In both fiction and nonfiction, **sequence** is the order of events.
- The time of day and clue words such as *before* and *after* can help you determine sequence.

Directions Read the following passage. Then complete the diagram by telling the sequence of events.

Rosa was babysitting when the tornado siren went off. She knew that meant a tornado had been spotted in the area. She gathered the children, and told them that they were all going to play in the basement for a while. Rosa made sure to appear as calm as possible. Before going downstairs, she took her cell phone out of her purse. Then she ran to the kitchen and took the radio from the counter. Rosa wanted to make sure she could get any updates about the tornado while in the basement. Once downstairs, Rosa guided the children away from the windows. They were upset, so she gathered them near her and sang them one of their favorite songs. Soon they began to sing with her.

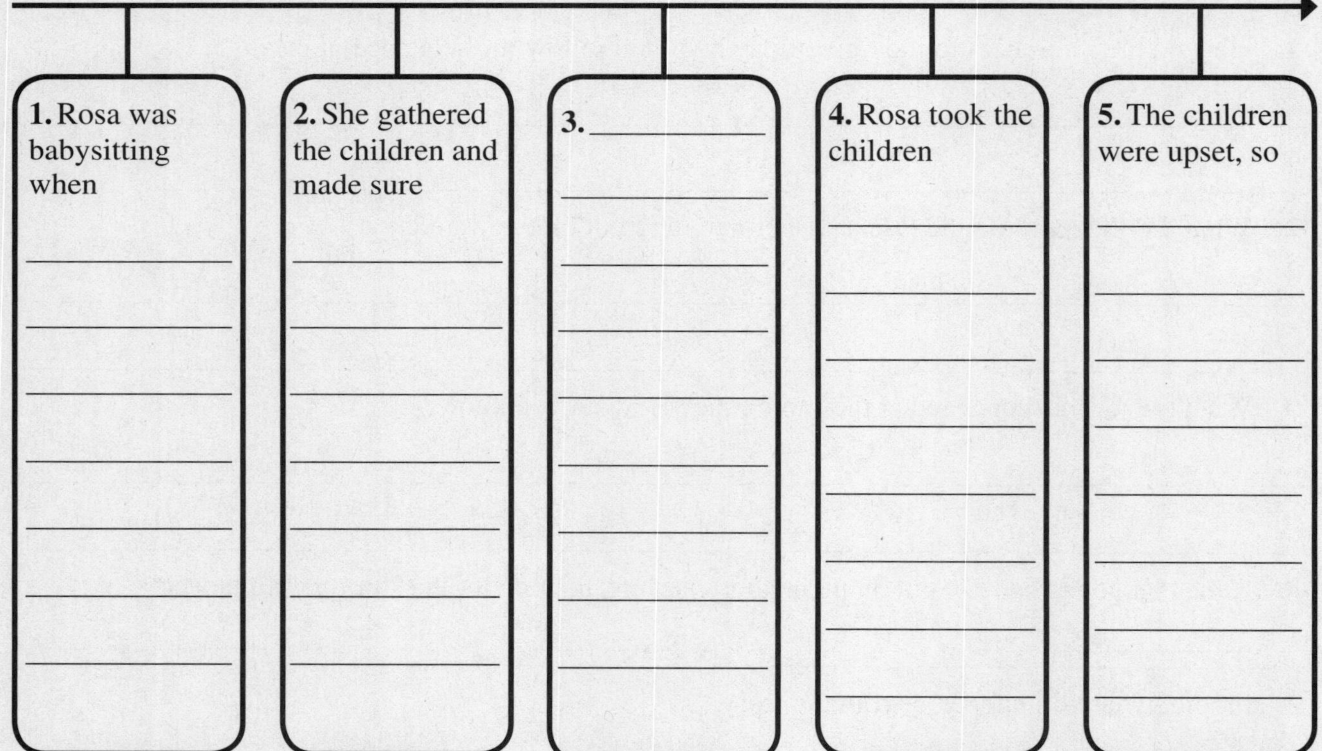

1. Rosa was babysitting when

2. She gathered the children and made sure

3. ____________

4. Rosa took the children

5. The children were upset, so

Home Activity Your child identified the sequence of events in a story, using a graphic organizer. Together, use a time line to write down the sequence of events in a typical school day.

Name ______________________

Study Strategies

- Use **study strategies** to help you save time and avoid reading irrelevant information. You can make a KWL table, a two-column comparison table, or you can follow the steps of SQP3R.
- CD-ROM resources can help you gather information on a particular topic. You might use a CD-ROM dictionary, encyclopedia, or a topic-related CD-ROM. You can use search CD-ROMs to find specific information or click on underlined links to find related information.

Directions Use the following study strategies to answer the questions below.

Topic ______________________

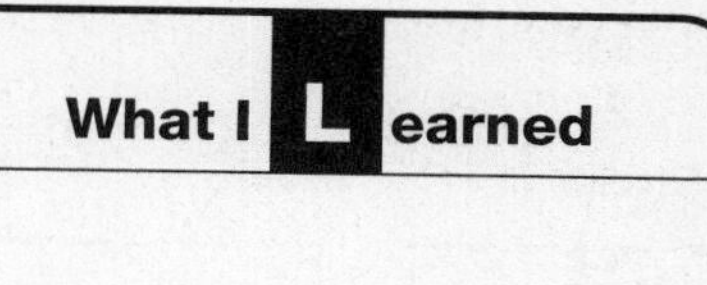

SQP3R

- **Survey** the text.
- Formulate **questions** about it.
- **Predict** what the text will be about.
- **Read** the text.
- **Recite** what you have learned.
- **Review** what you have learned.

Details About "A"	Details About "B"

1. In the comparison table, what would you write in the two columns?

____

2. How do you think reciting what you have learned might help you?

____

3. For what reason is it helpful to write down what you already know about a topic?

____

____

4. What do you do when you survey a text?

____

____

5. Which strategy do you find most helpful? Explain.

____

____

Name ____________________

Directions Use the two CD-ROM sample screens to answer the following questions.

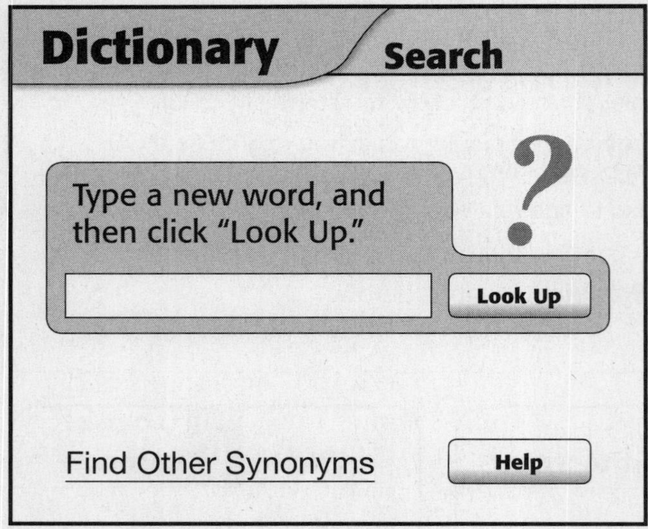

Encyclopedia Search Results

Swimming
Swimming (Olympic Sport)
Water Safety
Lifeguard

Choose a topic above or type in key words for a new search.

Search for: ____________________

6. How would you use one of the above media sources to make a two-column table to compare *riptides* and *ebb tides*?

____

____

7. Imagine you are researching *Swimming (Olympic Sport)* and using a KWL chart to organize your information. Write a sentence you might put in the K column.

____

____

8. Imagine you are researching *Swimming (Olympic Sport)* and using a KWL chart to organize your information. Write a question you might put in the W column.

____

____

9. When you go to the Encyclopedia Search Results for *Swimming (Olympic Sport)* and find text for this topic, if you are using SQP3R, what are your next two steps?

____

____

10. When using SQP3R, after you predict what the text will be about, what should you do?

____

____

Home Activity Your child learned about several study strategies. Choose a nonfiction article to read together. Have your child apply one of the study strategies to the reading. Work through the article together, using the study strategy. Then discuss how the strategy helped with understanding the topic.

Name

Family Times

Summary

Juan Verdades: The Man Who Couldn't Tell a Lie

Juan Verdades, the foreman on don Ignacio's ranch, has never told a lie. One day don Arturo bets don Ignacio his ranch that he can make Juan tell a lie. Don Arturo's daughter, Araceli, tempts Juan to give her don Ignacio's greatest possession—the apples from his apple tree. Juan loves Araceli and so he does it. In the end, Juan confesses to his boss and don Arturo loses the bet. Don Ignacio gives Juan the ranch he won. Juan proposes to Araceli, so don Arturo's ranch stays in the family after all.

Activity

Truth or Lies? Take turns telling either a truth or a lie to family members. Have them ask you questions about the statement to see if they can figure out if it is a truth or a lie.

Comprehension Skill

Generalize

To **generalize** is to make a broad statement or rule that applies to several examples. Sometimes an author uses words such as *all*, *many*, or *in general* to signal a generalization.

Activity

An Experiment Design a mini-experiment, such as whether a paper airplane will fly more than five feet. Make observations about each trial run, for example: *Trial 1 was a success.* Then make a generalization about the experiment, for example, *Most of the trials were successful.*

Lesson Vocabulary

Words to Know

Knowing the meanings of these words is important to reading *Juan Verdades: The Man Who Couldn't Tell a Lie*. Practice using these words.

Vocabulary Words

confidently certainly; surely; with firm belief
dismounted got off something, such as a horse or bicycle
distressed in great pain or sorrow
flourish to grow or develop well; thrive
fulfill to perform or carry out a duty or command
permission consent; leave
repay to do or give something in return for something received
vigorously strongly; actively; energetically

Grammar

Troublesome Verbs

Troublesome verbs are verbs that look so much alike and are so similar in meaning that it is easy to use one when you mean the other. Consult the chart below for examples.

Troublesome Verb	Definition
lie	rest or recline
lay	put or place
sit	take a sitting position
set	put or place
let	allow or permit
leave	go away

Activity

Picture Cards Sometimes it is easier to remember a verb's definition if you have a visual image to go with it. Write some troublesome verbs on squares of paper and draw pictures of the verbs in action on the other side. Use these picture cards whenever you forget how to use a troublesome verb.

Practice Tested Spelling Words

____________	____________	____________	____________
____________	____________	____________	____________
____________	____________	____________	____________
____________	____________	____________	____________
____________	____________	____________	____________

Name ______________________________

Generalize

- A **generalization** is a broad statement or rule that applies to many examples.
- Valid generalizations are supported by examples, facts, or good logic. Invalid generalizations are not supported.

Directions Read the following passage. Then complete the diagram below by making a generalization about Jung and supporting it with examples.

After Jung lost her grandmother's brooch, she wasn't sure what to do. She feared telling her grandmother the truth because it would break her heart. So, Jung took all of her savings and went downtown to see if she could find a similar brooch to replace the lost one. She found one with beautiful emerald stones, but it was too expensive. She found another one that she could afford, but it paled in comparison to the original.

Jung decided to tell her grandmother the truth. She crept up the stairs to her grandmother's room and softly knocked on the door. When her grandmother answered it, she was wearing the brooch! Jung told her what had happened anyway. Her grandmother was pleased that Jung had been honest and allowed Jung to borrow the brooch again. Jung realized it's always best to tell the truth.

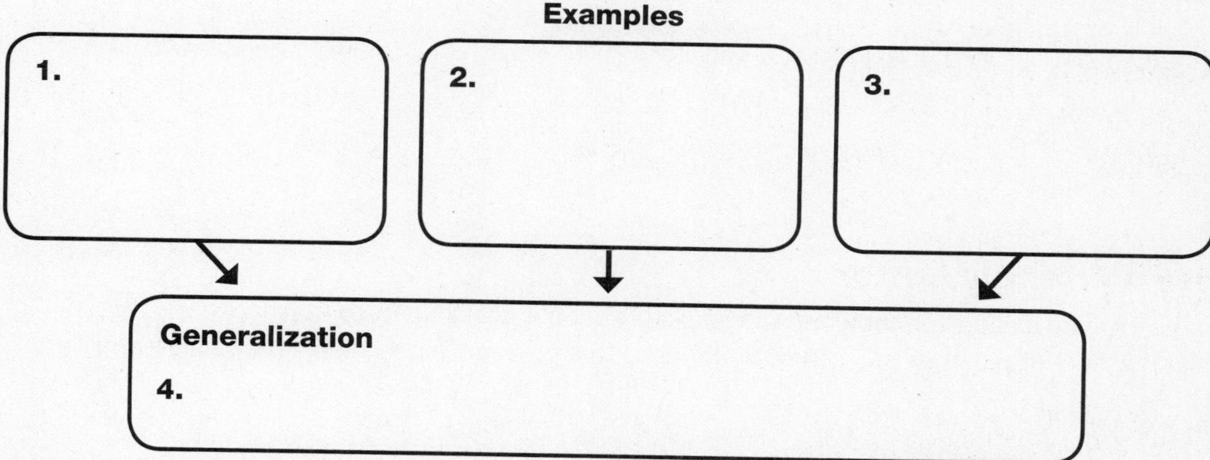

5. Make a prediction about whether or not Jung will lose the brooch the next time.

____

____

____

Home Activity Your child made a generalization based on examples in a story. Have your child make a generalization about his or her personality or behavior. Discuss examples from your child's life that would support this generalization.

Name ____

Vocabulary

Directions Draw a line to connect each word on the left with its definition on the right.

1. repay	in great pain or sorrow
2. distressed	to do something in return
3. fulfill	got off a horse
4. dismounted	to grow or develop well
5. flourish	to perform or carry out a duty

Check the Words You Know

- ___confidently
- ___dismounted
- ___distressed
- ___flourish
- ___fulfill
- ___permission
- ___repay
- ___vigorously

Directions Circle the word that has the same or nearly the same meaning as the first word in each group.

6. permission	consent	disagreement	response
7. repay	cheat	keep	refund
8. confidently	with certainty	unsurely	timidly
9. vigorously	weakly	strongly	sadly
10. flourish	decrease	thrive	decline

Write a Friendly Letter

Imagine you are asking for someone's permission to do something or to borrow something. On a separate sheet of paper, write a friendly letter to this person. Use as many vocabulary words as you can.

Home Activity Your child identified and used vocabulary words from *Juan Verdades*. Together, write a creative tall tale using all the vocabulary words from this selection.

Vocabulary • Word Structure

- A **prefix** is added to the beginning of a base word and changes the base word's meaning.
- The prefix *re–* means "again" or "back"; the prefix *dis–* means "to remove" or "the opposite of."

Directions Read the following passage. Then answer the questions below.

Pete dismounted from Shadow's saddle and led his beloved horse toward the stable. He was distressed. Shadow was clearly too sick to run in the race next week. He knew he would never fulfill his dream of winning the Crescent City Classic now. When Pete entered the stable, he found Tyler, the stable's owner, waiting for him. "Pete," said Tyler, "I want you to enter the Classic with Dale."

"Dale?" Pete shook his head, recalling the last time he had seen Dale race. "But he's the fastest horse here! Why me?"

"I can say confidently that you and Dale will work well with each other," Tyler said. "I think it's a great match."

"But ... how will I ever repay you?"

"Do your best at the Classic and that will be more than enough."

1. How does the prefix change the meaning of the base word in *dismounted*?

2. What is the prefix in *recalling*? What does the word mean?

3. Can you apply the rules of prefixes with finding the meaning of the word *distressed*? Why or why not?

4. For what does Pete want to *repay* Tyler?

5. What is the meaning of *dishonor*? Give an example of how Pete could dishonor his agreement with Tyler.

Home Activity Your child identified prefixes to help determine the meanings of words. Make a two-column chart on a piece of paper. In the first column, write the prefixes *dis–* and *re–*. In the second column, write as many base words as the two of you can think of that would make sense when added to these prefixes.

Name ____

Cause and Effect

Directions Read the story. Then answer the questions below.

Dan told a lie to get out of cutting the grass. He said he twisted his ankle while playing basketball at school. His mom offered to take him to the doctor, but Dan said if he just rested and put some ice on it, he'd be fine. Dan sat in his room reading comic books while his older sister cut the grass. About an hour later, the phone rang. It was Dan's friend Keith. Keith wanted to know if Dan could go skateboarding.

Dan really wanted to go. He decided to tell his mother that he was feeling better, and that he was only going to watch his friends skateboard. Before going downstairs, Dan decided to fake a limp to be more convincing. While pretending to limp, Dan lost his footing and slid down the stairs. His ankle hurt as he stood up. When his mom asked what happened, Dan just said ,"I think I need some more ice," and hobbled back up the stairs to his room.

1. What were some of the immediate effects of Dan's lie?

____

____

2. What caused Dan to decide to tell his second lie?

____

____

3. What caused Dan to fake a limp?

____

____

4. What effect did Dan not intend to happen because of his lie?

____

____

5. On a separate sheet of paper, write about a time when you or someone you know got caught up in a lie. What were the causes and effects of the lie?

Home Activity Your child has answered questions about cause and effect. Look through a newspaper or magazine. Try to find a news event in which several causes led to several effects. Ask your child to create a graphic organizer to represent the causes and effects.

Name ____________________

Generalize

- A **generalization** is a broad statement or rule that applies to many examples.
- Valid generalizations are supported by examples or facts. Invalid generalizations are not supported by examples or facts.

Directions Read the following passage. Then answer the questions below.

The perfect chance for me to make some money had arrived. The Feldmans in apartment 2B were going away on vacation. They needed a trustworthy person to take care of their two miniature poodles. I had never taken care of pets before, but I really wanted this job. I could tell they were the kind of people who cared more about their pets than anything else, so I knew getting them to trust me was no easy task. On Saturday morning, I stopped by their apartment for an interview. The meeting was my suggestion. When I came through the door, I greeted the dogs with lots of loving pats on the head. Then I sat down with the Feldmans. I handed them a resume and a number of references from people in the building who I knew well. I even told them that they could interview my parents if they wished. The Feldmans were astonished and at first said nothing.

1. What generalization might be made about the narrator's personality?

____

2. Name an example from the passage that supports this generalization.

____

3. What generalization does the narrator suggest about the Feldmans?

____

4. Is this a valid or invalid generalization? How do you know?

____

____

5. What do you predict the Feldmans will do next?

____

____

Home Activity Your child identified generalizations in a passage and made a prediction. Read a story together. During the story, challenge your child to predict the upcoming actions of the main character based on a generalization about the character's personality and previous actions. Read on to see if the prediction comes true.

Name ____

Generalize

- A **generalization** is a broad statement or rule that applies to many examples.
- Valid generalizations are supported by examples or facts. Invalid generalizations are not supported by examples or facts.
- Clue words such as *all, most, always, usually,* or *generally* signal generalizations.

Directions Read the following passage. Then complete the diagram below.

Raven knew she could always trust the members of her swim team. Shauna was usually very quiet and kept secrets well. She never told another soul about Raven's fear of heights. Jade was especially dependable. She helped Raven study for the geometry test even though Jade had plenty of other things to do. Then there was Abby. Raven could not come to practice one day because she was feeling ill and told Abby to deliver the message to the coach. Abby did just that, and even called to check up on Raven later that evening. Raven knew she was very lucky.

Examples

1. Shauna never ____________________

2. Jade was ____________________

3. Abby ____________________

Generalization

4. The girls on Raven's team ____________________

5. Based on the generalization, predict how Raven's swim team would respond if she told them she needed their help planning a surprise party for their coach.

____

____

____

____

School + Home **Home Activity** Your child identified a generalization and examples to support it. Together, make a generalization about your town or community. Come up with examples to support this generalization.

Name ______________________________

Outline

An **outline** is a plan that shows how a story, article, report, or other text is organized. You can use an outline to better understand how a text is organized or as a way to organize your own thoughts before you write something of your own. Outlines contain a title, heads, subheads, and details.

Directions Study the following outline. Then answer the questions below.

My Two Best Friends

I. Luis
   A. Personality
      1. funny
      2. trustworthy
      3. intelligent
   B. Why we are friends
      1. We're lab partners in science class.
      2. We play on the soccer team together.
      3. He's an older brother to me.

II. Mandy
   A. Personality
      1. serious
      2. athletic
      3. understanding
   B. Why we are friends
      1. We walk to school together.
      2. We have Spanish and math classes together.
      3. We think the same way about the world.

1. What might be the purpose of this outline?

____

____

2. What are the two topics?

____

3. What is similar about why the author is friends with Luis and Mandy?

____

4. What is one major difference between the personalities of Luis and Mandy?

____

5. Why do you think it is important to have about the same number of subtopics under each topic?

____

____

____

Name ______________________

Directions Read the following essay. Then fill in the missing sections of the outline below.

Ellen and I met when we were two years old. She and I were in daycare together. I remember playing in the sandbox with Ellen, and I know we had a lot of fun. Later on, we attended the same elementary school and junior high.

Ellen is always cheerful and friendly. On my birthday, she baked me a cake and made a card for me. I am friends with Ellen because I know that I can tell her anything, and she won't laugh at me. It is nice to have a friend like that.

Lionel just moved to town this year. I remember on the first day of school, he was wearing a Tigers jersey. I was wearing one, too. When we saw each other in math class, we both started cracking up about it. I invited Lionel over to my house to watch the Tigers game one Saturday afternoon, and after that we have never missed a game.

Lionel is intelligent and fun to hang out with. We can talk about sports, school, or just about anything. He wants to be an archaeologist when he grows up, and his stories about ancient civilizations are always interesting.

Friends

6. I. ______________________

A. How we know each other

1. Daycare when we were two

7. 2. ______________________

B. Personality

1. cheerful

8. 2. ______________________

3. good listener

II. Lionel

A. How we know each other

1. math class

2. watch all the Tigers games

9. B. ______________________

1. intelligent

2. fun to hang out with

10. 3. ______________________

Home Activity Your child learned how to use an outline. Have your child pretend he or she is going to write an essay comparing two family members. Have your child make an outline of information about his or her subjects in preparation for writing the essay.

Name

Family Times

Summary

Elizabeth Blackwell: Medical Pioneer

Elizabeth Blackwell became the first woman to receive a degree in medicine in the United States, but it was not easy. Many people were against the idea of women practicing medicine, which made it difficult for Elizabeth to get into medical school. Later, she caught an eye infection that resulted in blindness in one of her eyes. But not even that would stop her. Eventually, Elizabeth opened her own clinic and continued to be a role model for women of the age.

Activity

Times Have Changed Discuss with your family how times have changed since the days of Elizabeth Blackwell. How are women's lives different today than years ago?

Comprehension Skill

Draw Conclusions

When you **draw a conclusion**, you form a reasonable opinion about something you have read. When you draw a conclusion it should make sense. Ask yourself, "Is the conclusion based on facts? Does the information I have read support the conclusion?"

Activity

A Job I'd Like to Have With a family member, look up an occupation you are interested in on the Internet or in a reference book or magazine. Draw a conclusion about this occupation based on the details you have found.

Lesson Vocabulary

Words to Know

Knowing the meanings of these words is important to reading *Elizabeth Blackwell: Medical Pioneer*. Practice using these words.

Vocabulary Words

absurd plainly not true; ridiculous
behalf side, interest, or favor
candidate person who seeks some position
dean head of a division or school in a college or university
delirious wildly excited
diploma a printed paper given by a school that states that someone has graduated from a certain course of study
hovers waits nearby
obedient doing what you are told
reject to refuse to take; to turn down

Grammar

Prepositions

Prepositions are words that show certain relations between other words. The words *with*, *for*, *by*, and *in* are prepositions in the sentence, "Someone *with* flowers *for* sale walked *by* our house *in* the morning."

A **prepositional phrase** is a phrase that includes a preposition and its object:

during lunch
next to you
on the beach

During, *next to*, and *on* are prepositions. *Lunch*, *you*, and *beach* are the objects of the prepositions.

Activity

Preposition Hunt Read an article with a family member and locate the prepositional phrases. Discuss what each phrase modifies.

Practice Tested Spelling Words

____	____	____	____
____	____	____	____
____	____	____	____
____	____	____	____
____	____	____	____

Draw Conclusions

- When you **draw conclusions,** you form opinions or make decisions about what you have read.
- Your conclusions should be reasonable and make sense. They should be based on details and facts from the reading and your own experiences.

Directions Read the following passage. Then complete the diagram with facts or details from the passage and a reasonable conclusion.

Women were not always thought of as equal to men. Many people believed that women should take care of the family and stay at home. At one time, they were unable to own land or go to college. Eventually, groups of women began organizations to help them fight for equal rights.

After years of struggle, women were given the right to vote in 1920. Women today have benefited from the dedication and work of generations of women who have come before them.

Fact or Detail
1.

Fact or Detail
2.

Fact or Detail
3.

Fact or Detail
4.

Conclusion
5.

Home Activity Your child drew a conclusion from facts or details found in a reading passage. Tell your child a short story about an event that happened in your life. Have your child single out two or three details from the story and form a conclusion about it.

Name ____________________

Vocabulary

Directions Choose the word from the box that best matches each definition. Write the word on the line shown to the left.

Check the Words You Know

- ___absurd
- ___behalf
- ___candidate
- ___dean
- ___delirious
- ___diploma
- ___hovers
- ___obedient
- ___reject

____________ **1.** to turn down someone or something

____________ **2.** a person who seeks some position

____________ **3.** doing what you are told

____________ **4.** waits nearby

____________ **5.** wildly excited

____________ **6.** plainly not true; ridiculous

Directions Choose the word from the box that best completes the sentences below. Write the word on the line shown to the left.

____________ **7.** On ____ of the organization, I want to say thank you for your donations.

____________ **8.** The ____ of students gave a speech to the graduating class.

____________ **9.** It is ____ to think that women are less capable of learning than men.

____________ **10.** On the wall of the doctor's office is a ____ that shows where she studied medicine.

Write a Scene from a Play

On a separate sheet of paper, write a short scene from a play about a woman who tried to run for president 100 years ago. Use as many vocabulary words as you can.

Home Activity Your child identified and used vocabulary words from *Elizabeth Blackwell: Medical Pioneer.* Make up a story with your child, taking turns adding sentences containing one vocabulary word each.

Name ______________________________

Vocabulary • Context Clues

- **Antonyms**, or words with opposite meanings, may provide clues that give you a hint about the meaning of an unfamiliar word.

Directions Read the following passage about medical schools. Then answer the questions below. Look for antonyms as you read.

It can be difficult to get into medical school. Each year, medical schools reject half the students that apply to them. However, they accept the other half. That is why it is not absurd but reasonable to apply. Good medical school candidates should be obedient and not defiant of their teachers' instructions. A good candidate must be single-minded as well, because medical school is very difficult. When observing patients, a medical student hovers behind a doctor for hours at a time and cannot wander. For anyone who applies to medical school, waiting to get a school's reply is a tense experience. Those who get into a school are delirious. Those who do not are often miserable.

1. What does *reject* mean? What is its antonym in the passage?

____

2. What does *absurd* mean? What is its antonym in the passage?

____

3. Why is an *obedient* person a good candidate for medical school?

____

4. Based on the passage, what does *hovers* mean? How do you know?

____

____

5. What clues give you the meaning of *delirious?* What is the definition of *delirious?*

____

____

____

Home Activity Your child identified and used antonyms to understand new words in a passage. Help your child select some unfamiliar words in a newspaper article. Then give your child antonyms for the words until he or she can guess the words' meanings.

Name ____________________

Sequence

Directions Read the scene. Then answer the questions below.

DR. GOMEZ: When did your throat start hurting?

JANET: Last Thursday after the swim meet.

DR. GOMEZ: Why did you wait so long to come and see me?

JANET: I wasn't sure why it started hurting. I thought it was because I was cheering for my team during the meet. Then last Saturday my friend Lena canceled her birthday party because she was sick.

DR. GOMEZ: I see. Was Lena also at the swim meet?

JANET: Yes, she swam in the race before mine.

(Dr. Gomez takes Janet's temperature. Then she looks at Janet's throat.)

DR. GOMEZ: I'm writing a prescription for some medicine for your throat. It looks like Lena passed her sickness to you.

JANET: Does this mean I won't be able to go to swim practice tomorrow?

DR. GOMEZ: I'm afraid not. But don't worry, you'll be back in the pool by the end of the week.

1. Which event took place first, the swim meet or Lena canceling her party? Explain how you know.

____

____

2. Would it have mattered to the understanding of the scene if Dr. Gomez had written out the prescription before talking to Janet?

____

____

3. Is it necessary to know that Lena swam the race before Janet?

____

4. Based on the scene, what will most likely happen next?

____

____

5. On a separate sheet of paper, create a time line that shows the order of all the events that occur in the scene as well as those that occurred prior to the scene.

Home Activity Your child read a fictional scene and placed its details in the order in which they occurred. Read a short story with your child. Discuss the sequence of events and have your child explain whether or not the sequence affected the story's outcome.

Name________________________________

Draw Conclusions

- When you **draw conclusions,** you form opinions or make decisions about what you have read.
- Your conclusions should be reasonable and make sense. They should be based on details and facts from the reading and your own experiences.

Directions Read the following passage. Then answer the questions below.

Lucy Hobbs Taylor would not let the rules of society keep her from fulfilling her goals. After an Ohio medical school rejected her admission, she decided to do something different. Instead of becoming a medical doctor, she would study dentistry. She applied to a dental school, and once again was told she could not attend because of her gender.

Lucy started studying and practicing dentistry on her own. She moved to Iowa and soon won the support of the Iowa State Dental Society. They helped her get into the Ohio College of Dental Surgery. Upon graduation, Lucy became the first woman in the United States to receive a diploma from a dental college.

1. What conclusion can you draw about Lucy's personality from the passage?

____

2. What is one important detail that helped you draw this conclusion?

____

____

3. What is a second detail that helped you draw that conclusion?

____

____

4. What conclusion can you draw about how the Iowa State Dental Society felt about Lucy?

____

5. Describe the structure of this passage.

____

____

____

Home Activity Your child drew conclusions from facts or details found in a passage and identified the structure of the passage. Read an article from an encyclopedia or reference book about a famous woman. Then have your child use the structure of the passage and its details in order to draw a conclusion.

Draw Conclusions

- When you **draw conclusions,** you form opinions or make decisions about what you have read.
- Your conclusions should be reasonable and make sense. They should be based on details and facts from the reading and your own experiences.

Directions Read the following scene. Then complete the diagram by finishing the statements.

RUTH: I am here to tell you that I am going to run for governor.

CHAIRPERSON: A woman governor? Don't be absurd.

RUTH: I am just as smart as any male candidate. I have a diploma from the best women's college in the country. I have been a leader in my community for ten years.

CHAIRPERSON: But what will you do for our state?

RUTH: I know how to save our state money, how we can clean up our cities, and how we can give all our children an education.

CHAIRPERSON: There's no reason to reject your idea, Ruth. On behalf of the party, we'll support you as our candidate.

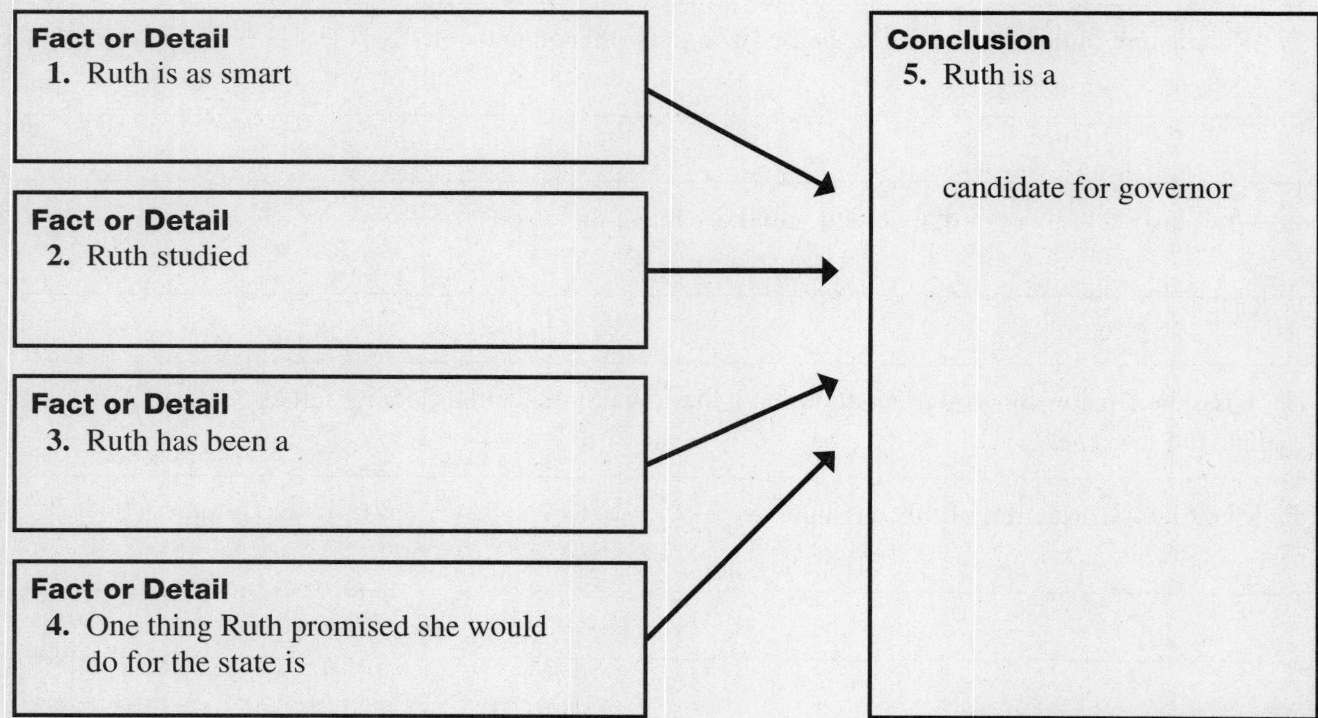

Home Activity Your child identified details of a scene to draw a conclusion about it. Read a short story with your child. Have your child draw a conclusion about the attitude of the main character. Ask your child to explain the details that support the conclusion.

Name________________________________

Print Sources/Media

- Libraries contain many sources of information. You can use a library database or a card catalog to identify and locate these materials. In both cases, you can search for materials by author, title, or subject.
- **Print sources** include encyclopedias, newspapers, magazines, dictionaries, and other reference books, including the *Readers' Guide to Periodical Literature.*

Directions Study the following examples of reference sources.

Newspaper article

Female Enrollment in Local Medical Schools On the Rise

by Jessica Humphry

According to enrollment reports released Tuesday by area colleges, the number of women studying in medical school has risen since last year. In fact, the reports show a 25% increase in female students enrolled in programs in the medical field. One university official cautioned, however, that enrollment in medical school does not guarantee that all students will graduate and go on to practice medicine. Nonetheless, she said that the new figures do signal a change in women's attitudes toward medical school.

Encyclopedia entry

Medicine is the study of the body and how to prevent disease. Medicine is a large subject that is discussed in several different encyclopedia entries (see list of topics below). The study and practice of medicine is crucial to the existence of human beings. It is a field that depends on constant research to update knowledge and methods. (See also: *history of medicine, disease, diet, childhood diseases, life, biology, cell, aging, cancer, organs, growth and development, body systems, pregnancy, prescription drugs*)

Card Catalog Entry

MEDICINE—BIOGRAPHY
Florence Nightingale: a life / Christine Argyle.
New York: Mammoth Publishing Co., 2003.

Biography of famed nineteenth century nurse and social reformer.

1. Medicine—Biography. 2. Medicine—Women in Medicine. 3. History—Women

Magazine Article

My Life in Medicine

by Flo Passerine

I have always respected people who have gone into medicine. I decided to do it myself after several years of reading about the work done by doctors and nurses around the world. As I began my training, I was both thrilled and frightened: there was so much to learn, and so many things that could go wrong if

Name ____

Directions Imagine that you are writing a report on women in medicine. Use the samples of print resources on the preceding page, and your prior knowledge to answer the questions below.

1. Which of the four entries would you start with to begin your report?

____

2. How would you broaden your base of information?

____

3. What would be a good strategy to find the information you need in the print encyclopedia?

____

4. How could magazine articles enrich your report?

____

5. Does the encyclopedia entry shown relate to your report?

____

6. What is the topic of the newspaper article?

____

____

7. How would you go about finding appropriate magazines for your research in a library?

____

____

8. What topics would you look for in the *Readers' Guide to Periodical Literature*?

____

9. Compare the advantages and disadvantages of using newspapers and encyclopedias.

____

____

10. Why is it a good idea to use a variety of sources when possible?

____

____

Home Activity Your child answered questions about print sources. Discuss what print sources are available in your home. Decide which sources your child could use for a future report, and make a plan to visit your local library to become familiar with their sources as well.

Name

Family Times

Summary

Into the Ice: The Story of Arctic Exploration

Many people in history tried to become the first human to reach the North Pole. Some of the most daring and interesting attempts include the journey of Fridtjof Nansen, the balloon flight of Salomon Andrée, and the first officially successful expedition by Robert Peary. These men faced disappointment, disaster, and controversy on their journeys.

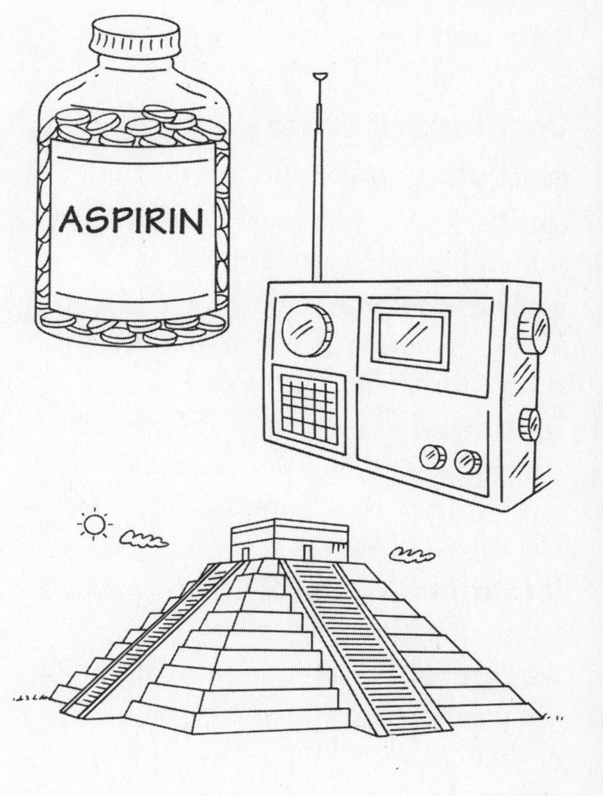

Activity

The First Discuss with your family why people have the need to become the first one to discover something. How does discovery affect the discoverer and others? Talk about what processes, places, or information you would have liked to have discovered and why.

Comprehension Skill

Cause and Effect

A **cause** is what makes something happen. An **effect** is what happens as a result of a cause. To find a cause, ask yourself "Why did this happen?" To find an effect, ask yourself "What happened because of this?" Sometimes an effect can have more than one cause.

Activity

How Many Causes? Read a nonfiction article with a family member about a current event or discovery in our world today. Record the effect of the event or discovery and list as many causes as you can identify.

Lesson Vocabulary

Words to Know

Knowing the meanings of these words is important to reading *Into the Ice: The Story of Arctic Exploration*. Practice using these words.

Vocabulary Words

conquer to overcome; get the better of

destiny what becomes of someone or something; one's fate or fortune

expedition journey for some special purpose, such as exploration, scientific study, or military purposes

insulated lined or surrounded with a material that does not conduct energy; protected from the loss of heat, electricity, or sound

isolation the state of being separated from others, of being alone

navigator person in charge of finding the position and course of a ship, aircraft, or expedition

provisions a supply of food and drinks

verify to prove to be true; confirm

Grammar

Subject and Object Pronouns

A **subject pronoun** is used as the subject of a sentence. *I*, *you*, *he*, *she*, *it*, *we*, and *they* are subject pronouns. An **object pronoun** is used as a direct object or the object of a preposition in a sentence. Only these pronouns can be used as object pronouns: *me*, *you*, *him*, *her*, *it*, *us*, and *them*.

Activity

Pronoun Color Game Create a chart with twelve numbered spaces. Fill the spaces with the following pronouns: *I*, *him*, *we*, *it*, *they*, *her*, *me*, *us*, *she*, *them*, *he*, *you*. Take turns with a family member at rolling a number cube and moving a game piece along the numbered spaces on the chart. Read the pronoun, decide whether it is an object or subject pronoun, and make up a sentence that uses it correctly. If you are correct, color the space with the color of your choice. If you are incorrect, the other player takes a turn. The winner is the person who has the most squares in his or her color when both players reach the twelfth space.

Practice Tested Spelling Words

____________	____________	____________	____________
____________	____________	____________	____________
____________	____________	____________	____________
____________	____________	____________	____________
____________	____________	____________	____________

Name ________________________________

Cause and Effect

- A **cause** is what makes something happen. An **effect** is something that happens as a result of a cause. To find a cause, ask yourself, "Why did this happen?" To find an effect, ask yourself, "What happened?"
- Clue words such as *because, so,* and *due to* can help you spot cause-and-effect relationships.

Directions Read the following passage. Then complete the graphic organizer.

The northern lights are beautiful lights that dance in the northern sky at night. They are most visible in the northern states. They occur due to large explosions on the sun. The explosions release particles that travel through space and are attracted to Earth's magnetic poles. Because of a collision between these particles and Earth's atmosphere, light particles are released. These particles are what form the northern lights.

Cause		Effect
What makes something happen 1.	→	**What happened** 2.
What makes something happen 3.	→	**What happened** 4.

5. Write a one-sentence summary of this passage.

____

____

Home Activity Your child identified causes and effects in a passage about the northern lights. Read another article about the northern lights with your child and discuss the cause of the different colors of the northern lights.

Name ____

Vocabulary

Directions Choose the word from the box that best matches each definition. Write the word on the line.

Check the Words You Know

- ___conquer
- ___destiny
- ___expedition
- ___insulated
- ___isolation
- ___navigator
- ___provisions
- ___verify

_______________ **1.** to overcome; get the better of

_______________ **2.** to prove to be true

_______________ **3.** what becomes of something or someone

_______________ **4.** person in charge of finding the position and course of a ship or aircraft

_______________ **5.** a supply of food and drinks

Directions Choose the word from the box that best matches each clue. Write the word on the line.

_______________ **6.** This is a journey taken for a special purpose.

_______________ **7.** This is done to keep something from losing heat by wrapping it with special material.

_______________ **8.** This is a state of being separate from the rest of the group.

_______________ **9.** A witness is often called to do this to a person's statement in a trial.

_______________ **10.** This is what you try to do to your enemy in a war.

Write a Description

Imagine you have just explored the North Pole. On a separate sheet of paper, write a description of your trip there. Use as many vocabulary words as you can.

Home Activity Your child identified and used vocabulary words from *Into the Ice.* Write a poem together about exploring. Use the vocabulary words from the selection.

Name ____________________

Vocabulary • Context Clues

- When you are reading and see an unfamiliar word, use context clues, or words around the unfamiliar word, to figure out its meaning.
- Context clues include definitions, explanations, and synonyms (words that have the same or nearly the same meaning as other words).

Directions Read the following passage. Then answer the questions below.

Jared was preparing for their expedition. He was very excited about this journey. He packed their provisions: plenty of water and multigrain bars. He put their water in an insulated jug so it would stay cold. Tonight, his older brother would verify their route with their father, making sure it was the safest one possible. Tomorrow, Jared and his brother would leave early on their fishing trip. His brother would be the navigator of their fishing boat, because he knew the best fishing spots. Jared felt it was their destiny to catch enough fish for their dinner.

1. What does *expedition* mean? What clues help you to determine its meaning?

2. Give examples of *provisions* mentioned in the passage. What is another example of a *provision*?

3. What does *verify* mean? What clues help you to determine its meaning?

4. What does *navigator* mean? Why is Jared's brother the *navigator*?

5. Rewrite the sentence with the word *destiny* in it so that it contains a context clue.

Home Activity Your child identified and used context clues to understand new words in a passage. Work with your child to identify unfamiliar words in an article using context clues. Have your child come up with original context clues that could be added to the article to help the reader understand the unfamiliar words.

Name____

Main Idea and Details

Directions Read the following article. Then answer the questions below.

Glaciers exist on every continent, but most glaciers are found near the North and South Poles. Glaciers require high snowfall in the winter and cool summers. Glaciers are formed when, after a long time, snow becomes tiny grains separated by air spaces. Then more snow falls, compressing the lower layers of snow. Then the bottom layers mix with ice crystals and air pockets. These ice crystals continue to grow in size, squeezing out the air. It takes a long time for glaciers to form. At the South Pole, it takes an even longer time to form a glacier, because the amount of snowfall is smaller.

1. Where do glaciers exist?

____

____

2. Give two conditions necessary for the formation of a glacier.

____

____

3. Explain why it would take longer for a glacier to form at the South Pole.

____

____

____

4. What is the main idea of this passage?

____

____

5. On a separate sheet of paper, draw a picture of a forming glacier and label the parts.

Home Activity Your child has read information about the formation of a glacier. Read an article about climates, and have your child identify the main ideas in it.

Name ______________________________

Cause and Effect

- A **cause** is what makes something happen. An **effect** is something that happens as a result of a cause. To find a cause, ask yourself, "Why did this happen?" To find an effect, ask yourself, "What happened?"
- Clue words such as *because, so,* and *due to* can help you spot cause-and-effect relationships.

Directions Read the following passage. Then answer the questions below.

There are still some wild areas for modern explorers to investigate. One such area is Polar Bear Provincial Park in Ontario, Canada. Most of the area has not been explored in depth because it is very isolated. The only way into the park is by boat or plane. There are no roads, only tundra. Tundra is a treeless area with frozen subsoil, low-growing vegetation, and spongy wet soil. These are not the best conditions for walking and exploring. When the weather finally warms in July, hordes of mosquitoes make exploration more difficult. Most exploration of the park has been done by airplane, where it is not unusual to fly over herds of caribou, nesting golden eagles, and polar bears. But there is still a lot of land exploration to do.

1. Why is it difficult to reach this park?

____

2. What causes exploration to be difficult in this park?

____

____

3. What causes exploration during the summer to be even more difficult than at other times?

____

____

4. What is the effect of these harsh conditions?

____

____

5. Write a one-sentence summary of the passage.

____

____

Home Activity Your child identified cause-and-effect relationships in a nonfiction passage to write a summary of it. Read an article about a wilderness area with your child. Work together to write a short summary of the article.

Name ______________________________

Cause and Effect

- A **cause** is what makes something happen. An **effect** is something that happens as a result of a cause. To find a cause, ask yourself, "Why did this happen?" To find an effect, ask yourself, "What happened?"
- Clue words such as *because, so,* and *due to* can help you spot cause-and-effect relationships.

Directions Read the following passage. Then complete the graphic organizer.

Many athletes who work hard to set new records are often called modern explorers because they enter areas that have never been entered before. Tanya Streeter is one of these modern explorers. She is a freediver. Freediving, or breath-hold diving, is done without breathing devices. These athletes must train their bodies and their minds so they can swim underwater for several minutes on a single breath. It is difficult training because the diver needs to focus her mind on holding her breath and dealing with ear pressure. Tanya is a world record holder. She has broken both men and women's records. A magazine even called her "The World's Most Perfect Athlete" in 2002.

Cause		Effect
Why something happens 1. Athletes have ______________	→	**What happened** 2. They are called ______________
Why something happens 3. They must ______________	→	**What happened** 4. They can ______________

5. Write a one-sentence summary of this passage.

____

____

____

School + Home

Home Activity Your child identified cause-and-effect relationships in a nonfiction passage to write a summary of it. Discuss times when you or your child has tried to do something challenging. Answer these questions: Why did you do it? What happened because of it?

Name______________________________

Diagram/Scale Drawing

- A **diagram** is a drawing, usually with parts that are labeled. A diagram shows how something is put together, how an object's parts relate to one another, or how something works. Sometimes a diagram must be looked at in a certain order—left to right, top to bottom, or bottom to top. Diagrams often have text that explains how different parts in a diagram work.
- A **scale drawing** is a diagram that uses a mathematical scale, such as *1 inch on the drawing equals 1 foot in real life.*

Directions Use this diagram to answer the questions below.

A Home Weather Station

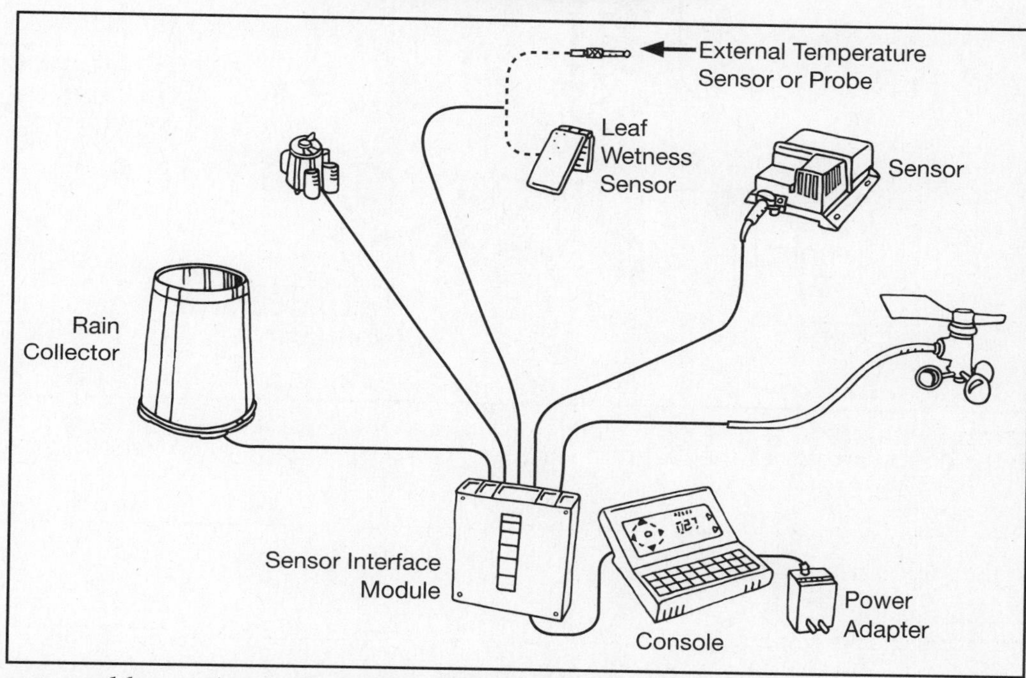

1. What part would you plug into an electrical outlet?

____

2. What part is placed outside to read the temperature and humidity?

____

3. What part is placed outside to determine the amount of rainfall?

____

4. What seems to be missing from this diagram?

____

5. What kind of information would you expect to see accompanying this diagram?

____

____

Name ____________________

Directions Use this diagram of a thunderstorm to answer the questions below.

The diagram below is a cross-section of a thunderstorm moving from right to left. Warm, moist air fuels updrafts. As the air rises, it cools and falls as rain in downdrafts.

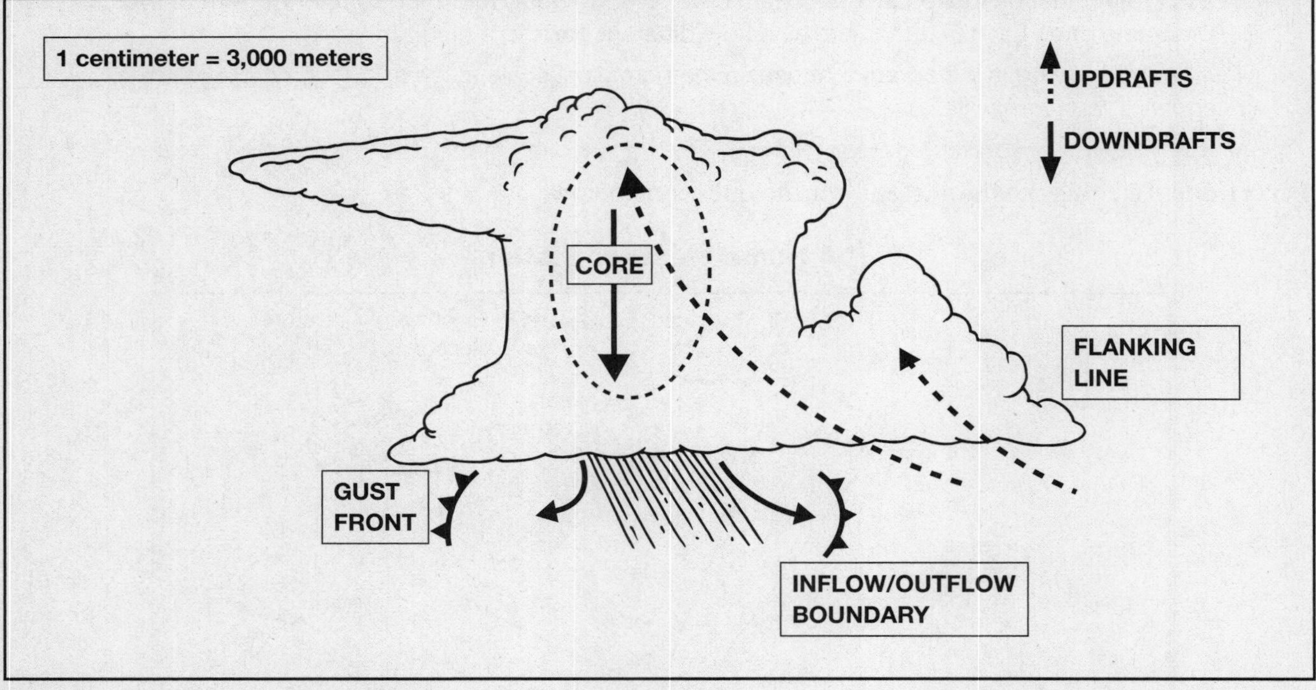

6. What do the dotted arrows of the diagram show?

7. What do the solid arrows show?

8. Where does the rain form in the thunderstorm cloud?

9. If the thunderstorm cloud is five centimeters tall on the diagram, what is its actual height?

10. How are diagrams helpful to readers?

Home Activity Your child learned about using diagrams as resources. Find a scale drawing on the Internet or in a reference book. Have your child explain to you the actual measurements of the item in the scale drawing.

Name ______________________________

Family Times

Summary

The Chimpanzees I Love: Saving Their World and Ours

Chimpanzees are smart and emotional creatures just like humans. Yet many chimpanzees living in captivity at zoos and circuses are mistreated. Chimpanzees living in the wild are also in danger because of hunting practices and forest destruction. It is important to learn about chimpanzees in order to find solutions to these problems.

Activity

Endangered Animals Discuss with your family the types of animals that are in danger of losing their habitats and their lives. What are some of the problems these animals face? Design a poster that explains the need to save endangered animals.

Save Endangered Animals!

Comprehension Skill

Author's Purpose

The **author's purpose** is his or her reason(s) for writing. Authors may write to persuade, inform, express ideas or feelings, or entertain. If you know the author's purpose, you can adjust the way you read. If the purpose is to entertain, you may choose to read faster. If the purpose is to inform, you may want to read more slowly.

Activity

What's the Purpose? Imagine you are writing an article for the school newspaper about an event at your school. Plan your article with a family member and determine your purpose. What do you want to write about? What will your purpose be?

Lesson Vocabulary

Words to Know

Knowing the meanings of these words is important to reading *The Chimpanzees I Love: Saving Their World and Ours.* Practice using these words.

Vocabulary Words

captive kept in confinement
companionship friendly feeling among companions; fellowship
existence condition of being
ordeal a severe test or experience
primitive very simple
sanctuaries places of refuge or protection
stimulating lively; engaging

Grammar

Pronouns and Antecedents

A **pronoun** takes the place of one or more nouns. The **antecedent** is the noun or nouns to which the pronoun refers. *For example: Jacob said he would help out.* The *pronoun* "he" refers to the *antecedent* "Jacob." Pronouns and antecedents must agree. *For example: Bob and Whitney said they would bring their dog.* Because "Bob and Whitney" indicates more than one person, the pronoun "they" must *agree* and be plural as well.

Activity

What's Next? Have a family member write or say a sentence. *For example: Sue has a new car.* Then write or say a logical sentence that could follow using pronouns. *For example: She is very excited about it.* Point out the pronouns and their antecedents.

Practice Tested Spelling Words

______	______	______	______
______	______	______	______
______	______	______	______
______	______	______	______
______	______	______	______

Name________________________________

Author's Purpose

- The **author's purpose** is the reason or reasons the author has for writing. Authors may write to persuade, inform, express ideas or feelings, or entertain.
- As you preview a selection, predict the author's purpose. After reading, ask if the author met his or her purpose.

Directions Read the following passage. Then complete the graphic organizer.

During the 1960s and 1970s, polar bears were a threatened species, so a landmark agreement was reached to stop sport hunting of the bears. However, a bigger threat to the polar bear today is global warming. The warmest temperatures in four centuries have reduced the ice cover over the Arctic waters. If there is more open water, younger bears may not be able to swim far enough to reach solid ice for their food. Warmer springs also lead to more rainfall, which can cause bears' dens to collapse. These conditions lead to lower fitness and reproduction.

Before Reading

What is the author's purpose?

1.

↓

During Reading

What are three clues to the author's purpose?

2.

3.

4.

↓

After Reading

Was the purpose met? How?

5.

Home Activity Your child identified the author's purpose of a nonfiction passage. Work with your child to identify the author's purpose in a magazine or newspaper article. Ask your child to identify some clues that revealed the author's purpose.

Name ______________________________

Vocabulary

Directions Choose the word from the box that best matches each definition. Write the word on the line.

Check the Words You Know

- ___captive
- ___companionship
- ___existence
- ___ordeal
- ___primitive
- ___sanctuaries
- ___stimulating

______________ **1.** very simple

______________ **2.** kept in confinement

______________ **3.** a severe test or experience

______________ **4.** places of refuge or protection

______________ **5.** friendly feeling among companions

Directions Choose the word from the box that best completes each sentence. Write the word on the line shown on the left.

______________ **6.** Margaret really enjoyed the ___ among her friends.

______________ **7.** Karl did not believe in the ___ of ghosts.

______________ **8.** She joined the Film Club so she could meet people who liked ___ conversations about movies.

______________ **9.** The class survived the ___ of taking the hardest test they had ever had.

______________ **10.** The science class went to visit several wildlife ___.

Write a Newspaper Article

On a separate sheet of paper, write a newspaper article about a person who is trying to save an endangered animal. Use as many vocabulary words as you can.

Home Activity Your child identified and used vocabulary words from *The Chimpanzees I Love.* Read a story or nonfiction article with your child. Have him or her point out unfamiliar words. Use a dictionary to look up the unfamiliar words.

Vocabulary • Dictionary/Glossary

- **Dictionaries** and **glossaries** provide alphabetical lists of words and their meanings.
- Sometimes looking at the words around an unfamiliar word can't help you figure out the word's meaning. If this happens, use a dictionary or glossary to find the meaning.

Directions Read the following passage. Then answer the questions below.

Mary found the little bird on the ground after it had fallen from its nest. It survived the ordeal of the fall, but now needed someone to take care of it. Mary took it home and made a primitive shelter out of a shoebox. She called a bird sanctuary to ask what to do. They gave her feeding instructions and told her to keep the bird captive until it was strong enough to fly on its own. Mary enjoyed the bird's companionship for the two weeks she took care of it, but it was time to release the little bird to its wild existence.

1. Find the word *ordeal* in a dictionary or glossary. What does it mean?

____

2. Find the word *primitive* in a dictionary or glossary. Why is a shoebox a *primitive* nest?

____

____

3. Find the word *sanctuary* in a dictionary or glossary. What is the plural form of the word?

____

4. What does the word *captive* mean? Why would the bird experts want Mary to keep the bird captive until it could fly on its own?

____

____

5. What does the word *existence* mean? What is a wild existence?

____

____

Home Activity Your child used a dictionary or glossary to understand new words in a passage. Work with your child to identify unfamiliar words of an article. Then use a dictionary to look up the meanings of these unfamiliar words.

Name ________________________________

Fact and Opinion

Directions Read the article. Then answer the questions below.

Women scientists have contributed to society since the sixth century B.C., but many people did not think that women had the ability to be scientists. Women who studied science received horrible treatment from others. For example, Agloanike was a Greek astronomer during the fifth century B.C. She was able to predict the times and locations of lunar eclipses. But because she was a woman, her skills were attributed to witchcraft.

During the fourth century B.C., Aglodike had to dress like a man in order to practice medicine. When she was found out, she was put on trial. Today most people accept women scientists, but there are still a few prejudiced people who think women do not have the ability to be scientists.

1. Write a statement of opinion from this article.

____

____

2. How do you know the statement you wrote above is a statement of opinion?

____

____

3. Write a statement of fact from this article.

____

____

4. How could you prove the statement of fact you wrote above as true or false?

____

____

5. Why is "Sue should become a scientist when she grows up" a statement of opinion?

____

____

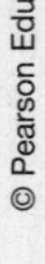

Home Activity Your child has read a passage about early women scientists and identified statements of facts and opinions. Read an article about a woman scientist and have your child identify the statements of facts and opinions in the article.

Name ______________________________

Author's Purpose

- The **author's purpose** is the reason or reasons the author has for writing. Authors may write to persuade, inform, express ideas or feelings, or entertain.
- As you preview a selection, predict the author's purpose. After reading, ask if the author met his or her purpose.

Directions Read the following passage. Then answer the questions below.

Human beings have been one of the main reasons the bald eagle was put on the endangered species list. In the first half of the twentieth century, more than a hundred thousand eagles were killed in Alaska because the salmon fishermen thought they were a threat to the salmon population. DDT, a poisonous insecticide, was also a major cause of death in bald eagles. It was sprayed on plants that were eaten by small animals that the eagles hunted. As a consequence, the eagles were poisoned. Also, as people keep expanding into the eagles' natural habitats, the eagles are losing their nesting areas.

1. What is the author's purpose in writing this passage?

____

2. What is the main idea of this article?

____

____

3. What is one important detail about the author's purpose?

____

____

4. What is another detail about the author's purpose?

____

____

5. Did the author achieve his purpose? How?

____

____

Home Activity Your child identified the author's purpose in a nonfiction passage. Work with your child to identify the author's purpose in an article about an endangered species. Ask your child to identify some clues that reveal the author's purpose.

Name ______________________________

Author's Purpose

- The **author's purpose** is the reason or reasons the author has for writing. Authors may write to persuade, inform, express ideas or feelings, or entertain.
- As you preview a selection, predict the author's purpose. After reading, ask if the author met his or her purpose.

Directions Read the following passage. Then complete the graphic organizer.

Bats are one of the most misunderstood animals in the United States. Because they are associated with vampires in the movies and are often depicted trying to get into people's hair, most people do not like bats. But bats are very beneficial to humans. They are the only major predators of night-flying insects. One bat can eat almost 1,000 mosquitoes and other pests in just one hour. They are a natural insecticide. Unfortunately, many of the 45 species of bats in the United States are either on the endangered or threatened species list. People need to be more educated about the benefits of bats in our environment.

Before Reading

What is the author's purpose?

1. The author is writing to ______________________________

During Reading

What are three clues to the author's purpose?

2. Bats are ______________________________
3. ______________________________
4. People should ______________________________

After Reading

Was the author's purpose met? How?

5. ______________________________

____

Home Activity Your child identified the author's purpose in a passage. Read an article from the editorial page of a newspaper. Have your child identify the clues to the author's purpose.

Name ____________________

Electronic Media

- **Electronic media** includes online newspapers, magazines, encyclopedias, and other sources on the Internet.
- Noncomputer electronic media sources are audio tapes, videotapes, films, filmstrips, television, and radio.

Directions Use the following list of possible electronic media to answer the questions below.

- *The Rain forest Project* (Public Television documentary about saving endangered species in the Brazilian rain forest)
- A Rain Forest of Flowers (Internet site developed by a 2nd grade class about the flowers found in the rain forest)
- *Forest Voices* (CD of various rain forest animal sounds)
- "Rain Forest for the Future" (Taped interview with several rainforest experts about the future of the rain forest)
- *The Rain forest Encyclopedia* (CD-ROM with general information about the flora and fauna of the rain forest)
- Natural Habitat (Internet site about endangered primates in the Brazilian rain forest)

1. Which source would be least helpful in writing a report on endangered animals in the rain forest? Why?

____

____

2. How would you find a video copy of *The Rain forest Project*?

____

____

3. If you were doing an Internet search, what keywords would you type into the search engine to find the Web site Natural Habitat?

____

4. Which source would be most helpful if you needed sound effects for a class presentation about the rain forest?

____

5. Which source would you start with if you needed to decide on a subtopic for a report on the rain forest?

____

Name ____________________

Directions Use the following Internet search results found on a search engine to answer the questions below.

Search Results

Rain Forest Monkeys
University of Brazil's official site for rain forest monkey information. Natural habitats, eating and sleeping habits, scientific studies.

The Eroding Environment
University of Brazil Professor Winston Soela's five-year study of the effect of the disappearing habitat on the spider monkey, its population, food and water sources, social habits.

Fight for the Rain Forest
Sao Paolo Endangered Species Protection Society site. Information about endangered species, monkeys, reptiles. Updates on preservation efforts, fundraising efforts, Brazilian government decision deadlines.

The Brazilian Rain Forest
Our trip to the Brazilian rain forest was fantastic! We saw monkeys, all kinds of insects. Photos.

6. What does the information below the underlined links tell you?

____

7. What keywords might have been used to get these search results?

____

8. Which sites are university sites regarding rain forest monkeys?

____

9. Which site would be the least reliable if you were doing a report for school? Why?

____

____

10. Why might the *Fight for the Rain Forest* site be valuable if you wanted to help preserve endangered species?

____

Home Activity Your child answered questions about electronic media. With your child, look around your house and see how many different types of electronic media you have on hand. Talk with him or her about how each of the various electronic media sources could be valuable in his or her studies.

Name

Family Times

Summary

Black Frontiers

After the Civil War, many African Americans moved out to the open land of the West. Land was free and plentiful there, and people truly lived off it. During this time period, the first all-African American communities were established. African American soldiers, nicknamed Buffalo Soldiers, protected frontier outposts for the U.S. Army.

Activity

Frontier Times Imagine moving to the open plains of the West with nothing but your family and a few personal items. How would you survive? Discuss how your life would change if you were living back in frontier times.

Comprehension Skill

Cause and Effect

A **cause** is why something happens. An **effect** is what happens. To find a cause, ask yourself "Why did this happen?" To find an effect, ask yourself "What happened because of this?"

Activity

Moving Matters Think about why people move from one place to another. Discuss the answers to the following questions with your family: What have you learned about the settlers and immigrants in this country? Why did they move? What did they find when they moved? Have you ever moved? What was the cause of the move?

Lesson Vocabulary

Words to Know

Knowing the meanings of these words is important to reading *Black Frontiers*. Practice using these words.

Vocabulary Words

bondage being held against your will under the control of another; slavery

commissioned holding the rank of second lieutenant or above in the U.S. Army

earthen made of ground, soil, or earth

encounter meet unexpectedly; meet in a battle

homesteaders people who own and live on land granted by the U.S. government

settlement group of buildings and the people living in them

Grammar

Possessive Pronouns

Possessive pronouns show ownership. They do not use apostrophes. *My/mine, your/yours, his/hers, its, our/ours,* and *their/theirs* are possessive pronouns. Use *my, your, her, our,* and *their* before nouns. *For example: This is my dog.* Use *mine, yours, hers, ours, theirs* after nouns. *For example: The dog is mine. His* and *its* can be used both before and after nouns.

Activity

Before and After Make two two-column charts with one column labeled *Before* and the other *After*. Give one chart to a family member. In the *Before* column, write five sentences using a possessive pronoun before a noun. In the *After* column, write five sentences using the possessive pronoun after a noun. Try to see who can complete their chart first.

Practice Tested Spelling Words

Cause and Effect

- A **cause** is what makes something happen. An **effect** is something that happens as a result of a cause. Sometimes several causes lead to one effect.
- Clue words and phrases such as *consequently, as a result,* and *therefore* can help you spot cause-and-effect relationships. Sometimes, though, there are no clue words.

Directions Read the following passage. Then complete the graphic organizer below.

The tornado destroyed everything we had: our sod house, our windmill, and our barn. Even though the tornado touched down a mile away, the ferocious winds affected all the farms in the area. Also, this wasn't your ordinary tornado. According to witnesses, two funnel clouds came together to produce one strong force of nature. Pa still believed we could have avoided such a disastrous outcome, though. He said if we had had sturdier materials to build our home with, then maybe things would've been different. Because our house and the barn were made from the resources of the earth, they didn't stand a chance against the mighty tornado.

Cause (What makes something happen)
1.

Cause (What makes something happen)
2.

Cause (What makes something happen)
3.

Effect (What happened)
4.

5. What prior knowledge did you use to help you understand the passage?

____

____

Home Activity Your child identified causes and effects in a passage while using prior knowledge to better understand its contents. Together, discuss the causes and effects of natural disasters in your area.

Name ______________________________

Vocabulary

Directions Choose the word from the box that best matches each definition. Write the word on the line.

Check the Words You Know
___bondage
___commissioned
___earthen
___encounter
___homesteaders
___settlement

______________ **1.** to meet unexpectedly; meet in a battle

______________ **2.** group of buildings and the people living in them

______________ **3.** people who own and live on land granted by the government

______________ **4.** being held against your will

______________ **5.** made of the ground or soil

Directions Choose the word from the box that best matches each clue. Write the word on the line.

______________ **6.** This is what a town or city of today once was.

______________ **7.** A mud house could be described as this.

______________ **8.** This describes someone who holds the rank of second lieutenant or higher.

______________ **9.** Enslaved people experienced this condition.

______________ **10.** Two soldiers on opposite sides in a war might be involved in this.

Write a Friendly Letter

Imagine what it would be like living on the frontier. Write a friendly letter to someone back home about your experiences as a pioneer. Use as many vocabulary words as you can.

Home Activity Your child identified and used vocabulary words from *Black Frontiers.* With your child, write a story set back in the pioneer days. Use your family members as characters. Include as many vocabulary words from the selection as possible.

Name ____________________

Vocabulary • Context Clues

- When you are reading and see an unfamiliar word, you can use **context clues,** or the words around the unfamiliar word, to figure out its meaning.

Directions Read the following passage. Then answer the questions below.

Today I found out more about my family's history. I thought we had always lived in Kansas, but that wasn't the case. My ancestors were enslaved people in Alabama. When they were no longer held in bondage by white plantation owners, they decided to move as far away from the South as they could. They became homesteaders, moving to the open lands of the West that they bought from the government. My ancestors joined other African Americans who started their own settlement. Their community was a group of homes and buildings made out of earthen materials, such as sod, mud, and grass at first. I found it very strange that the towns and cities I know of today were once crude and small. I also found out that my great-great-great-uncle Thomas was a commissioned officer. I had no idea that my family's history was so interesting!

1. What is the definition of *bondage*? What context clue helps you figure out its meaning?

____

____

2. What context clue helps you figure out the definition of *homesteaders*?

____

3. How do you know a *settlement* is unlike the towns and cities of today?

____

4. What are some examples of *earthen* materials? What is another example not used in the passage?

____

5. The sentence containing the word *commissioned* does not have a context clue. Rewrite the sentence so that a context clue appears. (You may write it as more than one sentence.)

____

____

____

Home Activity Your child identified the definitions of unfamiliar words by using context clues. Read a story or article together. Have your child underline or highlight the context clues that suggest the meanings of unfamiliar words.

Name ____________________

Author's Purpose

Directions Read the following passage. Then answer the questions below.

The Life You Dreamed Of

Do you want the life you have dreamed of? Do you want to own your own land, grow your own food, and build your own home? Do you want to live in a community with other people who have similar backgrounds and experiences? If you answered "yes" to any of the above questions, then you should join Charles Washington as he travels to the open lands of Nebraska. When we arrive, we will all work as a team to construct a town free of Jim Crow laws and prejudiced behavior. We will learn together how to use the resources of the land to give us everything we could possibly need or desire. We will establish a community that is safe and comfortable. This is the time to take action and find a better life for you and your family. If you are interested, please contact Charles Washington at his home at 43 Main Street. We plan on moving starting in early March, so please act promptly.

1. What is the author's purpose for writing this passage?

____

2. How is the passage organized?

____

____

3. What kinds of ideas are used in the passage to meet the author's purpose?

____

____

4. Do you think the author was successful in getting across his or her purpose? Explain why.

____

____

5. On a separate sheet of paper, write an advertisement that convinces the reader to do something.

Home Activity Your child has identified the author's purpose in a passage. Have your child write a short piece with a specific purpose in mind. See if you can guess the intended purpose after reading the piece.

Name ____________________

Cause and Effect

- A **cause** is what makes something happen. An **effect** is something that happens as a result of a cause. Sometimes several causes lead to one effect.
- Clue words and phrases such as *consequently, as a result,* and *therefore* can help you spot cause-and-effect relationships. Sometimes, though, there are no clue words.

Directions Read the following passage. Then answer the questions below.

As more and more settlers came to live on the open plains of the West, the need for new technology arose. People used fences to keep animals in certain areas and to mark their plots of land. But these fences were made out of wood, mud, or stone that sometimes was hard to find on the open plains. There was a need for inexpensive fencing. As a result, barbed wire was invented. When the use of barbed wire spread throughout the plains, people thought their problems were solved. Instead, other problems surfaced. States had to make laws against those farmers who still let their animals roam freely. Soon the open lands that the pioneers sought when they first came to the West were divided up into independently owned plots. With the expansion of railroads, cattle drives between long distances were no longer necessary, and the unclaimed West was a thing of the past.

1. Why did people build fences in the first place?

____

2. What was a cause of the invention of barbed wire?

____

3. What clue words helped you find this cause?

____

4. What were some effects of barbed wire?

____

____

5. What prior knowledge helped you to understand this article?

____

____

Home Activity Your child determined causes and effects in a passage while activating prior knowledge. Make a plan to help your child increase his or her general knowledge about the world. The plan could include checking books out from the library, reading the newspaper on a regular basis, or getting a subscription to a magazine.

Name ______________________________

Cause and Effect

- A **cause** is what makes something happen. An **effect** is something that happens as a result of a cause. Sometimes several causes lead to one effect.
- Clue words and phrases such as *consequently, as a result,* and *therefore* can help you spot cause-and-effect relationships. Sometimes, though, there are no clue words.

Directions Read the following passage. Then complete the diagram below.

Howard was restless. He was tired of working as a farmer on land that he didn't own. Plus he found the work incredibly dull and boring. One day, he saw a poster advertising cowboy jobs. The cowboys would drive cattle across long distances. These cowboys would have to work long days without a single day off for months. He would be alone for much of the time. Yet the idea of being on a horse, riding across the open plains of the country, was thrilling to Howard. The next day, Howard packed his few belongings and headed West.

Cause (What makes something happen)

1. Howard was tired of ______________________

____

Cause (What makes something happen)

2. Howard saw a poster that ______________________

____

Cause (What makes something happen)

3. ______________________________

____

Effect (What happened)

4. ______________________________

____

5. If Howard never saw the poster, do you still think he would have left for the West? Why or why not?

____

____

School + Home **Home Activity** Your child identified causes and an effect in a passage. Discuss an instance or moment in your child's life in which several causes led to one effect.

Name ____________________

Note Taking

- **Note taking** can help you when you are collecting information for a report. It can also help you keep track of information in a story and remember what you have read for a test.
- When you take notes, paraphrase, or put what you read into your own words. Synthesize, or combine, information so that you include only important details. Use keywords, phrases, or short sentences.

Directions Read the following passage. Takes notes as you read on the lines to the right.

As a kid, I believed cowboys had only existed in myths, legends, and movies. I wanted to think that people really roamed across the countryside and involved themselves in all kinds of adventures, but it just sounded like the stuff of bad novels to me. Then as I grew older, I began to do a little research into the subject, and, boy, were my eyes opened.

One of the cowboys I researched was Nat Love. Nat Love was born into slavery in 1854. He lived as an enslaved person until all such people were given their freedom in 1865. When he was 15, he decided he would try the cowboy life. He moved to Dodge City, in Kansas, where he found a job as a cowboy. Nat Love spent twenty years of his life driving cattle across the open lands of the country. He won a contest in 1876 for his cowboy skills (such as roping cattle, shooting, and riding a horse).

Eventually, Love decided to record his thoughts and stories about life as a cowboy in a book. The book was published as Love's autobiography in 1907. Books like these included the stories that I remember hearing as a child—the wild adventures of cowboys. Yet, experts believe many of Love's stories are tall tales and not very close to the truth. We may never know how exciting the cowboy life in the Old West really was, but we have the freedom of letting our imaginations run wild.

NOTES

Name ______________________________

Directions Answer the questions below using the article and your notes.

1. Synthesize the information in the first paragraph and write it as a single sentence.

2. Paraphrase the first sentence in the third paragraph of the article.

3. How long was Nat Love's cowboy career?

4. What fact about Nat Love's childhood is most important to write down?

5. Why would writing your notes into a table or diagram help you understand the article?

6. What did Nat Love do in 1876 that led to his fame?

7. For what purpose would you want to take notes on the author's opinions of cowboy stories?

8. Why should you only write down important ideas when taking notes?

9. Is there only one way to take notes?

10. Name two ways taking notes can help you study for a test.

Home Activity Your child learned how to take notes, synthesize, and paraphrase information. Read an article or story with your child. Help your child experiment to find a method of note-taking he or she is most comfortable with (traditional, chart, web, outline etc.).

Name

Family Times

Summary

Space Cadets

In order to explore a new planet and establish peace, the Captain sends his serious First Officer and two space cadets, Harold and Tom, to investigate. The three characters encounter a space cow and two aliens. The humans act more afraid of the cow than the actual aliens, who they assume to be harmless space dogs. After the humans get scared and leave the planet, the aliens discuss how there truly is no intelligent life out there.

Activity

Space Scene Imagine living in outer space in the future. What would people be like? What would your home be like? Talk about what you think a typical day would be like.

Comprehension Skill

Draw Conclusions

When you **draw a conclusion,** you form a reasonable opinion about something you have read. When you draw a conclusion it should make sense. Ask yourself, "Is the conclusion based on facts? Does the information I read support the conclusion?"

Activity

What's the Conclusion? Think of a subject you know about and write a statement about it without showing anyone. Say two or three facts that support your statement, and see if a family member can draw the same conclusion that you wrote down.

Lesson Vocabulary

Words to Know

Knowing the meanings of these words is important to reading *Space Cadets.* Practice using these words.

Vocabulary Words

aliens imaginary creatures from outer space

barge a large, strongly-built boat or ship for carrying freight or waste

hospitable friendly; receptive

molten made liquid by heat; melted

ore rock containing enough of a metal or metals to make mining profitable

refrain to keep yourself from doing something

universal existing everywhere, for all purposes

version a special form or variant of something

Grammar

Indefinite and Reflexive Pronouns

Indefinite pronouns do not always have definite antecedents. *For example: No one answers when I call. No one* does not have a particular antecedent in the example. It is an indefinite pronoun. Some singular indefinite pronouns include *someone*, *no one*, and *anyone*. Plural indefinite pronouns include *everyone*, *several*, *both*, *others*, and *many*.

Reflexive pronouns reflect the action of the verb back onto the subject. They end in *-self* or *-selves.*

Activity

The Truth About Our Family With a family member, take turns creating true statements about your family and the people in it. Each statement should include an indefinite or reflexive pronoun. *For example: Nobody in our family has ever been to Buenos Aires. Sarah made herself breakfast this morning.*

Practice Tested Spelling Words

______	______	______	______
______	______	______	______
______	______	______	______
______	______	______	______
______	______	______	______

Name________________________________

Draw Conclusions

- When you **draw conclusions**, you form reasonable opinions about what you have read. Use what you know about real life to help you draw conclusions.
- Be sure that there are enough facts or information in the text to support your conclusions.

Directions Read the following passage. Then complete the diagram.

I think in the future people will live on other planets in our solar system. They will have grown tired of the crowded cities on Earth and will manage a way to build smaller communities on other planets. Life will be slower on these planets. People won't feel like they have to compete with each other for space, jobs, and resources since the whole solar system will be opened up for their use. People will spend their days exploring the universe and learning about new life forms instead of being consumed with day-to-day details.

Fact or Detail
1.

Fact or Detail
2.

Fact or Detail
3.

Conclusion
4.

5. How did you visualize the future described in the passage?

____

____

Home Activity Your child visualized the details in a passage to draw a conclusion about it. Look through books or magazines for a detailed illustration or photo. Have your child study the picture and draw a conclusion about what is going on in it.

Name ___________________________

Vocabulary

Directions Draw a line from the words on the left to their definitions on the right.

1. **barge**	friendly; receptive
2. **refrain**	existing everywhere
3. **hospitable**	made liquid by heat; melted
4. **universal**	to keep yourself from doing something
5. **molten**	boat or ship carrying freight

Check the Words You Know

___aliens
___barge
___hospitable
___molten
___ore
___refrain
___universal
___version

Directions Choose the word from the box that best completes each sentence. Write the word on the line shown on the left.

________________ 6. They mine iron ___ here.

________________ 7. Her ___ of the story was hilarious.

________________ 8. Do you believe that ___ exist?

________________ 9. I hope they are ___ beings.

________________ 10. Please ___ from exiting the space ship while in flight.

Write a Story

Write a science fiction story set in outer space. Use as many vocabulary words as you can.

School + Home **Home Activity** Your child identified and used vocabulary words from *Space Cadets*. With your child, have a conversation about what you perceive the future to be like. Try to use the vocabulary words from the selection while conversing.

Name ____________________

Vocabulary • Context Clues

- When you are reading and see a word that has more than one meaning, you can use **context clues**, or words around the multiple-meaning word, to figure out its meaning.

Directions Read the following passage. Then answer the questions below.

Before we could start on the mission, we had to obtain a permit to land on the planet Apollo. The planet had recently been added to the Dangerous Zone by the Space Council. There was evidence that the environment of Apollo was dangerous to humans. Since we were on a special mission to extract molten lava for research purposes, we were granted permission. It took a full day to gather the material into canisters and load them onto the space barge, the vehicle that would take us back to Earth. We had to refrain from bringing any other substance from Apollo onboard with us for fear of contamination. So when I noticed some planet Apollo dust on my elbow, I had to be quarantined immediately. I was not allowed to return to work until the foreign dust was contained and proven harmless.

1. What is the definition of *permit* in this passage? What is another definition of the word?

____

2. How do you know *barge* does not mean "to enter quickly" in the passage?

____

____

3. What is the definition of *refrain* as it is used in the passage? How do you know?

____

____

4. What is another meaning of *elbow*?

____

____

5. Use one of the multiple-meaning words in an original sentence. Make sure to include a context clue in the sentence, so that the intended meaning of the word is clear.

____

____

Home Activity Your child identified the definitions of multiple-meaning words by using context clues. Make a list of words that have multiple meanings. Have your child pick a word from the list and draw an illustration of its meaning while you try to guess which word it is. Switch roles, and repeat the activity.

Name ____

Sequence

Directions Read the fictional article. Then answer the questions below.

Space exploration and settlement has increased at a rapid rate in the last century. In 2055, Dr. B.R. Slater invented the single-family space shuttle. This vehicle included all the latest space navigation technology as well as many of the comforts of home that families had enjoyed on Earth. Then, in 2077, space explorer Marsha Tewillinger became the first person to walk on the new planet Zeus. During her mission she was able to record signs of life on the planet in the form of grass-like plants and simple, grazing creatures that we know now as the yook and the pellilope. Of course, as we know now, this discovery encouraged settlers from Earth to hop into their space shuttles and settle Zeus. They built large ranches on the blue plains and raised animals. While the communities on Zeus were still being developed, the hospitable aliens from Mars began to settle the hilly lands of Helio, one of Zeus's several moons. Helio has proven to be a popular vacation area for beings from all around the universe.

1. How do you know the sequence of events in this article?

____

____

2. When did Marsha Tewillinger walk on Zeus?

____

3. What event did the invention of the single family space shuttle lead to?

____

____

4. What events happened simultaneously?

____

____

5. Predict events that could happen in the future of space exploration. On another sheet of paper, draw out a time line that shows the order of the events.

Home Activity Your child has identified the sequence of events in a fictional article. Have your child tell a funny story about an event that happened in his or her life. Ask your child to tell it out of order. Compare the original story to the rearranged one.

Name ______________________________

Draw Conclusions

- When you **draw conclusions**, you form reasonable opinions about what you have read. Use what you know about real life to help you draw conclusions.
- Be sure that there are enough facts or information in the text to support your conclusions.

Directions Read the following scene. Then answer the questions.

COMMANDER 1 I think we need to be aware that the aliens on Zolta may be dangerous.

COMMANDER 2 Why do you think that? Just because they're different from us doesn't mean they are dangerous.

COMMANDER 1 Do you want to take that chance? I sure don't want to risk my life because I'm afraid I may hurt some unknown being's feelings.

COMMANDER 2 I am only trying to give them the benefit of the doubt. *(The two commanders prepare to leave the ship and explore. COMMANDER 1 takes a ray gun and tranquilizing devices. COMMANDER 2 packs a translator and space ice cream meant to be a gift to the aliens.)*

COMMANDER 2 Let me do the talking.

COMMANDER 1 Fine, but don't say I didn't warn you!

1. What conclusion can you draw about Commander 1's personality?

____

2. What details from the scene support this conclusion?

____

____

3. What conclusion can you draw about Commander 2's personality?

____

4. What details from the scene support this conclusion?

____

____

5. How did you visualize this scene taking place?

____

____

Home Activity Your child drew conclusions by visualizing the details in a scene. Read a story together. Have your child pretend he or she is going to make a movie out of the story. Ask your child to draw out a few of the scenes based on the details he or she visualized.

Name ____________________

Draw Conclusions

- When you **draw conclusions**, you form reasonable opinions about what you have read. Use what you know about real life to help you draw conclusions.
- Be sure that there are enough facts or information in the text to support your conclusions.

Directions Read the following article. Then complete the diagram by drawing a conclusion about the possibility of life as we know it on Mercury.

Mercury is a small planet. It is not very far from the sun. Its surface temperature varies greatly from side to side. The side of Mercury that is closer to the sun is extremely hot (427 degrees Celsius). The other side is very cold (about –183 degrees Celsius). That's quite a difference!

As opposed to Earth, Mercury has a thin atmosphere made of sodium and helium. Scientists have concluded that craters, plate movement, and volcanoes are responsible for shaping the surface of the planet.

Fact or Detail
1. Mercury is too close

Fact or Detail
2. The temperature

Fact or Detail
3. The atmosphere

Conclusion
4. There is no

5. What did you visualize the surface of the planet Mercury to look like?

____

Home Activity Your child drew a conclusion based on details in an article. Have your child visualize what a planet would look like if he or she could create it. Ask your child to draw a conclusion about what life would be like on this planet based on his or her description of it.

Follow and Clarify Directions

- **Following directions** involves doing or making something. **Clarifying directions** means writing clear directions for others to use.
- Directions usually are numbered. The numbers tell you the sequence of the steps. Read all directions before starting to act on the first direction given. Visualize the purpose or the end result of the directions while reading.

Directions Read the following set of directions.

How to Make a Papier-Mâché Planet

1. Gather the following items: all-purpose flour; water; balloon; old newspapers; large mixing bowl; measuring cups; mixing spoon; old newspapers; paint brush.
2. In a large mixing bowl, combine three cups of water to one cup of flour. Stir together until you have a smooth mixture. (You may double or triple this recipe depending upon size and number of your papier mâché planets.)
3. Cut the old newspapers into two-inch-wide strips. Cover designated work space with the rest of the newspaper.
4. Blow up your balloon to the desired size of your planet. Tie a knot at the bottom of it.
5. Place strips of paper into the mixing bowl. Use a paintbrush or your hands to wet the strips with the mixture. Place the strips of paper onto your balloon. Try to crisscross the strips of paper (or overlap them to form X's) as you add them to the balloon. Cover the entire balloon.
6. Allow the balloon to dry thoroughly before advancing on to the next step.
7. Gather the following items: clean paintbrush; paints of desired colors; paper towels; water; small bowl.
8. Choose the appropriate colors to paint your planet. You may want to consult an encyclopedia or another reference book with pictures or illustrations of the planets to get a good idea of what they look like. Paint your planet accordingly. Make sure to rinse your paintbrush in the small bowl of water between colors. Use the paper towels to wipe off your paintbrushes after painting.
9. Let the balloon dry completely. Cut a small slit into your papier-mâché surface. Insert a needle to pop the balloon. Pull the popped balloon out of the papier-mâché mold.
10. Display your planet for all to see and admire.

Name ______________________________

Directions Use the directions to answer the following questions.

1. If you were actually going to make a papier-mâché planet what is the first thing you need to do?

2. In what step do you blow up the balloon?

3. How could popping the balloon too early change your end result?

4. How could the directions in step 6 be clarified?

5. Why do you think the directions include two steps in which you gather materials?

6. How could the directions in step 3 be clarified?

7. Will this project always take the same amount of time to complete?

8. How does visualizing help you to follow directions?

9. Is there any way the steps in this process could be changed while getting the same final product?

10. Add a direction to the end of this set that explains how to display the papier-mâché planet.

Home Activity Your child answered questions about a set of directions. Have your child write a set of directions to perform a task that he or she knows well. Help your child to write as clear and accurate directions as possible.

Name

Family Times

Summary

Inventing the Future: A Photobiography of Thomas Alva Edison

While working at a telegraph office, Thomas Edison took an interest in inventions. Soon, he had quit his job and was designing and building inventions on a full time basis. Some of his inventions include a long-lasting light bulb, a movie camera, and a number of phonographs.

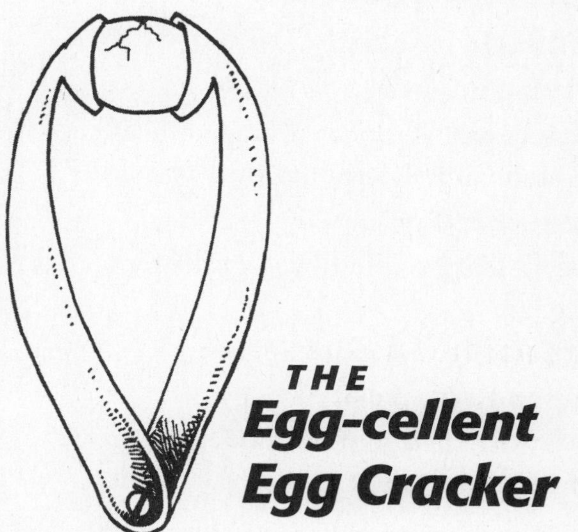

Activity

Be an Inventor Discuss with your family an invention you believe would help make people's lives easier. Draw a picture of your invention and name it.

Comprehension Skill

Author's Purpose

The **author's purpose** is his or her reason for writing. An author may write to persuade, inform, express, or entertain. Preview the title, headings, and pictures of an article to predict the author's purpose. As you read, you may need to adjust your ideas about the author's purpose.

Activity

Purpose Log Choose an article or story to read with a family member. Look at the text, pictures, and headlines or titles. Write what you believe the purpose is and how you know. Repeat this step halfway through the article and after reading it. Decide whether or not the author met his or her purpose.

Lesson Vocabulary

Words to Know

Knowing the meanings of these words is important to reading *Inventing the Future.* Practice using these words.

Vocabulary Words

converts changes
devise invent
efficiency ability to produce the effect wanted without waste of time or energy
generated produced
percentage allowance figured by percent
proclaimed declared publicly
reproduce to make a copy of
transmitted sent out signals by means of electromagnetic waves or by wire

Grammar

Who and Whom

Who and ***whom*** are pronouns. Use *who* as a subject, and use *whom* as the object of a preposition such as *to, for,* or *from. For example: Who is driving us to soccer practice? For whom are these flowers? Whom* is also used as a direct object, most often in questions. *For example: Whom did you see?*

Activity

***Who* and *Whom* Tic-Tac-Toe** On a sheet of paper, create a tic-tac-toe board. In each square, take turns with a family member writing down a sentence or question with a blank where *who* or *whom* should be. Then play tic-tac-toe. To claim a square, you must fill in the blank with the correct answer, *who* or *whom.*

Practice Tested Spelling Words

______	______	______	______
______	______	______	______
______	______	______	______
______	______	______	______
______	______	______	______

Name______________________________

Author's Purpose

- The **author's purpose** is the reason or reasons the author has for writing.
- An author may write to persuade, to inform, to entertain, or to express ideas and feelings. An author may have more than one reason for writing.

Directions Read the following passage. Then complete the diagram.

One very cool invention is the refrigerator. Before refrigeration, it was difficult to store and ship fresh food. In the early twentieth century, food was kept cold with a block of ice in a cabinet called an "icebox." The cooling process used in today's refrigerators dates back to Michael Faraday's experiments in the eighteenth century with liquefying ammonia. The first refrigeration machine was designed in 1805 by the American inventor Oliver Evans. Other inventors improved on this device. The first commercial home refrigerator was sold in 1911 by General Electric. Today, homes all over the world have refrigerators.

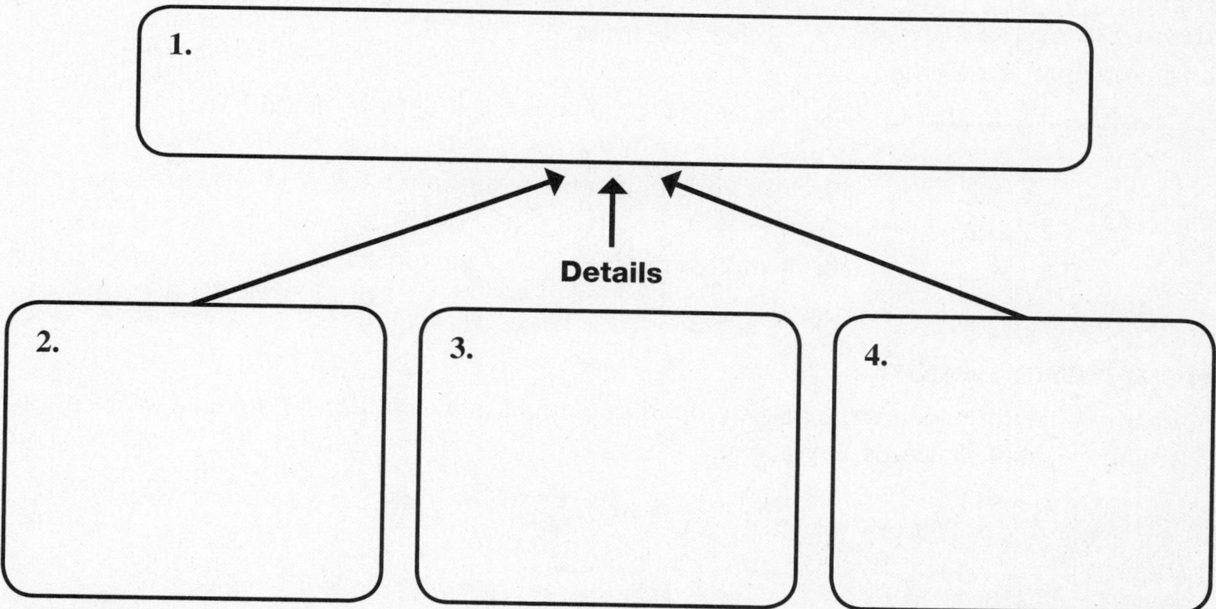

5. How did the author's language or style help meet the purpose?

____

____

Home Activity Your child identified the author's purpose and cited details to support this analysis. Work with your child to identify the author's purpose and supporting details of individual paragraphs in a magazine article about an innovation. Challenge your child to set his or her reading pace to match the purpose of the article.

Name ______________________________

Vocabulary

Directions Choose the word from the box that best matches each definition. Write the word on the line.

Check the Words You Know
___converts
___devise
___efficiency
___generated
___percentage
___proclaimed
___reproduce
___transmitted

__________ **1.** to invent

__________ **2.** allowance, figured by percent

__________ **3.** produced

__________ **4.** sent out signals by means of electromagnetic waves or by wire

__________ **5.** to make a copy of

Directions Choose the word from the box that best completes each sentence below. Write the word on the line shown to the left.

__________ **6.** The inventor ____ that he had a great invention.

__________ **7.** He claimed that his machine ____ food from one place to another, electronically.

__________ **8.** "It ____ food into electrical pulses," he declared.

__________ **9.** If it worked, it could result in more ____ by saving time.

__________ **10.** Although the idea ____ much interest, it turned out to be a fake.

Write a News Report

On a separate sheet of paper, write a news report you might make after observing a new invention. Use as many vocabulary words as you can.

School + Home

Home Activity Your child identified and used vocabulary words from *Inventing the Future.* Have a conversation about useful inventions. Why are they useful? What do they do? Use the vocabulary words from the selection while conversing.

Name ______________________________

Vocabulary • Word Structure

- If you see an unfamiliar word while you are reading, use word parts to figure out its meaning. **Prefixes** are word parts with their own meanings that are added to base words. They change the meanings of base words.
- The prefix *re-* means "again;" *pro-* means "before;" *trans-* means "over;" and *con-* means "together."

Directions Read the following article. Then answer the questions below.

Who deserves to be recalled as the inventor of the telephone? The principle behind the telephone is that it converts sound waves to electrical impulses that are then transmitted through a wire to reproduce the sound. Although Alexander Graham Bell claimed to be the inventor of the telephone, a little-known inventor named Elisha Gray also devised a telephone. Both men raced to the patent office to apply for a patent, and Bell beat Gray by only hours. Alexander Graham Bell will always be remembered, but not Elisha Gray. If Gray had arrived at the patent office a little bit earlier, he would be the famous one.

1. In the word *converts* how does the prefix *con-*, combined with the Latin root *vertere* for "turn," help you to determine the meaning of the word?

____

____

2. What does *transmitted* mean? How does the prefix contribute to the meaning?

____

____

3. How does the prefix in *reproduce* help you to determine the meaning of the word?

____

4. How would the prefix help you to determine the meaning of *proclaimed?*

____

5. What are two other words in the article that use the prefix *trans-, con-, re-,* or *pro-*?

____

Home Activity Your child identified and used prefixes to understand new words of a passage. Work with your child to identify unfamiliar words in another article. Then see if he or she can find prefixes to help with the understanding of the new words. Confirm the meanings with your child.

Name ___________________________

Cause and Effect

Directions Read the article. Then answer the questions below.

Strangely enough, some inventions are lost because people can't imagine their value. A use may need to be "invented" along with the invention. An example is the fax machine. The technology for faxing was invented in the 1800s. It took more than one hundred years, however, for the fax to be seen as useful. In 1843 Alexander Bain invented a machine to electrically transmit writing. At first, it was considered useless since few people thought there was a need for transmitting writing over wires. Eventually the value of the invention was realized, and it was improved for office use. By the 1980s, the fax machine became a piece of standard equipment in offices. The reason is that it can very quickly transmit written documents. Who knows how many other inventions just need to be recognized as valuable?

1. What clue words or phrases in the article indicate cause-effect relationships?

____

____

2. According to the author, why are some inventions lost?

____

____

3. Why did it take more than one hundred years for faxes to be widely used?

____

____

4. Why are faxes now considered to be pieces of valuable office equipment?

____

____

5. On a separate sheet of paper, explain what you think might happen if society does not recognize the value of a new invention.

Home Activity Your child has read information about an invention, including the causes for its rejection and acceptance. Read an article about another invention with your child. Challenge him or her to identify causes and effects related to the invention's acceptance.

Name____

Author's Purpose

- The **author's purpose** is the reason or reasons the author has for writing.
- An author may write to persuade, to inform, to entertain, or to express ideas and feelings. An author may have more than one reason for writing.

Directions Read the following passage. Then answer the questions below.

One summer day a walk through the woods led to a clever invention. George de Mestral was hiking the mountain paths of his native Switzerland with his dog in 1948. After he got home, he noticed burrs clinging to his pants and his dog's fur. Burrs are the prickly seed cases of certain plants. As he removed these burrs, he observed how their many curved arms stuck to fabric and fur. Studying them under the microscope gave him an idea for a new type of closure. He experimented with different materials and formats. Eventually, he invented a fabric covered with tiny hooks. This fabric sticks tight to any fabric with a fuzzy surface. His invention is manufactured to hold pockets, shoes, and clothing closed or to attach one thing to another. People should be glad de Mestral and his dog took a walk that day.

1. What was the author's main purpose for writing this passage?

____

2. What is one important detail that shows the author's purpose?

____

3. What is another important detail that shows the author's purpose?

____

4. How well do you think the author met this main purpose for writing? Explain.

____

____

5. To monitor your comprehension, take notes on the purpose of each sentence. Which sentence in the article has a different purpose from the main purpose of the passage? Explain.

____

____

Home Activity Your child identified the author's purposes in a nonfiction passage. Read a magazine article about a different invention with your child. Work together to identify the author's main purpose in the article. Talk about secondary purposes too. Challenge your child to monitor his or her comprehension and use fix-up strategies in order to understand the information in the article.

Name ______________________________________

Author's Purpose

- The **author's purpose** is the reason or reasons the author has for writing.
- An author may write to persuade, to inform, to entertain, or to express ideas and feelings. An author may have more than one reason for writing.

Directions Read the following passage. Then complete the diagram.

Thomas Edison's laboratory developed many inventions, but none was better than the motion picture machine. This 1893 invention led to modern movies, which are a great source of pleasure to many people. Movies allow people to imagine, dream, explore, and ponder. Surveys show that for many people movies are a major source of entertainment. Who doesn't have a favorite movie or look forward to seeing a new film? As the years go by, movies often become cherished memories. Movies help to make life interesting, and many people watch them over and over. While the light bulb is practical and the phonograph is astounding, the best to come out of his lab was a system for making motion pictures. Thanks to Thomas Edison, we can all go to the movies!

Author's Purpose

1. The author's purpose is to

Details

2. Edison's laboratory's best invention was

3. Modern movies are

4. Movies allow people to

5. Movies often become

Home Activity Your child identified the author's purpose of a nonfiction passage. Work with your child to use the proper reading pace while reading various articles that have different purposes.

Name ______________________________

Advertisements

Advertisements are designed to sell a product or service. Usually advertisements have four elements: a headline, image, body copy, and signature. When you read advertisements, watch for persuasive language and loaded words that appear to emotions. Also look for generalities that don't have any specific meaning, testimonials, and slogans.

Directions Use this advertisement to answer the questions below.

NEW! Have the music in you!

An exciting new invention lets you enjoy music all day long—even in the shower and as you sleep! No wires or headphones, just a tiny clip. For fabulous nonstop music. You have to hear it to believe it!

Music Magic. $49.95
at leading department stores

Love that music!

1. What is this advertisement selling?

____

2. Where are the four parts of this advertisement?

____

____

3. How do loaded words in the advertisement above appeal to emotions?

____

4. What is an example of a generality the advertisement contains? Explain.

____

____

5. What is the slogan in this advertisement? How does it appeal to the reader?

____

____

Name ______________________________

Directions Use this advertisement to answer the questions below.

Hello, Robot! Bye-Bye, Chores!

Teenage movie star Lindsay Cooper says, "I don't clean *my* room. Why should *you* clean yours?"

Have more time for fun! *Hello, Robot* will pick up, clean, dust, make your bed, and even prepare snacks. Let *Hello, Robot* do the work. Don't miss out! Get yours today!

Hello, Robot
Meet your fun machine!

6. Where are the four parts of this advertisement?

____

____

7. How is a testimonial used to persuade readers?

____

____

8. What loaded words does the advertisement use? How do they appeal to emotions?

____

____

9. What is an example of a generality the advertisement contains?

____

____

10. What is the slogan in this advertisement? How does it appeal to the reader?

____

____

Home Activity Your child learned about reading advertisements critically. Look at an advertisement together. Ask your child to explain what techniques are used to sell the product or service.

Name ______________________________

Family Times

Summary

The View from Saturday

Mix together a young boy, a visit to grandparents, and a bunch of off-beat oldsters. Then add a wedding where everybody pitches in. It's a recipe for laughs—and for bringing everyone closer together.

Activity

Spanning Generations Ask a grandparent, parent, or other older relative to tell stories about his or her childhood (it's a good idea to prepare questions in advance to get the stories rolling). Record these tales in a family scrapbook, along with a family tree. You'll be glad you did!

Comprehension Skill

Plot

The **plot,** or story line, is the series of related events in a story. It shows characters in action. After some **background,** the story starts when a character has a **conflict.** During the **rising action** this problem builds, and it comes to a turning point at the **climax.** During the **resolution** the conflict is usually solved. Plot events may be told out of order. A **flashback** tells events from the past.

Activity

Plotting Out Plots Share a funny story with your family. Then make a diagram outlining the story's plot: background, conflict, rising action, climax, and resolution. Try this process again with other stories that family members tell.

Lesson Vocabulary

Words to Know

Knowing the meanings of these words is important to reading *The View from Saturday*. Practice using these words.

Vocabulary Words

accustomed usual, customary; used to

decline process of losing power, strength, beauty, health, etc.; growing worse

former earlier, past

presence condition of being present in a place

unaccompanied not accompanied; alone

Grammar

Contractions and Negatives

A **contraction** is a shortened form of two words. *For example: do + not = don't.* In the example, the apostrophe shows that the letter *o* has been left out of *not.* Contractions formed with *not* such as *don't* are **negative words.** A negative word includes "no" or "not" in its meaning. Other negative words include *nobody, never, no,* and *none.* A phrase including either *no* or *not* and another negative word is called a **double negative** and should be avoided in your writing.

Activity

Bingo! Play Contraction Bingo with your family. Make cards with five squares across and five down. Then fill in the squares with different contractions. Now write different words used in making contractions on slips of paper. The caller pulls slips from the pile and calls the words out. Cross out a contraction on your card when you hear one of the words it is made from. Know your contractions, and yell "BINGO" when you get five in a row!

Practice Tested Spelling Words

____	____	____	____
____	____	____	____
____	____	____	____
____	____	____	____
____	____	____	____

Name ____________________

Literary Elements • Plot

- A **plot** includes (1) a **problem** or **goal,** (2) **rising action,** as a character tries to solve the problem or meet the goal, (3) a **climax,** when the character meets the problem or goal head-on, and (4) a **resolution,** or outcome.
- Sometimes a writer hints at an event that will happen later in the story. Such a hint is called **foreshadowing.** Sometimes a writer goes back in time to tell about an earlier event. The earlier event is called a **flashback.**

Directions Read the following passage. Then complete the diagram below.

Carrie and Carlos wanted to buy their parents an anniversary present, but they didn't have any money. "How can we get enough money in two weeks?" Carlos moaned. Just then, Carrie remembered something. "You know, our band didn't have any money, and we needed new music. We had a car wash, and we earned enough money," she told Carlos. Carlos liked the idea. So Carrie made signs, and Carlos put them up. On the big day, Carrie and Carlos were ready. The car wash was a big success. Their parents loved their anniversary gift. They loved the car wash coupon, too!

1. Problem: ____________________

Rising Action: Carrie suggests a car wash.

2. Rising Action: ____________________

3. Climax: ____________________

4. Resolution: ____________________

5. Carrie has a flashback of something that happened in the past. What is Carrie's flashback?

____

Home Activity Your child read a short passage and identified plot elements. Work with your child to identify the conflict, rising action, climax, and resolution in a short story that you read together.

Name ___________________________________

Vocabulary

Directions Choose the word from the box that best matches each definition. Write the word on the line.

Check the Words You Know
___accustomed
___decline
___former
___presence
___unaccompanied

_______________ **1.** process of losing strength or power

_______________ **2.** alone

_______________ **3.** usual, customary, used to

_______________ **4.** condition of being present in a place

_______________ **5.** earlier, past

Directions Choose the word from the box that best completes each sentence. Write the word on the line.

When Stan and Marie retired, Stan's health was in a state of **6.** _______________. They decided they needed a calmer life, **7.** _______________ by the noise and activity of the big city. They also thought that the **8.** _______________ of their grandchildren would make them happier. So they moved to a small town near where their son's family lived. Although they sometimes missed their **9.** _______________ home, they quickly grew **10.** _______________ to their new life. Stan and Marie felt better than they had for years.

Write a Journal Entry

On a separate sheet of paper write a journal entry about visiting your grandparents or some other older adults whom you know.

Home Activity Your child identified and used vocabulary words from the story *The View from Saturday.* Read a story or nonfiction article with your child. Have your child point out unfamiliar words. Work together to figure out the meaning of unfamiliar words by using other words that appear near them.

Name ____________________

Vocabulary • Context Clues

- An **antonym** is a word that means the opposite of another word.
- Look for clue words such as *unlike, no, but,* and *on the other hand* to identify antonyms.

Directions Read the following passage. Then answer the questions below.

My grandmother prefers lots of excitement, so she is disinclined to spend time alone. Unlike her current quiet life, her former life as a famous singer was thrilling. She still practices singing every day. However, her voice is deteriorating. It is not strong, the way it used to be. She's certainly not fragile, though. Her body may be frail, but her spirit is still robust.

I walked her to a doctor's appointment the other day. I was surprised at how excited everyone at the clinic was about my grandmother's presence. "We have missed your grandmother!" they exclaimed to me. "What a great singer!" Grandmother smiled and squeezed my hand.

1. Find the antonym in the passage for *disinclined.* How does this antonym help to define the word?

____

____

2. Find the antonym in the passage for *former.* How does this antonym help to define the word?

____

____

3. How does the antonym in the passage for *deteriorating* help to define the word?

____

____

4. How does the antonym in the passage for *robust* help to define the word?

____

____

5. Write a sentence or sentences using a word from the passage and its antonym.

____

____

Home Activity Your child read a short passage and identified and used antonyms to understand new words in a passage. Work with your child to identify unfamiliar words in an article. Ask your child to find antonyms and other context clues in the passage to help with understanding the new words.

Name ______________________________

Cause and Effect

Directions Read the following passage. Then answer the questions below.

No one will ever be able to forget Jim and Sue's wedding. Their wedding day started out sunny and beautiful. We were all thrilled, because the ceremony was being held outdoors, in my uncle's backyard. Shortly before the ceremony, though, huge black clouds began to fill the sky. Just as the ring bearer (my little cousin Charlie) brought the rings down the aisle, there was an enormous clap of thunder. He was terrified and ran screaming into the house, taking the wedding rings with him! As Charlie ran through the house, he tripped over my uncle's dog Flounder and fell into the wedding cake. Sue's father, Dan, jumped to try to save the cake. He caught it, but the cake was so heavy, he fell backward. Jim's mother, Anne, was behind him, and as Dan fell backward, the top of the cake hit Anne right in the face! Anne couldn't see anything because her face was covered in cake. As she tried to find a towel, she stumbled into the table and knocked all the food to the floor.

In the end, Sue and Jim did have a beautiful ceremony and we all ate pizza and cookies for dinner.

1. What caused the chain of events to begin? If that event hadn't happened, would the other events have happened?

____

____

2. What caused Charlie to fall into the cake?

____

3. What effect did the cake falling have on Dan?

____

4. What caused the guests to eat pizza and cookies for dinner?

____

____

5. On a separate sheet of paper, describe what effect the events in the story might have had on the bride, groom, and other guests at the wedding.

Home Activity Your child read a short passage and identified causes and effects. Read a short story with your child. Challenge him or her to identify causes and effects.

Name______________________________________

Literary Elements • Plot

- A **plot** includes (1) a **problem** or **goal,** (2) **rising action,** as a character tries to solve the problem or meet the goal, (3) a **climax,** when the character meets the problem or goal head-on, and (4) a **resolution,** or outcome. Sometimes a writer hints at an event that will happen later in the story. Such a hint is called **foreshadowing.** Sometimes a writer goes back in time to tell about an earlier event. The earlier event is called a **flashback.**

Directions Read the following story. Then answer the questions below.

For his birthday, Nathan's parents were sending him to Arizona to visit his grandparents. He dreaded it. His grandparents' idea of fun was listening to talk radio! After four days, he thought he was going crazy. He remembered going to the movies with his friends for his last birthday. He was threatening to walk home when his grandpa gave a knowing smile and said, "Before you start on your journey, I challenge you to a game of shuffleboard." "What's that?" Nathan asked. His grandpa taught him how to play. With a little practice, he got so good that other visiting grandkids wanted to see what was going on. They learned to play too. Nathan was really enjoying the daily tournaments—and the cookouts afterward. When it was time to return home, he didn't want to leave. But he was already planning his next birthday visit.

1. What conflict or problem gets the plot started?

____

2. What happens that make the problem worse for Nathan?

____

3. How can you tell that Nathan's trip to the movies is a flashback?

____

4. Grandpa does something that foreshadows, or gives a hint, about the resolution. What does he do?

____

5. What is the climax of the story?

____

Home Activity Your child read a short passage and identified its plot. Read a fable or short story with your child, and ask your child to identify the conflict, rising action, climax, and resolution. Discuss how effective the plot is.

Name ______________________________

Literary Element • Plot

- A **plot** includes (1) a **problem** or **goal,** (2) **rising action,** as a character tries to solve the problem or meet the goal, (3) a **climax,** when the character meets the problem or goal head-on, and (4) a **resolution,** or outcome.
- Sometimes a writer hints at an event that will happen later in the story. Such a hint is called **foreshadowing.** Sometimes a writer goes back in time to tell about an earlier event. The earlier event is called a **flashback.**

Directions Read the following passage. Then complete the diagram below.

Granny Sue was a stranger to me. When she said she was coming to my sister's wedding, I was surprised. She lived one thousand miles away, and she hated to fly! I picked her up the day before the wedding. At first glance, I thought she looked kind of boring. But meeting Granny Sue would teach me that first impressions can be wrong.

Granny Sue was quiet and uncomfortable. That first day, we sat in silence for hours. The next morning, I asked her what it was like for her growing up. She told me stories about her childhood in a coal-mining town. Her life was so hard, but her stories and jokes were really funny. By the time the wedding started, I felt like I had known Granny Sue all my life.

1. Problem:
Granny Sue is a ______________________

Rising Action:
I picked Granny Sue up at the airport.

2. Rising Action: ______________________

____

3. Climax:
Granny Sue told ______________________

____

4. Resolution:
Granny Sue's stories ______________________

____

5. What sentence foreshadows or gives a hint about the resolution?

____

____

Home Activity Your child analyzed the plot structure of a fiction passage about a family. Challenge your child to identify the conflict, rising action, climax, and falling action in another family story.

Schedule

A **schedule** is a kind of table. The **rows** are a series of horizontal boxes, and the **columns** are a series of vertical boxes. These boxes are also called **cells.** Schedules show times, dates, and locations for airplanes, trains, buses, activities, and sporting events.

Directions Look over this Alaska Cruise schedule for weeklong cruises between Whittier, Alaska, and Vancouver, British Columbia. Then answer the questions below.

DEPARTING	DAY	DATE	SHIP	COST
Whittier	Fri	7/06/07	*Ocean Dream*	$1,249
Vancouver	Fri	7/06/07	*Ocean Cloud*	$1,149
Whittier	Sun	7/08/07	*Ocean Whisper*	$949
Vancouver	Sun	7/08/07	*Ocean Breeze*	$849
Vancouver	Fri	7/13/07	*Ocean Dream*	$1,149
Whittier	Fri	7/13/07	*Ocean Cloud*	$1,249
Vancouver	Sun	7/15/07	*Ocean Whisper*	$849
Whittier	Sun	7/15/07	*Ocean Breeze*	$949

1. What information does this schedule tell about the Alaska cruises during ten days in July?

____

____

2. During this ten-day period, how many cruises depart from Vancouver? On what dates does the *Ocean Breeze* depart?

____

____

3. On which days of the week do cruises depart?

____

4. What is the name of the cruise ship that departs from Vancouver on July 15?

____

____

5. Which are the two most expensive cruises? What do they have in common?

____

____

Name ______________________________

Directions Use this activity schedule to answer the questions below.

FITNESS CENTER CLASSES							
Time	**Monday**	**Tuesday**	**Wednesday**	**Thursday**	**Friday**	**Saturday**	**Sunday**
6 A.M.	Run Club		Cardio		Cardio		Run Club
7 A.M.	Yoga	Strength	Yoga	Strength	Yoga		Yoga
8 A.M.	Tai Chi			Tai Chi		Yoga	
9 A.M.		Dance	Dance	Dance		Pilates	Yoga
11 A.M.	Cardio		Cardio		Cardio		
1 P.M.		Kickboxing		Kickboxing		Aerobics	Aerobics
3 P.M.	Water	Strength	Strength	Water	Strength		Strength
5 P.M.	Aerobics	Aerobics		Aerobics	Aerobics		Cardio
7 P.M.		Yoga	Cardio	Dance		Cardio	

6. What does this schedule show? How many classes does the fitness center offer each week?

____

____

7. On which days and at what times are aerobics classes offered? Kickboxing?

____

____

8. What kinds of classes are offered on Saturday? What is offered at 8 A.M. on Saturday?

____

9. On which day are the most classes offered? At what times?

____

10. Explain how you would use this schedule to find what class is offered at a specific time on a specific day.

____

____

____

Home Activity Your child learned about reading schedules. Look at a train or bus schedule together. Ask your child to figure out departure and arrival times at a specific station or stop.

Name

Family Times

Summary

Harvesting Hope

When young Cesar Chavez moves to California after his parents' farm fails, he works in the fields and sees injustice firsthand. Years later, Chavez leads farmworkers in protests to push for fairness.

Activity

Pull Together Think of something in your town or school that you think is unfair. Talk over with your family why you think it is unfair. Discuss how you think the situation can be changed.

Comprehension Skill

Fact and Opinion

A **statement of fact** can be proven true or false. A **statement of opinion** expresses someone's beliefs, judgments, or ideas and cannot be proven true or false. Statements of opinion are valid if they are supported by facts and expert authority.

Activity

You Be the Judge Get together with family members and talk over an issue you care about. Write down the statements that people make, and decide if they're facts or opinions. Then consider how valid the opinions are. How well are they supported by the facts?

Lesson Vocabulary

Words to Know

Knowing the meanings of these words is important to reading *Harvesting Hope: The Story of Cesar Chavez.* Practice using these words.

Vocabulary Words

access right to approach, enter, or use; admittance

authority power to enforce obedience; right to command or act

lush having thick growth; covered with growing things

obstacle something that prevents or stops progress; hindrance

toll tax or fee for some right or privilege

torment a cause of very great pain

wilt to become limp and bent down; wither

Grammar

Adjectives and Articles

Adjectives modify, or tell about, nouns or pronouns. Adjectives can tell what kind, how many, how much, or which one. *A*, *an*, and *the* are special adjectives called **articles.** *A* is used before a word that begins with a consonant sound. *An* is used before a word that begins with a vowel sound. An adjective formed from a proper noun is called a **proper adjective.** A proper adjective is capitalized. *For example: Spanish music, Asian art.*

Activity

Modifier Mix As a family game, clip out newspaper headlines. Then rewrite the headlines by adding different adjectives. Use surprising adjectives to make your headlines silly!

Practice Tested Spelling Words

Name ____________________

Fact and Opinion

- **Statements of opinion** are someone's beliefs or way of thinking about something. The statement *Cars are the best way to travel* is a statement of opinion.
- **Statements of fact** can be proved true or false. Statements of opinion cannot be proved, but can be shown to be valid or faulty. **Valid** statements of opinion are supported by facts or experts. **Faulty** statements are not supported by facts.

Directions Read the following passage and complete the diagram.

Everyone knows that Cesar Chavez was a major figure in American history. He was dedicated to an important struggle: the cause of migrant workers. His union drew attention to problems experienced by farm workers. A 1965 strike protested low wages for grape pickers, and a boycott of grapes started soon afterward. Chavez used marches and boycotts to protest unfair working conditions. In addition, he fasted to call attention to injustices. However, Chavez believed a protest should never become violent. At Cesar Chavez's funeral, President Bill Clinton spoke of him as "an authentic hero."

Statement of Opinion	Support	Valid or Faulty?
Everyone knows that Cesar Chavez was a major figure in American history.	**1.**	**2.**
However, Chavez believed a protest should never become violent.	**3.**	**4.**

5. Is the statement of opinion in the final sentence valid? Why do you think so?

____

____

____

____

Home Activity Your child identified valid and faulty statements of opinion in a nonfiction passage. Work with your child to identify the facts and opinions in a magazine article about a social issue. Discuss how well supported the opinions are.

Name ______________________________

Vocabulary

Directions Choose the word from the box that best matches each clue. Write the word on the line.

Check the Words You Know
___access
___authority
___lush
___obstacle
___toll
___torment
___wilt

______________ **1.** very great pain

______________ **2.** something that prevents or stops progress

______________ **3.** right to approach, enter, or use

______________ **4.** to become limp and bend down; wither

______________ **5.** power to enforce obedience

Directions Choose the word from the box that best completes each sentence. Write the word on the line shown to the left.

______________ **6.** The fields of southern California are ____ with growing fruits and vegetables.

______________ **7.** To harvest the crops, farm owners need ____ to a large supply of labor.

______________ **8.** One ____ for farm owners is the difficulty of finding a large labor supply.

______________ **9.** After many months, grueling farm labor can take a ____ on the workers.

______________ **10.** They may not have the ____ to change their working conditions.

Write a Newspaper Article

On a separate sheet of paper, write a newspaper article about a civic event you observed. Be sure to tell why, when, where, and how it occurred. Use as many vocabulary words as you can.

Home Activity Your child identified and used vocabulary words from *Harvesting Hope: The Story of Cesar Chavez*. Read a biography with your child. Have him or her point out unfamiliar words. Work together to try to figure out the meaning of each word by using other words that appear near it.

Name____

Vocabulary • Context Clues

- **Homonyms** are words that sound the same but have different meanings.
- When you see a homonym in your reading, use context clues around the word to figure out its meaning. Decide which meaning makes sense in the sentence.

Directions Read the following passage. Then answer the questions below.

The signing of the Declaration of Independance was like the toll of a funeral bell for British control of the American colonies. The United States was founded on principles including the right to free speech and freedom of assembly. The U.S. Constitution guarantees access to these rights. The framers of the Constitution wanted to avoid any obstacle to expressing these rights. As a result, today citizens can take part in protest marches and access articles that are critical of the government. While resulting disagreements can take a toll, there are many advantages to giving authority to the people.

1. *Toll* can mean "to announce by sounding a bell" or "something paid, lost, or suffered." Which meaning of the homonym is used in the first sentence?

____

2. How do context clues help you determine the meaning of the homonym *toll* in the last sentence? What does it mean there?

____

____

3. *Access* can mean "to make information available" or "right to approach, enter, or use." What does it mean in the fifth sentence? What helps you to determine the meaning?

____

4. How does the meaning of *access* help determine the meaning of *obstacle* in the fourth sentence?

____

5. *Authority* can mean "power to enforce obedience," "person who has such power," or "an expert on some subject." What does *authority* mean in the last sentence? How can you use context clues to determine the meaning?

____

____

Home Activity Your child identified and used context to understand homonyms and other new words in a passage. Challenge your child to find a homonym in an article. Then ask him or her to use context clues to help with the understanding of the homonym. Confirm the meanings with your child.

Name ______________________________

Sequence

Directions Read the article. Then answer the questions below.

An important date in the Civil Rights movement was December 5, 1955, when a bus boycott began in Montgomery, Alabama. The boycott was triggered by the arrest of Rosa Parks, who had refused to give up her seat to a white passenger. The day the boycott began, Dr. Martin Luther King, Jr., a Baptist pastor, spoke at a meeting. "If we are wrong, justice is a lie," he said. However, he also urged people to avoid violence. "We will be guided by the highest principles of law and order." Earlier that day, he had been named president of the community group overseeing the bus boycott. The boycott went on for many months. Finally, on November 13, 1956, the Supreme Court ruled that segregation on buses was illegal. Then Dr. King once again warned people to avoid violence as they returned to using the buses.

1. What are three clue words or phrases in the article that help you understand the sequence of events?

____

____

2. What are the first three events in the order they occurred?

____

____

3. What are the last three events in the order they occurred?

____

____

4. What do you think would have happened if Dr. Martin Luther King, Jr., hadn't stepped forward to lead the bus boycott?

____

____

5. How did what you already know about Dr. King help you to understand this article? Write your answer on a separate piece of paper.

Home Activity Your child has read information about Dr. Martin Luther King, Jr., and identified the sequence of events as well as applied prior knowledge. Read a biographical passage with your child. Ask him or her to explain the sequence of events.

Name ______________________________

Fact and Opinion

- **Statements of opinion** are someone's beliefs or way of thinking about something. The statement *Cars are the best way to travel* is a statement of opinion.
- **Statements of fact** can be proved true or false. Statements of opinion cannot be proved, but can be shown to be valid or faulty. **Valid** statements of opinion are supported by facts or experts. **Faulty** statements are not supported by facts.

Directions Read the following passage. Then answer the questions below.

Mohandas Gandhi was the world's most influential leader because of his philosophy of nonviolence. Born in India in 1869, he went to law school in England in 1888. For more than 30 years, he used peaceful resistance as a form of protest. Gandhi gave speeches, fasted, marched, and even went to prison in the name of human rights. Although he was gentle by nature, he fought hard against injustice. India's prime minister called him "the Father of the Nation."

Just one year before Gandhi died, India became independent from British rule. Gandhi was a great inspiration to many other leaders.

1. Is the first sentence a statement of fact or opinion? How do you know?

____

2. Write a statement of fact from the second paragraph.

____

____

3. Write a statement of opinion from the second paragraph.

____

____

4. Is the statement of opinion in the sixth sentence valid? Explain why.

____

5. What did you know about Gandhi before you read this passage? How did this prior knowledge help you to evaluate the opinions in the passage?

____

____

Home Activity Your child identified facts and opinions in a nonfiction passage. Read a biographical article with your child. Work together to identify facts and opinions, and discuss how well supported the opinions are.

Name ______________________________

Fact and Opinion

- **Statements of opinion** are someone's beliefs or way of thinking about something. The statement *Cars are the best way to travel* is a statement of opinion.
- **Statements of fact** can be proved true or false. Statements of opinion cannot be proved, but can be shown to be valid or faulty. **Valid** statements of opinion are supported by facts or experts. **Faulty** statements of opinion are not supported by facts.

Directions Read the following passage. Then complete the diagram by supporting statements and identifying the support as valid or faulty.

The women's rights movement in the 1960s took an important step toward gaining equal rights for women. At the time, women did not have the same access to credit, higher education, or athletics as men did. In addition, women who worked full-time on average made only 59 percent of what men made. The most important leader in the women's rights cause was Betty Friedan, whose powerful book *The Feminine Mystique* rallied women to protest. Many marches and court cases supported the women's rights movement. In time, the law recognized women's rights.

Statement of Opinion	Support	Valid or Faulty?
The women's rights movement in the 1960s took an important step toward gaining equal rights for women.	**1.** The women's movement was supported by ________ ________	**2.** ________ ________ ________
The most important leader in the women's rights cause was Betty Friedan.	**3.** There may have been other ________ ________	**4.** ________ ________ ________

5. Select another statement of opinion in the passage. Explain two ways that it could be supported. Be specific.

____

____

____

____

Home Activity Your child supported statements and identified the support as valid or faulty. Work with your child to identify facts and opinions in a magazine article about a social issue. Discuss how the opinions could be better supported.

Newsletter

A **newsletter** is a short publication containing news of interest to a particular group's members. Newsletters include news articles, features, and opinion pieces such as editorials. A news story, which has a headline and sometimes a byline giving the writer's name, tells who, what, when, where, why, and how something happened. Features, which are more informal, are written to inform in an entertaining way. Although news stories are intended to provide only facts, opinions can be expressed by leaving out certain facts.

Directions Use this article from a farm workers' newsletter to answer the questions.

FARM WORKERS MARCH IN PROTEST

by Ana Ortega

More than 400 people marched through Davis County on March 11 in support of local mushroom farm workers. Several film actors were among the group.

The march ended with a rally at Arojo Arena, where speakers demanded that local mushroom growers provide increased wages and benefits. "Immigrant workers deserve better treatment," a United Farm Workers spokesman told the crowd. Many workers carried signs or waved flags with the UFW emblem. Workers, who earn 80 cents per basket, are requesting a raise of 5 cents per basket. This would increase their wages to approximately $7.50 per hour.

Mushroom company officials did not comment.

"We need to give the farm workers our support," said actor Tim Bond, a marcher.

1. Is the article a news story, feature, or editorial? Why?

____

2. How does the article answer these questions: Who? What? When? Where? Why?

____

____

3. What is the headline? The byline?

____

4. What is one fact presented in the article?

____

5. Explain if you think the article has been slanted by leaving out facts.

____

____

Name ______________________________

Directions This is another article from the farm workers' newsletter about an event of interest to the group's members. Use it to answer the questions below.

JOIN THE CELEBRATION FOR CHAVEZ!

The week of April 21 to 28 has been named Cesar Chavez Week in Oxnard, California, and a special celebration on April 28 will cap off the festivities. Everyone should join in honoring the memory of Chavez, who did so much for the immigrant workers of California.

The day-long event will begin at 9 a.m. with a procession from Central Plaza to Chavez Park. Afterward, a ceremony will include speeches and songs. The mayor will give a memorable talk at 10 a.m., followed by a wonderful speech by a United Farm Workers representative. A Cesar Chavez scholarship will be presented. Dances, contests, songs, and theatrical performances will fill the day with fun.

This will be an event you will never forget. Be sure to attend—and bring your family.

6. What is the headline?

____

7. Is this article a news story, feature, or editorial? How do you know?

____

8. How does the article answer these questions: What? When? Where? Why? How?

____

____

9. What are two opinions given in the article?

____

____

10. Who is the audience for this newsletter? How is that audience reflected in the information this article contains?

____

____

Home Activity Your child learned about reading newsletters and the types of articles they contain. With your child, look at a newsletter for an organization. Ask him or her to locate news stories, features, and editorials and point out the facts and opinions they contain.

Name

Family Times

Summary

The River That Went to the Sky: A Story from Malawi

An old African myth explains how the Sahara came to be. It all starts when the River makes a wish. Then the Sun takes the River up to live in the sky, and many animals decide to live elsewhere.

Activity

Way Back When With your family, make up imaginative stories to explain the existence of something in nature. For example, what stories could explain storms, earthquakes, flowers, or stars coming to be? Take turns telling these tales and trying to make them as interesting as possible.

Comprehension Skill

Cause and Effect

A **cause** is why something happened, and an **effect** is what happened. Sometimes clue words, such as *since* and *therefore*, signal a cause-and-effect relationship. At other times, the cause-and-effect relationship is not stated directly. In many cases, an effect has multiple causes.

Activity

Just Because Look at advertisements with a family member and tell what cause-and-effect relationships they suggest. For example, an ad might suggest that if you use lipstick, you'll find love or be happier. But do these cause-and-effect relationships really exist?

Lesson Vocabulary

Words to Know

Knowing the meanings of these words is important to reading *The River That Went to the Sky: A Story from Malawi*. Practice using these words.

Vocabulary Words

densest most closely packed together; thickest

eaves lower edges of a roof that extend over the side of a building

expanse open or unbroken stretch; wide, spreading surface

moisture slight wetness; water or other liquid suspended in very small drops in the air or spread on a surface

ventured dared to come or go

Grammar

Demonstrative Adjectives

The adjectives *this, that, these,* and *those* are **demonstrative adjectives.** They tell which one or ones. Use *this* and *that* with singular nouns. *For example: this hat; that cow.* Use *these* and *those* with plural nouns. *For example: these pictures; those books. This* and *these* refer to things that are nearby. *That* and *those* refer to things that are far away. Avoid using *them* in place of *these* or *those.*

Activity

This and That Play the "This and That" game with your family. Point out places you know on a map. Tell about "this (something)" and "that (something)," using demonstrative adjectives correctly. For example, you could say, *This park is the one where we saw a bear.*

Practice Tested Spelling Words

______	______	______	______
______	______	______	______
______	______	______	______
______	______	______	______
______	______	______	______

Name____

Cause and Effect

- A **cause** is what makes something happen. An **effect** is something that happens as a result of a cause. Clue words such as *consequently, since, thus, as a result,* and *therefore* point to cause-and-effect relationships.
- When a cause is not directly stated, you must think about why something happened.

Directions Read the following myth from Polynesia. Then complete the diagram below.

Because he couldn't get enough done in a day, Maui the trickster wanted longer days. He set out to make the sun slow down. First, he made a lasso out of coconut fiber. But when he tied it to the sun, it burned. Then, he wove a rope out of his wife's long, sacred hair. At dawn, he tossed his noose and grabbed the sun. The sun pleaded to be released, but Maui wouldn't give in. As a result, the sun started losing more and more strength. Eventually, it couldn't race across the sky, but could only crawl. Consequently, Maui gave humans more daylight.

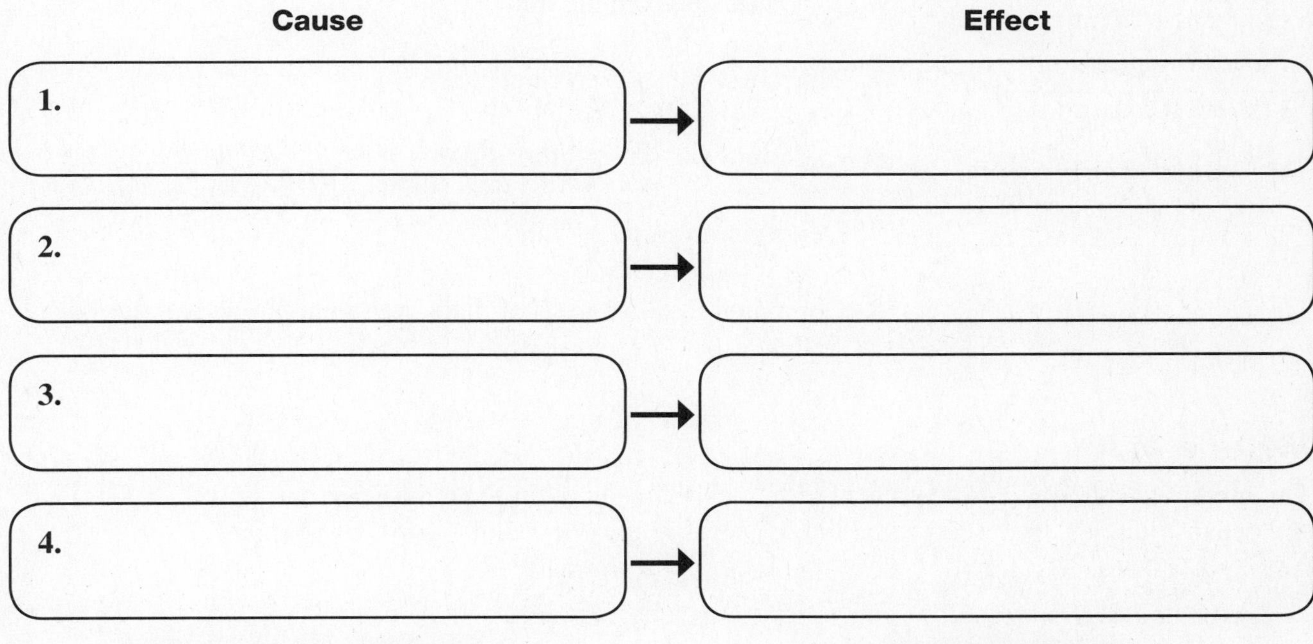

5. Create a graphic organizer of your own to show another cause-and-effect relationship in the myth. Also show what you think the effect would have been if Maui had pulled the sun down to Earth.

Home Activity Your child identified cause-and-effect relationships expressed in a myth. Work with your child to identify the cause-and-effect relationships in a story. Challenge your child to consider "what if" questions about the story.

Name ____

Vocabulary

Directions Choose the word from the box that best matches each definition. Write the word on the line.

Check the Words You Know
___densest
___eaves
___expanse
___moisture
___ventured

____________________ **1.** slight wetness

____________________ **2.** most closely packed together

____________________ **3.** dared

____________________ **4.** open or unbroken stretch

____________________ **5.** the lower edges of a roof that extend over the side of a building

Directions Choose the word from the box that best matches each clue. Write the word on the line.

____________________ **6.** This protects from the rain.

____________________ **7.** This could be a desert or ocean.

____________________ **8.** Explorers and adventurers did this.

____________________ **9.** Dew is an example of this.

____________________ **10.** Compared to other areas of plant growth, a jungle is described as this.

Write a Myth

On a separate sheet of paper, write a myth to explain something in nature, such as how the oceans, jungles, or deserts came to be. Use as many vocabulary words as you can.

School + Home **Home Activity** Your child identified and used vocabulary words from *The River That Went to the Sky.* Read a story or myth with your child. Have him or her point out unfamiliar words. Work together to try to figure out the meaning of each word by using other words that appear near it.

Vocabulary • Context Clues

- When you are reading and see an unfamiliar word, you can use **context clues,** or words around the unfamiliar word, to figure out its meaning.
- One kind of context clue is a **synonym,** a word that has nearly the same meaning as another word. Setting off a word with commas can indicate synonyms. Clue words like *such as* and *or* also signal synonyms.

Directions Read the following passage about the Sahara and answer the questions below. Look for context clues as you read.

The Sahara, in Africa, is a vast expanse, or stretch, of desert. All of it is very dry, but the Libyan part of the Sahara has the least moisture, such as rain or other water. If you ventured into the desert, you might ride a camel. Or, if you dared to go into the desert, you might look for an oasis. There you would see the densest population of people and animals; similarly, you would see the thickest groves of palms there. If you had a hut in the desert, sand cats and hedgehogs might gather in the shade of its eaves, or roof overhang. Now that you know about the Sahara, would you like to visit?

1. What is a synonym for *expanse*? What clue helps you to determine this?

____

2. What does *moisture* mean? What clues help you to determine the meaning?

____

____

3. How would you use context clues to determine the meaning of *ventured*?

____

____

4. What synonym is used for *densest*? How do you know it's a synonym?

____

5. What is the closest synonym for *eaves* in the context of the passage? What clues indicate a synonym?

____

Home Activity Your child identified and used synonyms as context clues to understand new words in a passage. Work with your child to identify unfamiliar words in an article. Then your child can find context clues to help with the understanding of the new words. Confirm the meanings with your child.

Name ___________________________________

Sequence

Directions Read this Japanese myth. Then answer the questions below.

The ruling god Izanagi put his son Susanowo in charge of the oceans and his daughter Amaterasu in charge of the heavens. Afterward, Susanowo got angry because he wanted a different kingdom. As a result, he started trouble everywhere, destroying trees, buildings, and rice paddies. Susanowo scared his sister Amaterasu so much that she shut herself inside a cave. The world became dark and chaotic. Meanwhile, the gods tried to tempt Amaterasu to leave the cave so there would be light. First they tried animals, then fire, and later music. Finally, one goddess danced in such a funny way that the gods starting laughing. Amaterasu was curious. When she asked what the gods found so intriguing, they held out a magic mirror for her to see her reflection. As she stared at her beauty, one of the gods pulled her out of the cave. In this way, the gods tricked her into leaving the cave. And ever since, the Sun has been in the sky.

1. What is the first event that occurs in the myth?

____

2. In order, what are three events that happen after Susanowo gets angry and before the world goes dark?

____

____

3. What is the sequence of the six methods the gods use to get Amaterasu out of the cave?

____

____

4. What is the myth intended to explain? Where does this event fit in the sequence of events?

____

____

5. On a separate sheet of paper, compare and contrast this myth with the tale of Maui (on page 223).

Home Activity Your child has read a Japanese myth and analyzed the sequence of events in the tale. With your child, read a short story. Challenge him or her to explain the order of events and how sequence makes a difference in the story.

Name________________________________

Cause and Effect

- A **cause** is what makes something happen. An **effect** is what happens as a result of a cause. Clue words such as *consequently, since, thus, as a result,* and *therefore* point to cause-and-effect relationships.
- When a cause is not directly stated, you must think about why something happened.

Directions Read the following passage. Then answer the questions below.

Water goes around our world in a cycle. Since the sun heats up water in lakes and oceans, some water evaporates and escapes into the air. As it rises, water vapor gets cold. Consequently, it condenses, or changes back into a liquid, forming clouds. Precipitation occurs when so much water condenses that the air can't hold it. This rain, snow, or hail falls back to Earth to soak into the land or collect in oceans and lakes. Then the cycle starts all over again.

1. In the water cycle, what is the cause of evaporation? What word indicates a cause-and-effect relationship?

____

2. What causes condensation in the air? What word indicates a cause-and-effect relationship?

____

3. What is the cause of precipitation?

____

____

4. Why does water collect in oceans and lakes?

____

____

5. Create a graphic organizer to show the cause-and-effect relationships in the water cycle. Use this graphic organizer to tell someone else about the water cycle.

____

____

Home Activity Your child identified the causes and effects in a nonfiction passage. Read a magazine article about a scientific process with your child. Work together to identify the causes and effects that are identified.

Name ______________________________

Cause and Effect

- A **cause** is what makes something happen. An **effect** is what happens. Clue words such as *consequently, since, thus, as a result,* and *therefore* point to cause-and-effect relationships.
- When a cause is not directly stated, you must think about why something happened.

Directions Read the following Greek myth that explains a process in nature. Then complete the diagram by identifying causes and effects.

Persephone was the beautiful daughter of Demeter, goddess of the fields. One day, Hades, god of the underworld, kidnapped Persephone. Demeter became so angry that she kept all the flowers from blooming and crops from growing. Earth became bleak and cold. Finally, the ruling god Zeus ordered Hades to return Persephone home. When Persephone reached home, Demeter was happy again, so she let the flowers bloom and crops grow. Zeus's final decision was that Persephone would have to spend six months a year in the underworld but could return home for the other six. Thus, winter turns to spring each year.

Cause		Effect
1.	→	Demeter became angry.
Demeter became angry.	→	2.
3.	→	Demeter was happy.
Demeter was happy.	→	4.
Zeus made Persephone spend six months in the underworld and six months at home.	→	5.
What makes it happen?		**What happened?**

Home Activity Your child identified the causes and effects in a myth. Challenge your child to identify cause-and-effect relationships in a magazine article about nature. Discuss whether there are multiple causes or effects.

Name ______________________________

Chart or Table

A **chart** or **table** usually is a box that contains words or numbers in rows and columns. Columns go down, and rows go across. These also are called cells. Most charts and tables have titles.

Directions Use this chart about Saharan animals to answer the questions below.

Animals of the Sahara				
Animal	**Type**	**Length**	**Food**	**Survival Features**
Addax	Mammal	4 ft	Plants	Wide hooves help walk on sand
Caracal	Mammal	3 ft	Jerboas, birds, squirrels	Nocturnal, jumps well
Desert hedgehog	Mammal	3 ft	Insects, frogs, eggs	Extracts water from prey
Desert monitor	Reptile	5 ft	Fish, frogs, snakes, eggs	Withstands heat, burrows
Fennec fox	Mammal	16–17 in.	Rodents, lizards, insects	Withstands heat, burrows
Golden eagle	Bird	30 in.	Rabbits, rats, reptiles	Has mountain nest
Houbara bustard	Bird	2 ft	Insects, lizards, seeds	Extracts water from prey
Jerboa	Mammal	2–6 in.	Plants, seeds, insects	Recycles breath moisture; jumps
Sand cat	Mammal	15–16 in.	Rodents, birds, reptiles	Burrows, extracts water from prey
Striped hyena	Mammal	3–4 ft	Lizards, birds, mammals	Stays in den, nocturnal

1. What is the longest animal listed in the chart? The shortest?

____

2. What do the Houbara bustard, desert hedgehog, and sand cat have in common?

____

3. Which is bigger, the addax (a type of antelope) or the caracal (a large cat)?

____

4. What is the food of the golden eagle? The striped hyena?

____

____

5. What do the survival features tell you about the ways Saharan animals have adapted to stay alive in the desert?

____

____

Name ______________________________

Directions Use this table about African lakes to answer the questions below.

Largest African Lakes

African Lake	Location	Area	Length	Maximum Depth
Victoria	Tanzania-Uganda-Kenya	26,828 sq mi	200 mi	270 ft
Tanganyika	Tanzania-Congo-Burundi-Zambia	12,700 sq mi	470 mi	4,708 ft
Chad	Chad-Niger-Nigeria-Cameroon	550 sq mi	—	23 ft
Rudolf	Kenya-Ethiopia	2,473 sq mi	154 mi	240 ft
Albert	Uganda-Congo	2,046 sq mi	100 mi	180 ft
Kioga	Uganda	1,700 sq mi	50 mi	about 30 ft

6. What is the largest lake in Africa?

____

7. What lakes are wholly or partially located in Uganda?

____

____

8. What is the deepest lake in Africa? The longest?

____

9. What are the area, length, and depth of Lake Albert?

____

10. Explain how to find the area of a specific lake on the chart above.

____

____

____

____

____

____

____

School + Home

Home Activity Your child learned about using charts and tables as resources. Find a chart or table in an almanac. Ask your child to explain what it tells. Challenge your child to find specific information in the chart or table.

Name

Family Times

Summary

Gold

Gold is a rare and precious metal with a fascinating history. Emblem of kings, envy of all, gold is found in many places around the world, including deep in the earth and the oceans. Not only is it beautiful, it also has countless uses because of its special properties.

Activity

Go for the Gold Ask your family, "What is your most precious treasure?" Compare and contrast everyone's responses, keeping track on a chart. Discuss why each precious treasure is so prized.

Comprehension Skill

Main Idea and Details

A **topic** is what a paragraph or article is about. The **main idea** is the most important idea about the topic. Supporting **details** are smaller pieces of information that tell more about the main idea. As you read, ask yourself what the main idea is and how well it is supported with details.

Activity

Find the Heart Talk about song lyrics with someone in your family. Try to pinpoint the topic and the main idea of each song. See if any details in the song support the main idea. You may be surprised at what you're hearing!

Lesson Vocabulary

Words to Know

Knowing the meanings of these words is important to reading *Gold*. Practice using these words.

Vocabulary Words

characteristic distinguishing one person or thing from another

corrode to wear or eat away gradually

engulfed swallowed up; overwhelmed

exploit to make use of

extract to pull or draw out, usually with some effort

hoard what is saved and stored away

Grammar

Comparative and Superlative Adjectives

An **adjective** describes a person, place, or thing. A **comparative adjective** is the form of the adjective used to compare two people, places, or things. *For example: clearer, heavier*. A **superlative adjective** is the form used to compare three or more people, places, or things. *For example: clearest, heaviest*. *More* and *most* usually are used with longer adjectives. *For example: more enjoyable, most delicious*. Never use *more* and *–er* together or use *most* and *–est* together. *For example: more better; most happiest*.

Activity

Adjective Action Make a three-column chart. In the first column, list at least ten adjectives. Then take turns with a family member filling in the comparative and superlative forms for each adjective. Write or say sentences that use them correctly.

Practice Tested Spelling Words

______	______	______	______
______	______	______	______
______	______	______	______
______	______	______	______
______	______	______	______

Main Idea and Details

- The **topic** is what a paragraph is about and can usually be stated in a word or two.
- To find the **main idea** of a paragraph, think about all of the important information the paragraph gives about the topic. The main idea is the most important of these. Sometimes it is stated directly, but sometimes it is not.
- **Details** tell more about the topic. They are less important pieces of information that support the main idea.

Directions Read the following passage. Complete the diagram below by telling the main idea of the paragraph. Then list supporting details that tell more about the main idea.

On January 24, 1848, gold was discovered at Sutter's Mill in California. What followed was a period of great turmoil and confusion. Settlers streamed in by wagon and by ship as the fever to make a fortune took hold. Very quickly, the population of San Francisco jumped from a few hundred to ten thousand.

However, at this time California was not a state and had no effective government. Consequently, there were few restrictions on the behavior of the people flooding the area. At Sutter's Mill, crops were destroyed and buildings were pulled down. Crime was everywhere. The California gold rush had begun!

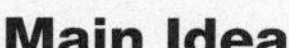

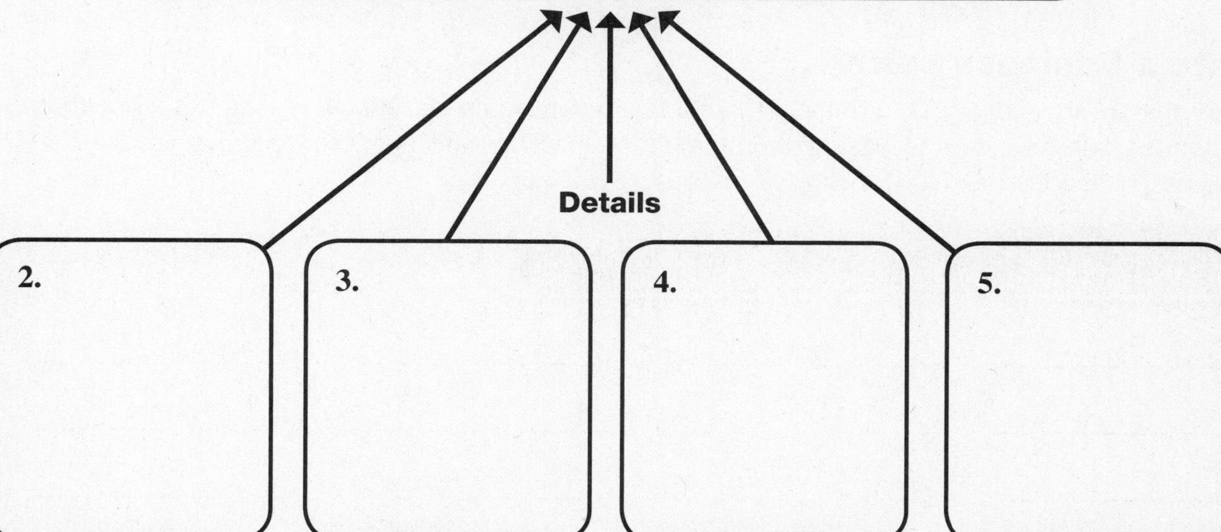

Home Activity Your child identified the main idea and supporting details of a nonfiction passage. Work with your child to identify the main idea and supporting details of individual paragraphs in a magazine article about wild animals. Challenge your child to summarize the entire article.

Name ______________________________

Vocabulary

Directions Choose the word from the box that best matches each definition. Write the word on the line.

Check the Words You Know

- ___characteristic
- ___corrode
- ___engulfed
- ___exploit
- ___extract
- ___hoard

______________ **1.** swallowed up; overwhelmed

______________ **2.** what is saved and stored away

______________ **3.** to make use of

______________ **4.** to wear or eat away gradually

______________ **5.** to pull out or draw out

Directions Choose the word from the box that best completes each sentence. Write the word on the line.

6. Gold is valuable as a metal because it does not ______________.

7. Many people are attracted by the ______________ shininess of gold.

8. A wave of fortune seekers ______________ the riverbed to search for gold.

9. New methods have been developed to ______________ gold from the earth.

10. Some people would enjoy having a ______________ of gold because of its value.

Write a Business Letter

On a separate sheet of paper, write a letter to a science museum about how to find out more about precious metals. Your business letter should identify specific aspects of the topic that you wish to research further. Use as many vocabulary words as you can.

School + Home

Home Activity Your child identified and used vocabulary words from *Gold*. Together, read a story or nonfiction article. Ask your child to point out unfamiliar words. Work together to figure out the meaning of each word by using other words that appear near it.

Name____________________

Vocabulary • Context Clues

- If you see an unfamiliar word as you read, use **context clues** to figure out the meaning of that word. Context clues are the words and sentences around an unfamiliar word.

Directions Read the following passage about gold mining. Then answer the questions below. Look for context clues as you read.

In 1848, thousands of hopeful people engulfed California, swarming into the state from around the world, to pan for gold. Today gold is mined in many countries, but South Africa is the world's largest source of this precious metal. Miners tunnel underground and use hydraulics and other advanced methods to extract, or pull out, gold from the earth. Human beings exploit this natural treasure of the earth, making use of it for various purposes. Some miners have been known to say that too much gold can corrode a person's soul, eating away at honesty and integrity. If you discovered gold, would you hoard it or give it away?

1. What does *exploit* mean? What clue helps you to determine the meaning?

____

____

2. What clues help you to determine the meaning of *engulfed*? What does this word mean?

____

____

3. Which words around the word *extract* give a clue to its meaning?

____

____

4. How do context clues help you determine the meaning of *corrode*?

____

____

5. What do you think *hydraulics* means? What clues help you decide on this meaning?

____

____

Home Activity Your child identified and used context clues to understand new words in a passage. As you read another nonfiction article with your child, have him or her identify unfamiliar words. Then work with your child to find context clues to help clarify the meanings of these words.

Name ____________________

Cause and Effect

Directions Read the following passage. Then answer the questions below.

The new goods produced during the Industrial Revolution brought about a great deal of new trade between nations. This new trade made it necessary to find ways to agree on how much a country's money was worth. To solve this problem, a gold standard was used. A gold standard is a system in which a country issues money for a set amount of gold. Many countries adopted a variation of a gold standard in the late 1800s. The huge cost of World War II helped bring an end to the gold standard.

1. What effect did the Industrial Revolution have on international trade?

____

____

2. How did this effect help cause the use of the gold standard?

____

____

____

3. What conflict could occur between two trading countries without a single standard for the value of each nation's money?

____

____

4. What factor helped cause the end of the gold standard?

____

____

5. On a separate sheet of paper, explain why you think the gold standard would be unnecessary for a nation that did not trade with other countries.

Home Activity Your child identified cause-and-effect relationships in a passage. With your child, read an article about another historical event that caused changes in the United States or in the world. Challenge your child to identify some of the causes and effects of this historical event.

Main Idea and Details

- The **topic** is what a paragraph is about and can usually be stated in a word or two.
- To find the **main idea** of a paragraph, think about all of the important information the paragraph gives about the topic. The main idea is the most important of these. Sometimes it is stated directly, but sometimes it is not.
- **Details** tell more about the topic. They are less important pieces of information that support the main idea.

Directions Read the following passage. Then answer the questions below.

Since the early 1500s, searchers have tried to find the mysterious Inca gold. The treasure was supposed to be ransom for an Inca king imprisoned by Spanish conquerors. However, one or more Inca soldiers hid the gold in the Llanganati Mountains in Ecuador. During the centuries since then, adventurers and fortune hunters have been searching for the gold. However, the Llanganati Mountains hold many dangers. The cliffs are steep, and heavy rains and earthquakes are common. Many searchers have not made it out alive. Currently, scientists are using new equipment such as radar in hopes of locating the ancient gold. Now thought to be worth about two billion dollars, it is the largest treasure that remains undiscovered in Latin America. Will the Inca gold ever be found?

1. In one or two words, tell what the passage is about.

____

2. What is the main idea of the paragraph?

____

3. What is one important detail that tells more about the main idea?

____

____

4. What is another detail that supports the main idea?

____

____

5. What text structure does the author use to organize the information in this passage?

____

Home Activity Your child identified the main idea and supporting details of an informational passage. With your child, read a magazine article about another intriguing mystery. Work together to identify the main idea and supporting details of the article. Then ask him or her to identify the text structure, such as cause-and-effect, problem-solution, or chronological order.

Name ______________________________

Main Idea and Details

- The **topic** is what a paragraph is about and can usually be stated in a word or two.
- To find the **main idea** of a paragraph, think about all of the important information the paragraph gives about the topic. The main idea is the most important of these. Sometimes it is stated directly, but sometimes it is not.
- **Details** tell more about the topic. They are less important pieces of information that support the main idea.

Directions Read the following passage. Then complete the diagram by finishing the sentence about the main idea and by naming four details that support the main idea of the passage.

A precious metal is a rare natural element of great value. Everyone knows about famous precious metals like gold and silver, but there are others. Platinum, in fact, is worth more than twice as much as gold.

To be considered precious, a metal must be in short supply. If new supplies of the metal are found, it becomes less valuable. For example, at one time aluminum was rare and considered more valuable than gold.

Precious metals are used to create jewelry, coins, and art. In the past, some precious metals were used in trade. Today, they are still important as investments.

Main Idea

1. A precious metal is ______________________________

____

Details

2. Three precious metals are ______________

3. Platinum is worth more than ______________

4. ______________

5. Precious metals can be used to create ______________

Home Activity Your child identified the main idea and details of a nonfiction passage. Together, read a magazine article about something precious. Work with your child to identify the main idea and details of each paragraph. Then challenge him or her to explain how the article is structured.

Type Formats

Recognizing **type formats** helps you understand the structure and design of what you read.

- **Bullets** are used to list details or parts of a topic.
- **Boldface** is darker than regular type. It is used to set off titles, headings, and subheadings.
- Underlining and ***italics*** (slanted type) may signal important words or ideas.
- **Type size** can be varied to make titles and headings stand out.

Directions Read this article about panning for gold and answer the questions that follow.

PANNING FOR GOLD

The simplest method of mining gold is *panning.* All that is needed is a circular dish or pan and a water source.

A three-step process. Panning for gold involves these steps:

- Fill a dish with sand or gravel.
- Hold it under a stream of water.
- Rotate the pan at the same time.

The water swirls away the lighter parts of the sand and gravel. If there are gold particles, they will be left near the center of the pan.

Panning for gold today. Even though the Gold Rush was over long ago, prospectors still pan for gold. The western United States is known to hold gold. In addition, travelers can go on gold panning trips to many other countries.

1. What is the topic of this article? How do type formats help you determine the topic?

____

____

2. Within the text of the article, how can you recognize the article's main ideas?

____

3. What does the use of italics indicate in the first paragraph?

____

4. What do the bullets signal in the second paragraph?

____

5. How do type formats help you to understand this article?

____

____

____

____

Name ______________________________

Directions Read this portion of an encyclopedia entry about rocks. Then answer the questions below.

ROCKS. Under a layer of soil, the earth is made of rock. Rocks tell the story of changes that have happened to the earth over time. The study of rocks is called *geology*.

Rocks and Minerals. Rocks are made up of minerals. Anything that is not an animal or a vegetable is a mineral. Rocks are solid mineral deposits. Some examples of rocks are gold, silver, salt, and quartz. Nonsolids such as water and gas are considered minerals but not rocks.

Types of Rocks. There are three main groupings of rocks, based on the ways in which they were formed. They are as follows:

- <u>Sedimentary rocks</u>. These rocks were formed by layers of lake, river, or ocean deposits.
- <u>Igneous rocks</u>. These rocks were produced by heating and cooling. Lava is an example of igneous rock.
- <u>Metamorphic rocks</u>. These formerly igneous or sedimentary rocks were produced when heat and pressure changed their form.

Hardness of Rocks. Some rocks are harder than others. In 1822, Frederick Mohs developed a scale to rate the hardness of rocks. Talc has the lowest rating, and diamond has the highest.

6. What is the topic of this entry? How do you know?

____

7. How do type formats signal main ideas in the entry?

____

____

8. For what purpose are italics and underlining used in this article?

____

____

9. What do the bullets signal in the third paragraph?

____

____

10. In what ways do type formats help you to understand this encyclopedia entry?

____

____

Home Activity Your child learned how recognizing type formats can help them understand the structure and ideas of a text. Together, look at a volume of an encyclopedia. Ask your child to explain the use of different typefaces. Challenge him or her to tell how the typefaces indicate topics, main ideas, details, and important terms.

Name

Family Times

Summary

The House of Wisdom

In ancient Baghdad, a great center of learning, Ishaq's father passes on his love of books. But Ishaq does not have the fire for learning and knowledge until he travels the world to collect books for Baghdad's House of Wisdom. Then he is inspired to connect with thinkers of the past—and the future.

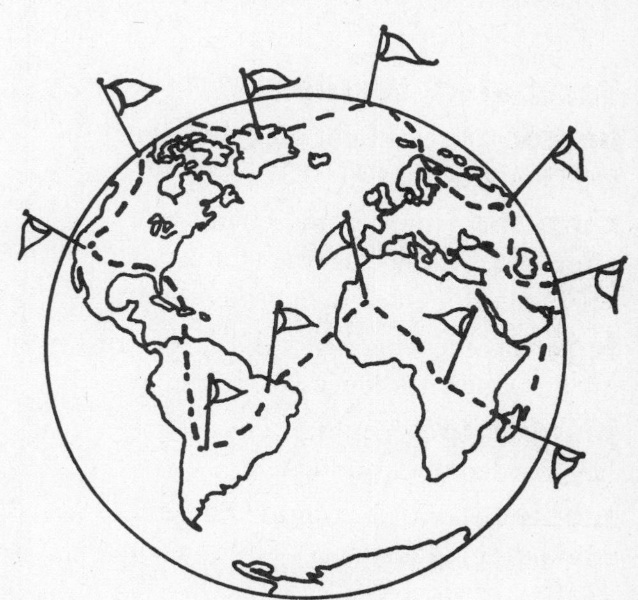

Activity

A World of Knowledge When we travel from place to place, we always learn new things. Using a globe, trace a journey that you would like to take. Tell a family member what you would like to learn in each place you visit.

Comprehension Skill

Sequence

When reading, it is important to keep track of the **sequence,** or order of events. Look for clue words, such as *then*, *first*, *next*, and *during*. Dates and times can help you to establish sequence too. Try to visualize events, or use a time line to help you recognize event order.

Activity

Searching for Wisdom Like the House of Wisdom, your local public library offers all kinds of knowledge. Describe to a family member the steps to follow in order to find and check out a library book. Make sure the steps are in order!

Lesson Vocabulary

Words to Know

Knowing the meanings of these words is important to reading *The House of Wisdom.* Practice using these words.

Vocabulary Words

beacon a fire or light used as a signal to guide or warn

caravans groups of merchants or pilgrims traveling together for safety through difficult or dangerous country

legacy something handed down from an ancestor or predecessor; heritage

manuscripts handwritten or keyboarded books or articles

medieval of or belonging to the Middle Ages (about A.D. 500 to about 1450)

observatory a building or room equipped with telescopes and other devices for watching and studying astronomical objects

patron a person who gives approval and support to some person, art, cause, or undertaking

Grammar

Adverbs

An **adverb** tells how, when, or where something happens. *For example: The caravan traveled quickly.* In the sentence, *quickly* is an adverb that modifies *traveled.* Usually adverbs modify verbs, but they can also tell about adjectives and other adverbs. A **comparative adverb,** which usually ends in *-er* or uses the word *more*, compares two actions. *For example: brighter, more mysterious.* A **superlative adverb** compares three or more actions. *For example: brightest, most mysterious.*

Activity

Adverb Attack Write short sentences on slips of paper and put them in a pile. Then write adverbs like these on slips of paper: *slowly, carefully, brightly, excitedly, too, very,* and *always.* Put these in another pile. Choose a piece of paper from each pile and see what happens if you add the adverb into the sentence.

Practice Tested Spelling Words

______	______	______	______
______	______	______	______
______	______	______	______
______	______	______	______
______	______	______	______

Name ______________________

Sequence

- **Sequence** refers to the order of events or the steps of a process.
- Dates, times, and clue words such as *first, finally, meanwhile,* and *then* can help you determine the order of events.
- Sometimes a text will present events out of order. In this case, you can read on, review, or reread the text in order to learn the correct sequence of events.

Directions Read the following passage. Then complete the diagram below.

In 2002, a new library opened in Alexandria, Egypt, named Bibliotheca Alexandrina. Although new libraries open all the time, this new library has a unique story to tell. Bibliotheca Alexandrina opened very near the site of the ancient Great Library of Alexandria. This ancient library dominated learning in the ancient world from approximately 300 B.C. until A.D. 400. It was home to up to 700,000 scrolls from all over the ancient world. It was partially destroyed when Julius Caesar set fire to the city in A.D. 48. Three centuries later, the library had completely fallen. The new Bibliotheca Alexandrina will house up to 5 million books and build special collections on Egypt, the Middle East, and Islam. It is also fireproof.

First Event	Second Event	Third Event	Fourth Event
1.	2.	3.	4.

5. How were you able to determine the order of events in this passage?

____

____

Home Activity Your child read a short passage and identified the sequence of events. Work with your child to write down the events from a historical passage on note cards. Scramble the note cards, and then have your child put them in the correct order.

Name ______________________________

Vocabulary

Directions Choose the word from the box that best matches each definition below. Write the word on the line.

Check the Words You Know
___beacon
___caravans
___legacy
___manuscripts
___medieval
___observatory
___patron

______________ **1.** a person who gives support to some person, art, or undertaking

______________ **2.** something handed down from an ancestor or predecessor

______________ **3.** a building equipped with telescopes for studying astronomy

______________ **4.** handwritten or keyboarded books or articles

______________ **5.** a fire or light used as a signal to guide or warn

Directions Choose the word from the box that best completes each sentence. Write the word on the line shown to the left.

______________ **6.** In _____ times, during the fourteenth and fifteenth centuries, scholars studied many subjects.

______________ **7.** _____ brought these treasures from Egypt to Europe.

______________ **8.** _____ were written by hand to record the scholars' ideas.

______________ **9.** These ancient writings are an important _____ for scholars today.

______________ **10.** Sometimes they guide scholars of ancient history like a _____.

Write a Story

On a separate sheet of paper, write a story about a character living in the Middle Ages in a faraway land. Use as many vocabulary words as you can.

Home Activity Your child identified and used vocabulary words from *The House of Wisdom.* With your child, read a story about a person who lived during a different historical period. Have your child point out any vocabulary words he or she sees in the story.

Name________________________________

Vocabulary • Dictionary/Glossary

- **Dictionaries** and **glossaries** provide lists of words and their meanings. Glossaries appear at the back of some books and list definitions for important words in the books. Dictionaries list many more words and provide pronunciations, parts of speech, and spellings as well as definitions.
- If you can't tell the meaning of a word from its context or structure, look it up in a dictionary or glossary. Try the meanings to see which one makes sense.

Directions Read the following passage. Then use a dictionary or glossary to answer the questions below.

Almost five thousand years ago in ancient Egypt, the earliest manuscripts were written on papyrus rolls. Papyrus continued to be used for thousands of years. Eventually, parchment replaced papyrus as the the preferred material for writing. Later, during medieval times, paper was introduced. Medieval manuscripts were often decorated with silver and gold to make them shine like a beacon. This process was expensive so a patron sometimes paid for the creation of a manuscript. Ancient manuscripts are part of a valuable legacy passed to our generation and generations to come.

1. Which context clues help you understand the meaning of *manuscript*? What other information is included in the dictionary or glossary entry for *manuscript*?

____

____

2. Which word from the passage would you find on a dictionary page with the guide words *battlement* and *beady*?

____

3. The dictionary gives these definitions for *patron:* "a regular customer," "a person who gives support," and "a guardian saint or god." Which meaning makes sense in the passage?

____

4. Where does a dictionary or a glossary say a *legacy* comes from?

____

5. Which word or words from this passage would you look up in a dictionary or glossary? Why?

____

____

Home Activity Your child read a short passage and used a dictionary or glossary to understand unfamiliar words. Work with your child to identify unfamiliar words in an article. Ask your child if he or she can understand the words using context clues. If not, then look up the meanings in a glossary or dictionary.

Name ______________________________

Literary Elements • Setting

Directions Read the following story. Then answer the questions below.

Menes put away the papyrus scroll as he finished his lesson for the day. His father had taught him many verses from the Books of Instruction, but this was the one he remembered: "Seek the advice of the untutored as much as the well-educated." Menes's father was a nobleman and owned many fields. After his lesson, Menes joined his father in the fields. One of the peasants was sowing seeds and told his father that the great Nile River was flooding. His father didn't believe him. "Maybe you should listen," Menes advised. "I listen only to the Pharaoh," said his father, who didn't give a second thought to protecting his fields. A day later, floodwaters engulfed their fields, and the seeds started to rot. "I should have listened to you, my boy," his father said. When Menes repeated the verse from the Books of Instruction, his father said, "I have learned a lesson too."

1. What time and place is this story set in?

____

2. What are some of the clues about the setting?

____

____

3. What does the story suggest about education at this time?

____

____

4. In a sentence or two, describe the setting for this story in your own words.

____

____

____

5. Imagine a new setting for this story that is familiar to you. In a sentence or two, on a separate piece of paper, describe the new setting.

Home Activity Your child read a short passage and has analyzed the setting. With your child, read a short story about family life. Ask him or her to explain the setting and how important it is to the story.

Name ____________________

Sequence

- **Sequence** refers to the order of events or the steps of a process.
- Dates, times, and clue words such as *first, finally, meanwhile,* and *then* can help you determine the order of events.
- Sometimes a text will present events out of order. In this case, you can read on, review, or reread the text in order to learn the correct sequence of events.

Directions Read the following passage. Then answer the questions below.

In the seventh century, Arab mathematicians began using Indian numerals. As early as A.D. 400, Indian mathematicians were using a system that represented zero. Other systems for representing numbers did not have a symbol for zero and were long to write. The Indian numerals made arithmetic much easier and, as a result, were adopted by Arab mathematicians.

It took a long time for Europeans to adopt this easier system, however. In 1202 Leonardo Fibonacci, an Italian mathematician working in Algeria, wrote *Liber Abaci.* This important book promoted the Hindu-Arabic system. But his book was not the first time the Hindu-Arabic system appeared in Europe. It had also been used in the tenth-century writings of a Spanish monk. In the fifteenth century, the invention of printing finally spread the use of Hindu-Arabic numerals throughout Europe.

1. Are the events in this passage written in sequence? What clues help you recognize this?

____

2. What is the first event in the passage? When did it take place?

____

3. What is the second event in the passage? When did it take place?

____

4. What is the first event to take place in Europe? When did it take place?

____

5. What is the last event in the passage? When did it take place?

____

____

Home Activity Your child read a short passage and identified its sequence of events. With your child, read a magazine article about an ancient culture. Work together to identify the sequence of events in the article.

Name ______________________________

Sequence

- **Sequence** refers to the order of events or the steps of a process.
- Dates, times, and clue words such as *first, finally, meanwhile,* and *then* can help you determine the order of events.
- Sometimes a text will present events out of order. In this case, you can read on, review, or reread the text in order to learn the correct sequence of events.

Directions Read the following passage. Then complete the diagram below.

The story of the struggle between the wise Ahura Mazda and his cruel twin Ahriman can explain the history of the world. First, Ahura Mazda created time, the Sun, the stars, the Moon, the wind, and the rain. He also created love. Next, Ahriman angrily rebelled against his brother. Ahura Mazda then sent Ahriman far away into the darkness. Meanwhile, Ahura Mazda created the first man. But Ahriman returned and caused trouble again. He burst through the sky and brought the pain of sickness and death to the world. To control his brother, Ahura Mazda trapped him in this world. Now Ahura Mazda still keeps the world lovely, but Ahriman spreads evil.

First Event	Second Event	Third Event	Fourth Event
1. Ahura Mazda first created	**2.** After Ahriman rebelled,	**3.** Ahriman returned with	**4.** Ahura Mazda keeps the world lovely, but

5. How were you able to determine the order of events in this passage?

____

____

Home Activity Your child read a short passage and identified the sequence of events. Work with your child to identify the sequence of events in an activity you do together, such as hanging a picture or making bread. Then ask your child to write out the steps in the process.

Name______________________________

Encyclopedia

Encyclopedias give general information about many subjects. An **entry** is an article. An **entry word** begins each entry by telling the subject. A **key word** will help you locate information in an encyclopedia. **Cross-references** help you find more information about the topic. **Visuals** help explain information too. **Electronic encyclopedias** may be quicker to use than printed volumes and may also contain more images and even sound.

Directions Read these entries about Aristotle from two different encyclopedias.

Entry from a print encyclopedia:

ARISTOTLE (384–322 B.C.) was a Greek philosopher and scientist who had great influence on Western thought for more than two thousand years.

Philosophy. Aristotle was one of the most learned philosophers of ancient Greece. He studied all of the Greek philosophers who came before him. His own work spanned many fields, including the sciences, political theory, psychology, ethics, and history. Aristotle is widely known for his system of logic and concepts of ethics. He wrote many books on these topics.

For 20 years, Aristotle was a student of the Greek philosopher Plato. Aristotle and Plato are thought to be the greatest of the Greek philosophers.

Life. Aristotle was born in Stagira, Greece. His father was the private physician of the king of Macedonia, Amyntas, who was the grandfather of Alexander the Great. Aristotle's parents died when he was a child. At the age of 18, he began studying at Plato's Academy in Athens. Plato recognized his brilliance and saw him as the promise of the school. Afer Plato's death, Aristotle became the tutor of the young Alexander. Later, he started his own school in Athens, the Lyceum. He taught there for 12 years. In 323 B.C., he died in Chalcis.

See also *Plato, Greek philosophers.*

Entry from an electronic encyclopedia:

Aristotle

born 384 B.C., Stagira
died 322 B.C., Chalcis

Aristotle was a classical Greek philosopher, author, and scientist whose thinking influenced fields from science to ethics to politics.

Aristotle was a student of the Greek philosopher Plato. Aristotle's father was physician to Amyntas, the king of Macedonia and grandfather of Alexander the Great.

At 17, Aristotle began studying at Plato's Academy in Athens. He remained there for 20 years. A scholar and reader, Aristotle was known for his knowledge of the history of philosophy.

Some time after Plato's death, King Philip II of Macedonia asked Aristotle to take charge of the education of his young son Alexander, who later became Alexander the Great. Afterward, Aristotle began his own school, the Lyceum, where he taught for 12 years. In 323 B.C. he died in Chalcis.

Aristotle, along with Plato, is one of the most famous ancient Greek philosophers. He is known for developing a system of logic. He also believed in gathering facts and information, and his approach laid the groundwork for modern science.

Aristotle's many writings include books on logic, science, ethics, and history.

Name ____

Directions Use the encyclopedia entries to answer the following questions.

1. The twenty-six volumes of a printed encyclopedia, are organized alphabetically. What letter would be on the volume of the printed encyclopedia for this entry? Why?

____

2. Would the entry for Aristotle appear before or after the entry for Arctic? Explain.

____

3. You find entries in an electronic encyclopedia by searching for key words. Other than Aristotle, what key words do you think you would use to locate this entry?

____

4. What illustrations or graphics do you think you would find in both entries?

____

5. Would an encyclopedia be a good reference for finding specific quotations from Aristotle? Why or why not?

____

____

6. What cross-references are included in the print version? How can you tell?

____

7. What cross-references does the online version contain? How can you tell?

____

____

8. What do you learn from these entries about Aristotle's greatest contributions?

____

____

9. In what way do the facts differ in the two articles?

____

____

10. Compare and contrast the format and organization of the two versions.

____

____

Home Activity Your child learned about using encyclopedias as resources. With your child, look at both a printed volume of an encyclopedia and an online encyclopedia. Ask your child to locate several entries using key words that you suggest.

Name

Family Times

Summary

Don Quixote and the Windmills

Meet a famous character, Don Quixote, who imagines himself to be a knight of the Middle Ages. In his own foggy but idealistic way, he mistakes windmills for giants and challenges them to a battle.

Activity

Invent Yourself Ask a member of your family what he or she would like to do to make the world a better place. Discuss characteristics such as kindness, bravery, strength, and imagination. What characteristics would each of you need to make the world a better place?

Comprehension Skill

Author's Purpose

The **author's purpose** is the reason or reasons an author has for writing. Authors may write to persuade, inform, entertain, or express ideas. Authors often have more than one purpose. As you read, think about why the author may have written the selection, and how well that purpose was met.

Activity

On Purpose Look at a magazine with a family member and try to predict the authors' purposes for different articles in the magazine. Check out advertisements, feature articles, news stories, columns, and editorials. You'll find plenty of purposes!

Lesson Vocabulary

Words to Know

Knowing the meanings of these words is important to reading *Don Quixote and the Windmills*. Practice using these words.

Vocabulary words

lance a long, wooden spear with a sharp iron or steel head

misfortune bad luck

quests expeditions by knights in search of something

renewed to have been made like new; restored

renowned famous

resound to echo

squire attendant

Grammar

Modifiers

Words that describe, or tell about, other words are **modifiers.** Adjectives and adverbs are modifiers. Remember to use modifiers correctly. To avoid confusion, keep your modifiers close to the words they modify. Sometimes misplaced modifiers change the meaning of a sentence. *For example: Tim only cooked the meal. Only Tim cooked the meal. Tim cooked only the meal.* The placement of the word *only* in the three example sentences gives each one a different meaning.

Activity

Misplaced Meanings Write a sentence with a modifier. Ask someone in your family to rewrite the sentence by moving the modifier somewhere else in the sentence. Discuss how the meaning of the sentence has changed. Take turns writing and rewriting sentences.

Practice Tested Spelling Words

Name________________________________

Author's Purpose

- The **author's purpose** is the reason or reasons an author has for writing.
- Authors may write to persuade, inform, entertain, or express thoughts and feelings. They may have more than one purpose for writing.

Directions Read the following passage. Then complete the diagram below.

Chivalry was a way of life for knights in the Middle Ages. Their code of conduct valued courage, honor, service, and the protection of women. Chivalry developed during the eighth and ninth centuries in Europe and peaked in the twelfth century. The system required a knight first to be trained as a page and then serve as a squire, or knight's aide. Chivalry inspired the popular legend of King Arthur and the Knights of the Round Table. Today when we speak of someone as chivalrous, we usually mean they are courteous.

Author's Purpose

1.

Fact from Text

2.

Fact from Text

3.

Fact from Text

4.

5. Do you think the author met his or her purpose? Why or why not?

____

____

Home Activity Your child read a short passage and identified the author's purpose. Work with your child to identify the purpose of an article in a newspaper. Ask you child to explain if the author met his or her purpose.

Name ______________________________

Vocabulary

Directions Choose the word from the box that best matches each definition. Write the word on the line.

Check the Words You Know
___lance
___misfortune
___quests
___renewed
___renowned
___resound
___squire

________________ **1.** made like new

________________ **2.** searches or hunts

________________ **3.** a long, wooden spear with a sharp iron or steel head

________________ **4.** to echo

________________ **5.** bad luck

Directions Choose the word from the box that best completes each clue. Write the word on the line shown to the left.

________________ **6.** Unknown is to _____ as dull is to shiny.

________________ **7.** Knight is to _____ as blacksmith is to apprentice.

________________ **8.** _____ is to restored as built is to constructed.

________________ **9.** Happiness is to _____ as brightness is to dullness.

________________ **10.** _____ are to searches as journeys are to trips.

Write a Description

On a separate sheet of paper, write a description of a knight. Show that you have visualized details about the knight's appearance and actions. Use as many vocabulary words as you can.

School + Home **Home Activity** Your child identified and used vocabulary words from *Don Quixote and the Windmills.* Read a story or nonfiction article with your child. Have your child point out unfamiliar words. Work together to figure out the meaning of each word by using other words that appear near it.

Vocabulary • Word Structure

- A **prefix** is a word part added at the beginning of a base word to change its meaning. Look for prefixes to help you figure out the meaning of unfamiliar words.
- The prefix *re-* means "again" or "do over." The prefix *mis-* means "bad" or "wrong."

Directions Read the following passage. Then answer the questions below.

A renowned knight came upon a family that had had the misfortune of meeting robbers on the road. Ronald, the knight's new squire, wanted the famous knight to be pleased with him. Ronald eagerly handed the knight his lance so he could do battle with the robbers. But Ronald tripped, causing the knight to fall from his horse. This mishap gave the robbers a chance to race off. Ronald renewed his courage. He charged off toward the robbers and overpowered them, retrieving the family's fortune. "Your deeds will resound through history," the knight told Ronald with a smile.

1. How does the prefix in *misfortune* help you to determine its meaning?

____

____

2. How does the prefix in *mishap* help you to determine its meaning?

____

____

3. How does the prefix in *renewed* help you to determine its meaning?

____

____

4. How does the prefix in *resound* help you to determine its meaning?

____

____

5. Why is it hard to use the prefix in *retrieving* to understand its meaning?

____

____

Home Activity Your child read a short passage and used prefixes to understand new words. Work with your child to identify unfamiliar words in an article. Together, see if any of the unfamiliar words have prefixes that can help with understanding the unfamiliar words. Confirm the meanings in a dictionary.

Compare and Contrast

Directions Read the following passage. Then answer the questions below.

Every windmill is slightly different, but there are three main types: post, smock, and tower windmills. The post windmill, which was developed in the twelfth century, was the earliest type. The tower windmill came next. Then in the seventeenth century, the smock windmill was developed.

All three windmills have between four and eight large sails and were built to catch the wind for power. However, they differ in shape. The tower windmill is cylinder-shaped, the post windmill is box-shaped, and the smock windmill is usually octagonal.

The windmills also differ in their building materials. Post and smock windmills are made of wooden boards, usually in a horizontal pattern. In contrast, the tower windmill is made of stone or brick. Of all the types, the post windmill is most common.

1. What is being compared and contrasted in this paragraph?

____

2. What are two ways that all the types of windmills are similar?

____

____

3. What is one way that the three types of windmills differ?

____

____

4. How do windmills differ in terms of building materials?

____

____

5. What question could you use to compare and/or contrast something about the windmills that is not discussed above?

____

____

Home Activity Your child read a short passage and compared and contrasted details. With your child, make a list of types of buildings. Discuss the similarities and differences among the buildings, including when they were built, what they are built from, their general shape, etc.

Name ______________________________

Author's Purpose

- The **author's purpose** is the reason or reasons an author has for writing.
- Authors may write to persuade, inform, entertain, or express ideas. They may have more than one purpose for writing.

Directions Read the following passage. Then answer the questions below.

Stories from the past can spark the imagination of readers today. Intriguing characters such as Huck Finn, Romeo and Juliet, or Odysseus make stories enjoyable and inspiring. Sometimes humor makes fictional characters charming. But it is more important for characters to seem real. Through characters, readers get involved with the story. These characters can represent a struggle, a yearning, or a relationship for readers to identify with. Their stories help readers to understand their own conflicts or escape their everyday lives. Over the years, imaginative tales have remained popular around the world, and millions of people watch plays and read books each year.

1. What is the author's purpose?

____

2. What are some things that make characters appealing to readers?

____

____

3. What is one reason the author gives for why characters appeal to readers?

____

____

4. What evidence does the author provide that shows that stories appeal to readers today?

____

____

5. Do you think the author met his or her purpose? Why or why not?

____

____

Home Activity Your child read a short passage and identified the author's purpose. Together, read a feature article in a newspaper or magazine Then determine what the author was trying to say, and identify the author's purpose. Evaluate whether the author successfully achieved his or her purpose.

Name ______________________________

Author's Purpose

- The **author's purpose** is the reason or reasons an author has for writing.
- Authors may write to persuade, inform, entertain, or express ideas. They may have more than one purpose for writing.

Directions Read the following passage. Then complete the diagram below.

Brett looked out the window. "How is that bird making its nest so quickly?" he wondered. He imagined a treetop "nest" for bored school children. Unfortunately, when his teacher called on him, she wasn't asking about nests. "Brett, please pay attention!" she said. It was the same thing his mother had said at breakfast when he spilled his cereal because he was so absorbed in designing an imaginary fort. In his room after school, he imagined a new game called "Goofalicious." It was silly and serious at the same time. In fact, it was so different and so much fun that his friends loved it. "This is terrific!" they said, and eventually, the world agreed. Brett's game became a favorite with kids. Brett went on to imagine lots more.

Author's Purpose

1.

Supporting Details

2. Brett imagined

____

____

____

3. Brett created

____

____

____

4. ______________________

____

____

____

5. Do you think the author met his or her purpose? Why or why not?

____

____

School + Home

Home Activity Your child analyzed the author's purpose for a fiction passage. Work with your child to identify the author's purpose in a sports article. Challenge your child to justify this analysis.

Name ____

Parts of a Book

Understanding the **parts of a book** can help you to use books more easily. The **title page** gives the title, author, and publisher, and the **copyright page** tells when the book was published. It can help you to know if information in the book is recent. The **table of contents** lists the chapters, stories, or other contents of the book.

Directions Read these four pages from a book.

The History of Sixteenth-Century Spain

Second Edition

by
Matthew Allison

Real History Publishing Company
New York and London

Printed in the United States of America
ISBN 0-333-44444-6

Contents

Name ______________________________

Directions Use the book pages you just read to answer the following questions.

1. What is the first page on the left? What is the page to its right?

2. Who is the author of this book? On what page would you learn about the author?

3. Who is the publisher of the book? Where does the publisher have offices?

4. What year was this book published? Who holds the copyright?

5. By looking at the table of contents, how can you tell where the main part of the book begins? What is the name of the first section of the main part of the book?

6. Would this book be a good source for a report on Spanish kings in the 1500s? Explain.

7. Which chapter would you read to find out about Spain's business and trade in the sixteenth century?

8. Does this book have illustrations? How can you tell?

9. How would you locate information about King Ferdinand in this book?

10. Explain how the chapters of this book are organized.

Home Activity Your child learned about using the parts of a book. Look at a reference book together. Ask your child to locate the publication date and publisher, as well as to explain what is on the table of contents page.

Name

Family Times

Summary

Ancient Greece

The civilization of the ancient Greeks, from the first Minoan palaces to Alexander the Great and beyond, lasted for thousands of years. Its influence can still be felt in the world today.

Activity

Ancient Us Imagine the world two thousand years in the future. Discuss with members of your family what you think will be remembered of the world we live in today: our cities? our books, movies, and art? Explain why you think your choices will be remembered.

Comprehension Skill

Graphic Sources

Maps, charts, tables, diagrams, graphs, pictures, and time lines are all examples of **graphic sources.** Graphic sources can help you to understand a text better, and they also can be used to preview a selection. The use of graphic sources is an important part of the reading process.

Activity

Picture This Imagine that your family will be traveling to a new part of the world. Together, look at maps, books, pictures, and brochures to help plan your trip. What do the graphic sources in these works tell you? Discuss how helpful graphic sources are for your planning.

Lesson Vocabulary

Words to Know

Knowing the meanings of these words is important to reading *Ancient Greece.* Practice using these words.

Vocabulary Words

architecture a style or special manner of building

democracy government that is run by the people who live under it

empire a group of countries or states under one ruler or government

ideal just as you would wish; perfect

mythology a group of legends or stories about a particular country or person

Grammar

Conjunctions

A **conjunction** is a word that joins words, phrases, or entire sentences, such as *and, but,* or *or. For example: you or me; beans and rice; not Wednesday but Thursday.* Conjunctions can also be used to combine sentences. *For example: I went to the bowling alley, but I didn't see anybody I knew.* The word *but* in the example is a conjunction joining two complete sentences.

Activity

Conjunction Functions Read an article in the newspaper with a member of your family. Write a short sentence about something that happened in the article, and write it in the first column of a three-column table. Then write a short sentence about what happened after that in the third column. Decide if a conjunction could be placed in the middle column to join the two sentences into a third sentence. Try again with other parts of the article.

Practice Tested Spelling Words

Name____

Graphic Sources

- A **graphic source** organizes information in a way that is easy to see. Graphic sources include maps, charts, tables, pictures, and time lines.
- Use graphic sources to help you understand what you read and to preview your reading.

Directions The following map shows regions in ancient Greece. Use it to answer the questions.

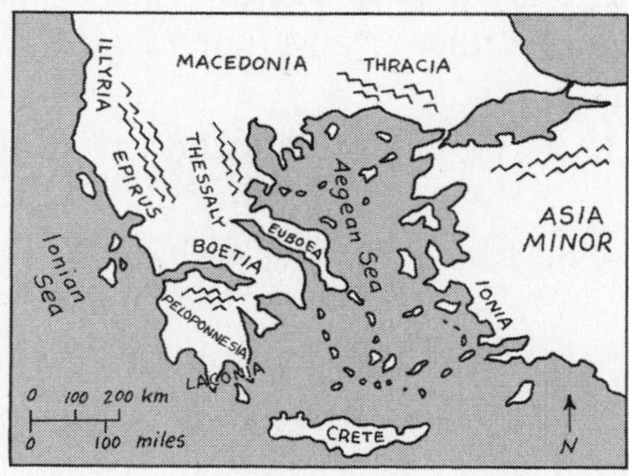

1. What does this map show?

____

____

2. What was the northernmost region of ancient Greece? The southernmost?

____

3. About how far was it from Macedonia to Crete? What bodies of water surrounded ancient Greece?

____

____

4. What can you tell about the geography and natural features of the land in ancient Greece?

____

____

____

5. The current border of Greece is south of Macedonia. It is also east of Thracia and west of Asia Minor. On a separate sheet of paper, draw your own map approximating Greece today. How does that map compare with the map of ancient Greece?

Home Activity Your child used a map to learn about ancient Greece. With your child, look over a map of an unfamiliar place, and challenge your child to explain what he or she can learn from it.

Name ______________________________

Vocabulary

Directions Choose the word from the box that best matches each definition. Write the word on the line.

Check the Words You Know

___architecture
___democracy
___empire
___ideal
___mythology

__________ **1.** a group of legends or stories about a particular country or person

__________ **2.** a group of countries or states under one ruler or government

__________ **3.** a style or special manner of building

__________ **4.** just as you would wish; perfect

__________ **5.** government that is run by the people who live under it

Directions Choose the word from the box that best matches each clue. Write the word on the line.

__________ **6.** Ancient Greece was the first example of this political system.

__________ **7.** The religion of ancient Greece included examples of this.

__________ **8.** Athens built up this kind of union of many territories.

__________ **9.** Ancient Greece made a large contribution in this field.

__________ **10.** The Greek philosopher Plato outlined this kind of government.

Write an Opinion

On a separate sheet of paper, write your opinion of an ideal civilization. Think about how it would look politically, economically, and artistically. Be specific in explaining your opinion.

Home Activity Your child identified and used vocabulary words from *Ancient Greece*. Read a story or nonfiction article with your child. Have him or her point out unfamiliar words. Work together to figure out the meaning of each unfamiliar word by looking at other words around it.

Name ____________________

Vocabulary • Context Clues

- When you are reading and see an unfamiliar word, use **context clues**, or words around the unfamiliar word, to figure out its meaning.
- Context clues include definitions, explanations, and synonyms (words that have the same or nearly the same meaning as other words).

Directions Read the following passage. Then answer the questions below. Look for context clues as you read.

Archaeologists study artifacts to understand the people, customs, and life of ancient times. They go to areas where ancient civilizations such as the Greek or Roman Empire existed, and they dig for artifacts. The shrines they find might tell them about the culture's religion or mythology. Remnants of buildings tell them about the architecture of the ancient culture. Weapons and tools may tell them about the hunting and farming practices of a culture. On an ideal dig, archaeologists quickly and easily find many artifacts telling a complete story of an ancient civilization.

1. Based on the passage, what is an empire?

____

2. What clues does the passage provide about the meaning of *mythology*?

____

3. How does a context clue tell you the meaning of *architecture*?

____

____

4. How do context clues help you determine the meaning of *democracy*?

____

____

5. What can you tell from context about the meaning of *ideal*?

____

____

Home Activity Your child identified and used context clues to understand new words in a passage. Work with your child to identify unfamiliar words in an article. Then have him or her find context clues to help with the understanding of the new words. Confirm the meanings with your child.

Name________________________________

Draw Conclusions

Directions Read the story. Then answer the questions below.

A famous tale of ancient Greece is Homer's *The Odyssey*. Its main character, Odysseus, has many adventures during his ten-year journey home from the Trojan War. In one episode, he and his men land their ship at Aeolia, the home of Aeolus, the god of the winds. As a parting gift, Aeolus seals all the harmful winds in a bag and gives it to Odysseus so he will have a safe journey home. Odysseus forbids his crew to open the bag of winds. However, they begin to suspect that the bag contains treasure. Because they can't resist having the treasure for themselves, they open the bag. Out burst the harmful winds, which create a terrible, deadly storm that blows Odysseus's ship off course. Eventually the ship lands at an island of half-giants called Laestrigonia. While some of the shipmates are devoured by the half-giants, most manage to escape. Odysseus then sails on to another adventure.

1. What conclusion do you draw about the characters' arrival at Laestrigonia?

____

____

2. From this story, how would you conclude the Greeks felt about gifts?

____

____

3. What can you conclude about Odysseus's crew from this story?

____

____

4. What lesson do you draw from the story of the bag of winds?

____

____

5. On a separate sheet of paper, explain what kind of story you think *The Odyssey* might be. What conclusions can you draw from this incident about the story and its characters?

Home Activity Your child has read about an adventure tale and drawn conclusions based on details in the story. Read a short story together. Challenge him or her to draw conclusions about the characters.

Name ____________________

Graphic Sources

- A **graphic source** of information is something that shows information visually. Graphic sources include maps, charts, tables, pictures, and time lines.
- Use graphic sources to help you understand what you read and to preview your reading.

Directions Read the following passage. Then answer the questions below.

Greek Gods and Goddesses

Aphrodite	goddess of love and beauty; daughter of Zeus and Dione
Apollo	god of poetry and music; son of Zeus and Leto
Ares	god of war; son of Zeus and Hera
Artemis	goddess of the moon and hunting; daughter of Zeus and Leto
Athena	goddess of wisdom; daughter of Zeus; sprang full-grown from Zeus' head
Demeter	goddess of agriculture
Dionysus	god of drink; son of Zeus and Semele
Eros	god of love; son of Aphrodite
Hades	god of the underworld; brother of Zeus
Hephaestus	god of fire, blacksmith, and husband of Aphrodite
Hera	goddess of marriage; wife of Zeus
Hermes	messenger god; son of Zeus and Maia
Poseidon	god of the sea; brother of Zeus
Zeus	chief Olympian god; husband of Hera

1. What does this chart tell?

____

____

2. What is the advantage of a chart for conveying this information?

____

3. According to the chart, who is the god of love? Who is the goddess of the moon?

____

4. Which gods, according to the chart, have the same mother and father?

____

5. On a separate sheet of paper, draw a family tree or web diagram showing how the Greek gods are related to each other.

Home Activity Your child analyzed a chart as a graphic source that can aid comprehension. Find a chart or graph that you can discuss with your child. Work together to discover what the graphic source reveals. Then make a chart together of your own showing family chores.

Name ______________________

Graphic Sources

- A **graphic source** organizes information in a way that is easy to see. Graphic sources include maps, charts, tables, pictures, and time lines.
- Use graphic sources to help you understand what you read and to preview your reading.

Directions Look at the map of Greece in the fifth century B.C. Then answer the questions.

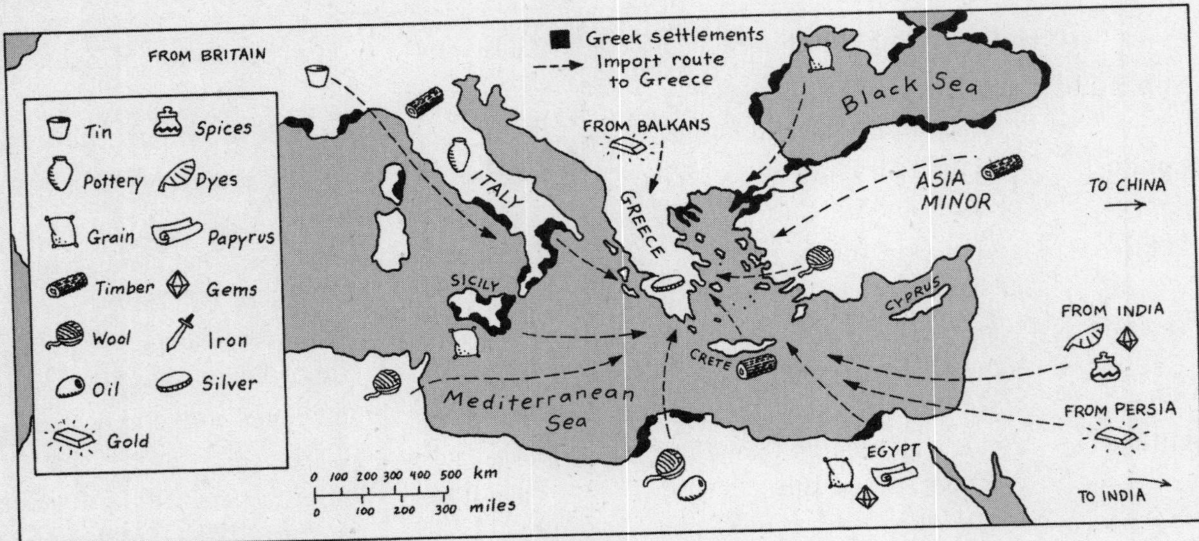

1. What does this map show about imports to ancient Greece in the fifth century B.C.?

____

2. From which countries did Greece import gold? From where did they import pottery?

____

____

3. What did Greece import from India?

____

4. Where are the Greek settlements in the fifth century B.C.?

____

5. What does this map suggest about the economic condition of Greece in the fifth century B.C.? Was it poor or prosperous?

____

____

Home Activity Your child used a graphic source to gain information about ancient Greece. With your child, look at pictures and diagrams in a magazine, and talk about the information they reveal.

Name_______________________________________

Time Line

Time lines are a way to visually present events in time order. The events may be in a story or in nonfiction information. Time lines can cover very general topics or very specific topics. There are many different designs for time lines, which may be read from left to right or top to bottom. Use time lines to help you understand time relationships and remember the order of events.

Directions Use this time line to answer the questions.

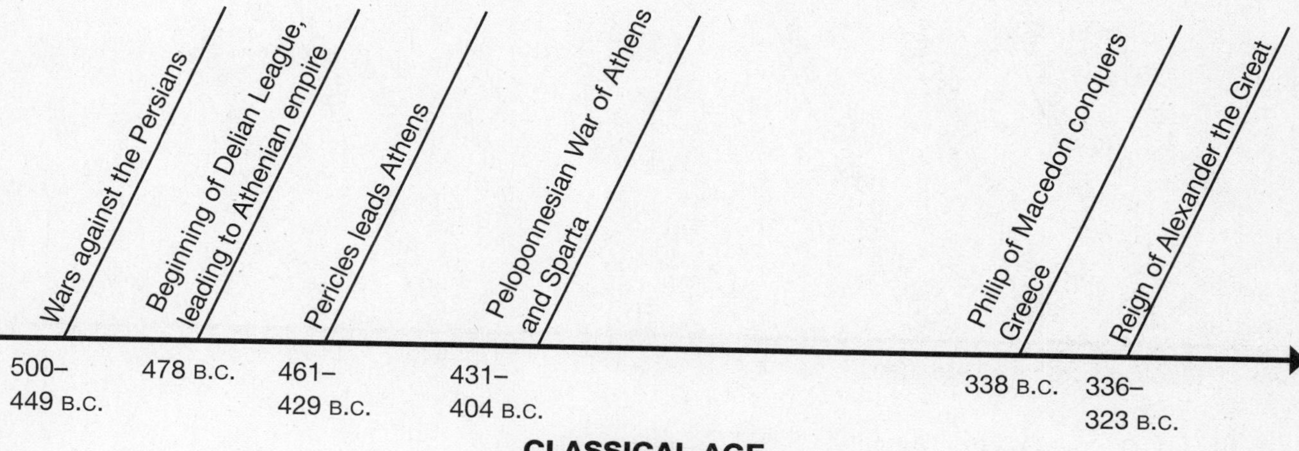

1. What does this time line show?

____

____

2. How is the time line organized? How is it read?

____

3. Who is the earliest Greek leader—Alexander the Great, Pericles, or Philip of Macedon?

____

4. How long of a time period does this time line cover?

____

5. How does the heading help in understanding the information?

____

____

Name ___________________________

Directions Use this time line to answer the questions.

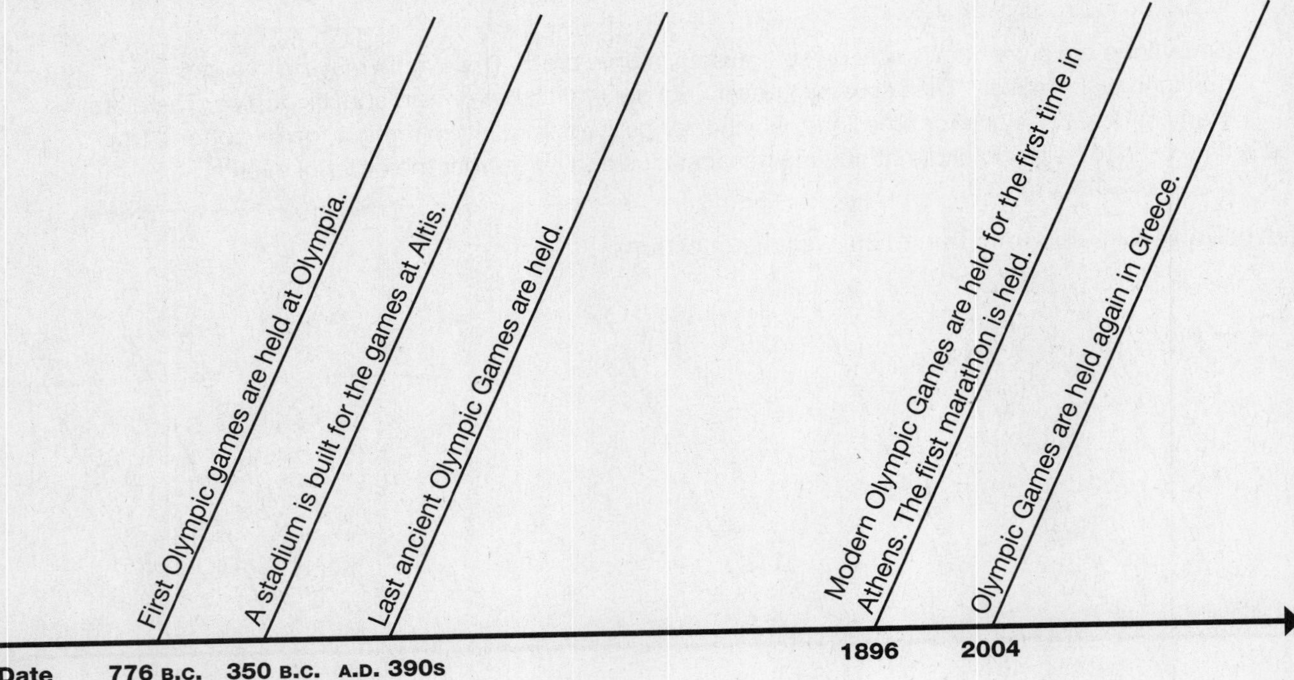

6. What does this time line show?

____

7. How is this time line read?

____

8. How many years does the time line cover? How long did the ancient Olympic Games last?

____

____

9. According to this time line, when were the modern Olympic Games held in Greece?

____

____

10. Explain how this time line can be used to improve understanding of the topic. What advantages does a time line have over text?

____

____

Home Activity Your child learned about using time lines as resources for improving comprehension. Together, look at a time line in an almanac or book. Ask your child to explain what the time line shows.

Name

Family Times

Summary

The All-American Slurp

The Lin family has just moved to America from China, and they find American table manners an amusing trial. But before long, the tables are turned, and the family has some realizations about American culture.

Activity

Culture Queries Imagine that your family moves to a new country where you don't speak the language or know the customs. Talk about what strategies you might use to learn about life in your new home.

Comprehension Skill

Compare and Contrast

To **compare** means to tell how two or more things are similar. To **contrast** means to tell how they are different. Sometimes clue words such as *similarly*, *instead*, *however*, and *like* signal comparisons and contrasts.

Activity

Family Food What are your family's favorite foods? Compare and contrast your family's favorite foods with the favorite foods of other families you know. Have others suggest examples, too.

Lesson Vocabulary

Words to Know

Knowing the meanings of these words is important to reading *The All-American Slurp*. Practice using these words.

Vocabulary Words

disgraced to have caused a loss of honor or respect
progress an advance or growth; development; improvement
promoted raised in rank, condition, or importance
relish a side dish to add flavor to food
retreat the act of withdrawing
revolting disgusting; repulsive
unison together; as one

Grammar

Commas

A **comma** is a punctuation mark used to set off words or groups of words. Use a comma after a person's name when you directly address that person. *For example: Mom, I'm home.* Use commas to separate three or more words in a series. *For example: I like fruit, vegetables, and eggs.* Use commas to set off an appositive, which is an explanation placed next to a word. *For example: Tamara, my cousin, is here.* A comma should never be used by itself to join two sentences—this is an error called a comma splice. *For example: I went to the door, it was my cousin.* Use a semicolon or a comma with a conjunction, instead.

Activity

Comma Quest Create a three-column table on a sheet of paper, with columns labeled "Direct Address," "Series," and "Appositive." With a family member, clip out examples from newspapers or magazines of commas used in these ways. See which of you can be the first to add three examples to each column.

Practice Tested Spelling Words

____	____	____	____
____	____	____	____
____	____	____	____
____	____	____	____
____	____	____	____

Name ____________________

Compare and Contrast

- When you **compare and contrast,** you tell how two or more things are alike and how they are different.
- Sometimes words such as *like, as, however,* and *unlike* signal comparisons or contrasts.

Directions Read the following passage. Then complete the chart below.

Schools in China and the United States are alike and different. In both countries, the school year is about 40 weeks long, however, in China students attend six days a week instead of five. Chinese elementary schools teach the same core subjects as U.S. schools, but politics, foreign language, and manual labor are taught too. In the United States, about the same amount of time is spent on English as on other subjects. However, in China, nearly forty percent of class time is spent on Chinese because it is so difficult. Unlike U.S. students, Chinese students must pass exams to move up to junior high school (called junior middle school) or high school (called senior middle school). Finally, in the United States all children attend junior high school, but in China less than half of all children attend.

	United States	**China**
Length of school year	40 weeks	40 weeks
Length of school week	Five days	Six days
Elementary school subjects	**1.**	
Time spent on language	**2.**	
Entrance exams	**3.**	
Junior high attendance	**4.**	
Names of schools	**5.**	

Home Activity Your child compared and contrasted information in a nonfiction passage. With your child, read about different holiday celebrations, and encourage your child to visualize the similarities and differences as you read. Challenge your child to compare and contrast the celebrations.

Name ______________________________

Vocabulary

Directions Choose the word from the box that best matches each definition below. Write the word on the line.

Check the Words You Know

- ___disgraced
- ___progress
- ___promoted
- ___relish
- ___retreat
- ___revolting
- ___unison

______________ **1.** together; as one

______________ **2.** raised in rank

______________ **3.** act of withdrawing

______________ **4.** repulsive; disgusting

______________ **5.** a side dish to add flavor to food

Directions Choose the word from the box that best completes each sentence below. Write the word on the line shown to the left.

______________ **6.** Appealing is to ____ as healthy is to sick.

______________ **7.** Defeat is to ____ as win is to advance.

______________ **8.** Criticized is to praised as ____ is to honored.

______________ **9.** ____ is to reduced as lifted is to dropped.

______________ **10.** Improvement is to increase as development is to ____.

Write a Journal Entry

On a separate sheet of paper, write a journal entry you might make after you attend a party or school event. Use as many vocabulary words as you can.

School + Home

Home Activity Your child identified and used vocabulary words from *The All-American Slurp*. Read a story or nonfiction article with your child. Have him or her point out unfamiliar words. Work together to try to figure out the meaning of each word by using other words that appear near it.

Name______________________________________

Vocabulary • Context Clues

- Some words have **multiple meanings,** or more than one definition.
- Try each of the meanings in the sentence. **Context clues,** or words around the unfamiliar word, can help you to figure out the correct meaning.

Directions Read the following story about a family meal. Then answer the questions below. Look for context clues as you read.

When I was promoted to junior high, my family had a party that I'll never forget. The guests had arrived and dinner was ready to be served when the cats jumped onto the table. They started munching on the tuna salad. "That's revolting!" Aunt Ida and Uncle Sid screamed in unison. The cats looked up and moved on to the relish plate filled with deviled eggs and pickles. Dad and I chased the cats, but already the guests had begun their retreat toward the door. Suddenly they all felt ill or had urgent work to do.

After they left, Mother moaned, "We can progress in every field of human life, but we can't keep the cats off the table!" She felt disgraced that the guests left without eating and upset that the meal was ruined. "Look at it this way," said Dad. "At least we don't have to buy cat food."

1. Two meanings of *promoted* have to do with "furthering a sale by advertising" and "raised in rank." What clue in the story above helps you to determine the correct meaning?

____

2. *Revolting* can mean "uprising" or "disgusting." What clues help you to determine its meaning in the story above?

____

3. In the passage does *relish* mean "good flavor" or "a side dish"? How do context clues help you determine the meaning?

____

4. Meanings for *retreat* include "the act of withdrawing" and "a retirement for religious exercises." How do context clues in the passage help you determine the meaning?

____

5. How does the context help you determine which meaning of *progress* is used in the story, "improvement" or "to move forward"?

____

Home Activity Your child identified and used context clues to determine the correct definition for words with multiple meanings. Read a story with your child. Encourage your child to figure out the meanings of unfamiliar words using context clues.

Name ______________________________

Draw Conclusions

Directions Read the article. Then answer the questions below.

On Ai's first day at an American school, she noticed everyone's clothes looked different from hers. But her biggest difficulty was that she couldn't understand anything they were saying. Nobody at her school spoke Chinese. When her teachers talked to her, she just stared back. In the lunchroom she sat alone with her fried dumplings and rice. By October she was playing on the soccer team, and she had gathered some friends who liked her easy smile. Then by November she could understand most of the chatter around her, with lots of concentration. At night after doing her homework and studying English, she tried hard to teach her mother the language. For her birthday in December, she was excited to have her friends over for a dinner that included ginger beef eaten with chopsticks.

1. What conclusion can you draw about the move that Ai's family has made?

____

____

2. What conclusion can you draw about how Ai's life changes over the four months the story takes place?

____

____

3. What details allow you to draw that conclusion?

____

____

4. What conclusion can you draw about Ai's personality?

____

____

5. On a separate sheet of paper, explain the conclusion you can draw about Ai's mother's adaptation to U.S. culture. Give a detail from the story to support your answer.

Home Activity Your child has read a story and drawn conclusions about the changes that occurred for the characters. Tell your child a story about a change you have experienced, and ask him and her to draw a conclusion from the details of the story.

Name ____________________

Compare and Contrast

- When you **compare and contrast,** you tell how two or more things are alike and how they are different.
- Sometimes words such as *like, as, however,* and *unlike* signal comparisons or contrasts.

Directions Read the following passage. Then answer the questions below.

Chinese and English are both difficult languages, but each is difficult in its own way. Written Chinese often uses both sound characters and meaning characters to form words. For example, a symbol for *river* combines the character for the sound of the word with the character for *water.* Written English, on the other hand, uses sound characters only, and its rules for pronunciation and spelling are very complicated and hard to learn. Although Chinese and English use mostly the same sounds, Chinese has sounds not found in English. It also uses varying tones that change words' meanings. One last difference is dialect. Dialects of English are different in different regions, but English speakers usually understand each other no matter where they are from. In Chinese, the regional dialects are so different that speakers from different areas often can't undertstand each other.

1. Does the first sentence in the passage make a comparison, a contrast, or both?

____

2. Contrast the ways written English and Chinese form words.

____

____

3. Compare the appearance of dialects in the two languages.

____

4. Compare and contrast the sounds used in the two languages.

____

____

5. Summarize the differences between English and Chinese described in the passage.

____

____

Home Activity Your child compared and contrasted two languages described in a nonfiction passage and visualized the details. With your child, read a magazine article about a different country. Work together to identify the similarities and differences between cultures.

Name ____________________

Compare and Contrast

- When you **compare and contrast,** you tell how two or more things are alike and how they are different.
- Sometimes words such as *like, as, however,* and *unlike* signal comparisons or contrasts.

Directions Read the following passage. Then complete the diagram.

In China, the most important festival is Spring Festival, which celebrates the new year. Families clean the house, which symbolizes a new start, and visit other family members. Fireworks are an old custom, in honor of a story about a beast that was scared off by fireworks. Another old custom is to hang pictures and poems on doors. Among the many foods served during this festival is New Year's cake. Dancing, music, gifts, and shows can be part of the celebration too.

Mid-Autumn Festival celebrates the brightest moon of the year. Its traditional date is the fifteenth day of the eighth lunar month. Unlike Spring Festival, it is a quiet celebration. People go out to look at the moon, and moon cake is served at a special dinner. A favorite story told at this time is about an empress who drank a potion to live forever and then went to live at the Moon Palace in the sky.

	Spring Festival	**Mid-Autumn Festival**
Date	Beginning of lunar new year	**1.**
Reason for	Celebration of lunar new year	**2.**
Activities	**3.**	Moon watching, dinner, storytelling
Food	**4.**	Moon cake

5. Compare and contrast the two Chinese holidays in one or two sentences.

____

____

____

Home Activity Your child compared and contrasted details of a nonfiction passage. Work together to compare and contrast information in a reference book about two historical events. Challenge your child to summarize the similarities and differences.

Name ______________________________

Instruction Manual

Instruction manuals are guidebooks that give instructions on how to do something. They may be intended for immediate use or for reference. They usually have several parts, such as table of contents, index, sections, and graphics. Read through instructions before following the procedures.

Directions Use this excerpt from an etiquette manual to answer the questions.

Table Manners

Eating is a social activity, which means that you need to think of others when you eat. Poor table manners can disgust other people. In contrast, good table manners show you respect them.

- Put your napkin on your lap.
- Sit up straight with your elbows off the table.
- Wait to eat until everyone is served.
- Don't talk with food in your mouth.
- Chew with your mouth closed.
- Don't make loud noises when you eat.
- Don't shovel in your food.
- Ask for something to be passed rather than reaching across the table for it.
- Don't lick your knife or eat off it.
- Don't lick your fingers.

1. How would this be used as a manual?

____

2. If you wanted to locate this information on table manners, how could you find it in the etiquette manual?

____

3. Would a manual on table manners be a good place to find out which fork to use or how to put butter on your plate? Why?

____

4. How might an etiquette manual on table manners be different in a different country?

____

____

5. What aspects of table manners are covered in this passage? Which items could graphics help you understand better?

____

____

____

Name ____

Directions Use these instructions to answer the questions.

How to Use Chopsticks

Chopsticks were developed about 5,000 years ago and are the most used utensil in China. Here are six easy steps for using chopsticks correctly.

1. Hold the chopsticks in the middle, with the ends even and not crossed.
2. Hold the top chopstick firmly between your thumb, index, and middle fingers, like a pen.
3. Rest the bottom chopstick on your ring finger and hold it down with your thumb. Always keep the bottom chopstick still.
4. Move the top chopstick by guiding it with your top two fingers.
5. Pick up food by moving the top chopstick outward, straightening your index finger. As you grab the food, bend your index finger to bring the top chopstick toward the bottom chopstick.
6. Lift food between chopsticks to your mouth.

Chopstick Etiquette

- Don't wave your chopsticks in the air.
- Don't transfer food from your chopsticks to someone else's.
- Don't stab food with them.
- Don't stick your chopsticks vertically in a dish.

1. What is the purpose of this passage?

____

2. Would the passage be for immediate use or reference? What would be a good way to use it?

____

____

3. How does the drawing improve your understanding of the procedure?

____

4. Which chopstick moves, and which one always stays still?

____

5. Does it matter if the instructions are followed in order? Why or why not?

____

____

____

____

Home Activity Your child learned about using manuals as resources. Look at a cookbook together, and ask your child in what ways it is a manual. Have your child demonstrate how to locate information and how to use the cookbook.

Name

Family Times

Summary

The Aztec News

News of battles, a city guide, entertaining features about business and fashion—it's all here in a fascinating mock newspaper covering the Aztec civilization.

Activity

A Nose for News Imagine that one thousand years from now reporters are describing today's civilization. What news would they report? See what your family members have to say, and make an outline of stories for a newspaper of the future.

Comprehension Skill

Draw Conclusions

A **conclusion** is a decision you reach when you think about facts and details. Your conclusions should be logical and well supported. Ask yourself if your conclusion makes sense and if it can be backed up with solid information.

Activity

Make a Leap With your family, look at the photographs in a book or newspaper. See what conclusions you can draw about the people in the photographs. Then read the text to confirm what you concluded. How can you avoid jumping to a mistaken conclusion?

Lesson Vocabulary

Words to Know

Knowing the meanings of these words is important to reading *The Aztec News.* Practice using these words.

Vocabulary Words

benefits things that are for the good of someone or something

campaigns a series of related military operations in a war

comrades fellow workers or soldiers

enrich to make rich or richer

foreigners persons from another country

invaders enemies who enter with force or attack

Grammar

Quotations and Quotation Marks

A **quotation** is the exact words a speaker says. In your writing, enclose a quotation in **quotation marks.** Use commas to set off the words that introduce a quotation. *For example: Joe said, "Has anyone seen my skateboard?"* Place the sentence's end punctuation, or the comma that ends the quotation, inside the quotation marks. *For example: "Listen to this news," Kelly said.*

Activity

Quotation Station Interview a family member, and write down the person's quotations correctly for a story in your "family newspaper." Be sure to keep your family "in the know."

Practice Tested Spelling Words

Draw Conclusions

- When you **draw** a **conclusion**, you form a reasonable opinion about something you have read.
- Evaluate whether your conclusions are valid. Ask yourself: Do the facts and details in the text support my conclusion? Is my conclusion valid, based on logical thinking and common sense?

Directions Read the following passage. Then complete the diagram below.

The Aztecs had many laws that covered issues from stealing to gambling to taxes. Laws even regulated the kinds of clothing Aztecs could wear. For example, nobles could wear clothes decorated in many colors, but commoners had to wear plain clothes. All laws were enforced by judges and police.

The punishment for many crimes, even lesser crimes, was death. For example, wearing the wrong type of clothing could lead to punishment of death. Anyone who broke laws protecting forests and crops could be killed as well. The laws applied to everyone—nobles, commoners, and slaves. However, since nobles were expected to behave better, they were punished more harshly for committing crimes. For example, while a commoner might have his head shaved for committing a crime, a nobleman might be put to death for the same crime.

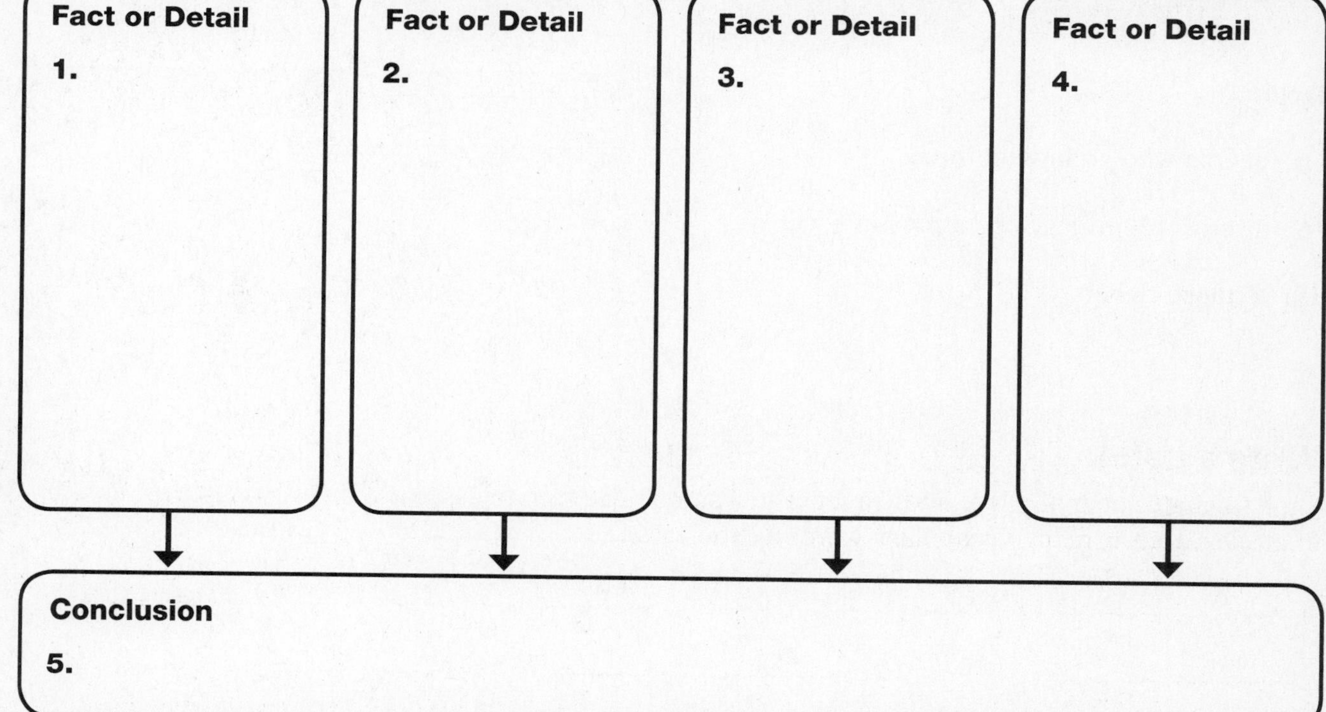

Home Activity Your child made a conclusion about a nonfiction passage and supported it with details. Work with your child to draw conclusions about information in the sports pages of the newspaper. Challenge your child to support his or her conclusions with specific details.

Name ______________________________

Vocabulary

Directions Choose the word from the box that best matches each definition below. Write the word on the line.

Check the Words You Know
___benefits
___campaigns
___comrades
___enrich
___foreigners
___invaders

__________________ **1.** things that are for the good of someone or something

__________________ **2.** enemies who enter with force or attack

__________________ **3.** people from another country

__________________ **4.** fellow workers or soldiers

__________________ **5.** to make rich or richer

Directions Choose the word from the box that best completes the crossword puzzle below. Write the word in the puzzle.

Across

6. partners

7. advantages

Down

8. people who go in with force

9. a series of military operations in a war

10. to make richer

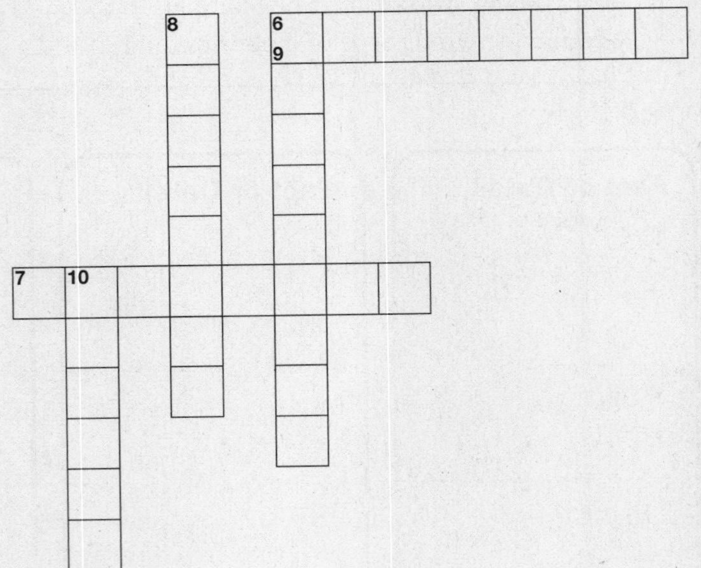

Write a Letter

On a separate sheet of paper, write a letter to a soldier. Be sure to ask questions you'd like the soldier to answer. Use as many vocabulary words as you can.

Home Activity Your child identified and used vocabulary words from *The Aztec News*. Together read a story or nonfiction article. Have him or her point out unfamiliar words. Work together to try to figure out the meaning of each word by using other words that appear near it.

Name______________________________

Vocabulary • Dictionary/Glossary

- **Dictionaries** and **glossaries** provide alphabetical lists of words and their meanings.
- While reading, sometimes a reader comes across unfamiliar words, or familiar words used in unfamiliar ways. If this happens, use a dictionary or glossary to find the meaning.

Directions Read the following passage. Then answer the questions below using a dictionary or glossary.

Tula was a young assistant to an Aztec warrior, and he and his comrades from school had been on many military campaigns. The Aztecs were often at war with other tribes. Conquering more lands would enrich the Aztec empire with more farmland. In addition, Tula knew that there were other benefits of war, such as the protection of trade, taking of prisoners, and gaining more goods and taxes from the people they ruled. In 1519, Tula and the rest of the Aztec army were surprised and confused by foreign invaders on horseback who spread disease across the land. "I have never seen such animals—they scare me," said Tula.

1. What is the meaning of *comrades* in this story?

____

2. What is the meaning of *campaigns* as it is used in the passage? What is another meaning for the word?

____

____

3. What meaning of *enrich* makes sense in this story?

____

4. In this passage, what is the meaning of the word *benefits*?

____

5. Choose a word with multiple meanings from the story. Write a sentence using the word in a different way from the way it is used in the passage.

____

____

School + Home

Home Activity Your child identified and used a dictionary or glossary to understand new words of a passage. Work together to identify unfamiliar words of an article. Then your child can use a dictionary or glossary to understand the meaning of the new words.

Name ______________________________

Author's Purpose

Directions Read the article. Then answer the questions below.

A popular Aztec game was a ball game called *tlachtli*. It was played by two teams on an I-shaped court with walls. A hard ball made from tree sap was used. The object of the game was to hit the ball through the opponent's goal, which was a stone ring hanging from the side of a wall. Instead of using their hands to hit the ball, players had to use their knees, elbows, and hips. Only noblemen were allowed to play the game, which was often part of religious celebrations. However, commoners could watch and cheer the teams.

Take a clue from the Aztecs and try *tlachtli*—it could become a new favorite. It has the same appeal as soccer, basketball, and volleyball. Like these games, it is quick-paced and involves teamwork. As in hockey, there is physical contact. The skills and strategy are a great challenge. And the cost of the game is minimal. Why not set up a *tlachtli* court in your neighborhood?

1. What is the purpose of the first paragraph?

____

2. Explain how details show the author's purpose in the first paragraph.

____

____

3. What is the purpose of the second paragraph?

____

4. Explain how some of the details show the author's purpose in the second paragraph.

____

____

5. On a separate sheet of paper, answer these questions: How do you think the playing of the Aztec game of *tlachtli* compares and contrasts with today's team sports? Aztec society is usually portrayed as warlike. With this in mind, why might an author write about Aztec games?

Home Activity Your child has read a passage about an Aztec game and analyzed the author's purpose. Read different passages from a magazine to your child. Challenge him or her to identify the author's purpose.

Name ____________________

Draw Conclusions

- When you **draw** a **conclusion**, you form a reasonable opinion about something you have read.
- Evaluate whether your conclusions are valid. Ask yourself: Do the facts and details in the text support my conclusion? Is my conclusion valid, based on logical thinking and common sense?

Directions Read the following passage. Then answer the questions below.

Archaelogists have found many remains and records of Aztec civilization. They can tell that the Aztec capital of Tenochtitlán had magnificent buildings. Great temples looked like stepped pyramids, and building them would have required engineering skill. The main source of information about Aztec society are *codices*. The Aztecs filled these books with drawings to show many aspects of family life, religion, and warfare.

One such aspect of Aztec life was farming. To grow crops for food, the Aztecs dug canals to bring water and built floating gardens on the lakes. Artifacts also include instruments such as different types of flutes and drums. In addition, their artistry was shown in pottery, jewelry, masks, and shields. One of the most famous artifacts was a huge carved stone showing the calendar that the Aztecs developed for measuring time.

1. What is one conclusion you can draw about Aztec civilization?

____

2. What support do you have for your conclusion?

____

____

3. Based on the buildings, what does the author conclude about Aztec civilization? Is this a sensible conclusion?

____

____

4. What do the books and instruments show about Aztec society?

____

5. What do the calendar and farming methods show about Aztec society?

____

Home Activity Your child drew conclusions based on a nonfiction passage about the Aztecs. Read a magazine article about a different culture with your child. Work together to draw conclusions based on the details of the article. Ask your child questions to challenge him or her to draw inferences.

Name ______________________________

Draw Conclusions

- When you **draw** a **conclusion**, you form a reasonable opinion about something you have read.
- Evaluate whether your conclusions are valid. Ask yourself: Do the facts and details in the text support my conclusion? Is my conclusion valid, based on logical thinking and common sense?

Directions Read the following passage. List facts or details you have learned. Then complete the diagram by drawing a conclusion.

In Aztec society it was easy to tell the nobles apart from the commoners. Although the houses of commoners could vary, many commoners had two-room houses. They lived in one room and slept in the other, and their homes had little furniture. In contrast, the noblemen lived in huge palaces with elaborate furniture. While commoners wore plain clothing and were not allowed to wear decorations, the clothing of the nobles was ornate and colorful, decorated with feathers and stitching. Noblewomen often wore jewelry and makeup too. There were several classes of nobles, from the very highest to lesser nobles and priests. Commoners were businesspeople, craftsmen, and farmers. Beneath them in the social order were the slaves. Commoners and slaves did most of the work of the society.

Fact or Detail	Fact or Detail	Fact or Detail	Fact or Detail
Commoners and nobles had different	Commoners and nobles wore	There were several	Commoners were

Conclusion

Aztec society had

Home Activity Your child drew conclusions based on the details of a nonfiction passage. Work with your child to draw conclusions from the details in a magazine article about a current trend.